## About the book

"This book is one of the most interesting I've read in the 20-odd years since I took up my profession [as an editor]. It is a high heroic counterattack on behalf of those people whose lives have been blighted by the overweening authoritarianism of prescriptive linguists. The author is clearly a skilled, intelligent and experienced writer, and in my opinion his heart's in absolutely the right place. [It is] a highly recommended book ... with treasures for any writer, editor or proofreader. Read it and learn from it!"

    Caroline Petherick, *Editing Matters*, July/August 2015, p. 13.

"*Correct English: Reality or Myth?* is an important book. As far as I know, it is the first of its genre that can justifiably be regarded as being significantly a work in applied philosophy. The issues it addresses, as well as those it hints at in passing (e.g. national policies for language), deserve further study and should become part of a more broadly envisaged philosophy of language."

    Professor Emeritus Karl Pfeifer, Department of Philosophy, University of Saskatchewan, *Metapsychology*, 2017, vol. 21, iss. 10.

GEOFFREY MARNELL

# Correct English

## Reality or Myth?

Burdock Books

Copyright © Geoffrey Marnell 2015

Geoffrey Marnell has asserted his right to be identified as the author of this work.

All rights reserved. No part of this book may be reproduced or transmitted by any person or entity, including internet search engines or retailers, in any form or by any means, electronic or mechanical, including photocopying (except under the statutory exceptions provisions of the *Australian Copyright Act 1968*), recording, scanning or by any information storage and retrieval system without the prior written permission of the publisher.

First published in Australia in 2015 by
Burdock Books
www.burdock.com.au
info@burdock.com.au

Second printing (with minor corrections): 2015

National Library of Australia Cataloguing-in-Publication entry

Creator: Marnell, Geoffrey R., author.

Title: Correct English : reality or myth? / Geoffrey Marnell.

ISBN: 9780994150202 (paperback)

Notes: Includes bibliographical references and index.

Subjects: English language--Usage.

English language--Errors of usage.

English language--Study and teaching.

English language--Written English.

Dewey Number: 427.9


Cover design by Lucian Marinescu


Printed and bound by China Gold Printing,
Shenzhen, China

To my wife *Melinda Lancashire,* whose generous dispensations afforded me the time to write this work.


And with special thanks to my mother, *Valerie Hickmore,* who, in hard times, scrabbled together enough money to buy her sickly, preschooler son a set of encyclopedias, thereby opening a world of enchantment and possibility that might otherwise have been viewed less dimly, if viewed at all.

## About the author

Geoffrey Marnell has a masters degree and doctorate from the University of Melbourne, gained by research in philosophy at the universities of Melbourne and Oxford. He has published widely— on such topics as language, technical writing, psychology and mathematics—and is the author of three books on recreational logic and mathematics.

Geoffrey tutored in philosophy at the University of Melbourne in the late 1970s and early 1980s before leaving academia to establish Abelard Consulting, a company that has, for close to 30 years, provided writing services, resources and training to organisations worldwide.

Geoffrey returned to the University in 2005 when, at the invitation of the English Department, he designed a course on technical writing and editing. He taught the course for nine years as part of the University's Publishing and Communications Program in the School of Culture and Communication.

In addition to language, Geoffrey's interests include literature, music, film and travel.

## By the same author

*Mindstretchers*
*Think About It!*
*Numberchains*

# Synopsis

*Chapter 1: The inevitable revolution*

Explores why the cultural warriors of the 1960s and 70s rejected the teaching of English (with numerous examples to show that much of what was taught was prejudiced, wrong or illogical).

*Chapter 2: The myth of correctness*

Analyses the concepts of *correctness* and *wrongness* and shows that language use, even if understood as following a mere convention, cannot be right or wrong, correct or incorrect.

*Chapter 3: Prescriptivists fight back*

Is the English language becoming corrupt? Is it losing its power to communicate effectively? This chapter considers various arguments put forward for keeping language pure (or at least stopping it from changing).

*Chapter 4: Taking language seriously*

If no-one owns the English language and no-one has the authority to control it, perhaps we need to rethink what makes good writing good. Perhaps the criterion should be not what is deemed correct, but what best meets our needs as *Homo sapiens*. By that criterion, is the absolutism of prescriptivism or the relativism of descriptivism the better approach?

*Chapter 5: The bedrock of good writing*

Explores the primacy of communication skills over knowledge of the rules of language use in ensuring writing that is not self-defeating. Illustrates the importance of clarity, familiarity, economy, conceptual lightness, neutrality and consistency in writing that meets the needs of both writer and reader.

### Chapter 6: Can the quality of writing be measured?

Writers have been sued for expecting their readers to understand documents that have a low readability score. This chapter considers the value of the readability scores provided in various word-processing software and concludes that there is none. The quality of writing cannot be measured.

### Chapter 7: Learning the lingo

If we are to prevent another backlash against teaching the basic mechanics of the English language—of the sort we saw in the 1960s and 70s—another approach to teaching is needed. This chapter discusses how active descriptivism is a better philosophy for developing the communicative prowess of students.

### Epilogue

Writing is a form of expression, as is painting and composing music. No-one has the right to tell artists to paint in a particular way nor to tell composers to compose in a particular way. So perhaps we have a right to talk and write as we please. But how can we accommodate creativity—or even improve the English language—if our primary purpose is to communicate and there are boundaries to communicative success?

# Contents

| | |
|---|---|
| Synopsis | 5 |
| Introduction | 9 |
| 1: The inevitable revolution | 17 |
|    Too much of what was taught was blatant prejudice | 19 |
|    Too much of what was taught was simply wrong | 25 |
|    Too much of what was taught was illogical | 32 |
|    The old school crumbles | 47 |
| 2: The myth of correctness | 51 |
|    Prescriptivism and descriptivism | 55 |
|    Change and difference: our restless language | 57 |
|    Language and knowledge | 68 |
|    Sources and types of knowledge | 71 |
|    Truth and mood | 88 |
|    Correctness and standards | 97 |
|    Can natural conventions be incorrect? | 103 |
| 3: Prescriptivists fight back | 123 |
|    Some usage is unnecessary | 125 |
|    Some usage is necessary | 128 |
|    Some usage is inconsistent | 132 |
|    Some usage is non-standard | 137 |
|    Change is necessarily diminution | 142 |
|    Chaos is just around the corner | 148 |
|    Universal grammar supports prescriptivism | 152 |
|    Etymological purity should be preserved | 156 |
|    Writing was better in the old days | 158 |
|    Effective teaching requires absolutism | 160 |

## 4: Taking language seriously — 163
- Prescriptivism and conventions — 165
- Descriptivism and conventions — 171
- Nudging change — 183
- Needs, morality and justice — 186

## 5: The bedrock of good writing — 195
- Clarity — 205
- Familiarity — 212
- Economy — 214
- Conceptual lightness — 215
- Neutrality — 220
- Consistency — 222

## 6: Can the quality of writing be measured? — 227
- The Flesch reading ease score — 230
- Correlation, volatility and validation — 236
- The irrelevance of readability formulas — 246

## 7: Learning the lingo — 249
- Communication as part-science, part-art — 251
- The variant of English to be taught — 258
- Language and literature — 262
- Clear thinking — 263

## Epilogue — 273

## Bibliography — 281

## Index — 285

# Introduction

There is much lament at the state of writing these days. Managers complain that the writing of their staff is indigestible, university lecturers wrinkle a brow at the poverty of expression in students' essays, pre-baby-boomers write letters to editors bemoaning the inelegance of much spoken and written discourse. Many see the origin of this expressive ineptitude in the neglect the mechanics of the English language got in school curricula from the 1970s until recently. Some call this period the *Dark Ages of English Language Teaching*.

This Dark Ages came about largely as a revolt against a particular view of language. This view, known as *prescriptivism*, holds that the rules of English usage are absolute and inviolable, to be followed by all and passed on from generation to generation in much the same way as we pass on the rules of gravitational attraction, chemical bonding and calculus. These rules were often taught with such priestly fervour that failure to follow them easily invited ridicule and shame (the memory of which coalesced into an anxiety that for many continued into adulthood). This view, and the methods of teaching it prescribes in the classroom, were hardly likely to survive the great cultural revolution of the 1960s and 70s, with its suspicion of authority and denial of absolutes. And sure enough it didn't.

Those cultural warriors of the 1960s and 70s who went on to become educational bureaucrats were certain to make changes, to reorient the teaching of English away from the seemingly groundless conservatism of the past. They had before them at least two novel approaches to teaching English. First, they could replace the stultifying prescriptivism of the past with a more logical, scientifically based approach (perhaps after determining what about language was most valuable to the wellbeing of students, or to the adults they will become). Or they could downplay, or even remove, the mechanics of language from the English curriculum. The latter approach, it appears, was the one most widely preferred.

This new breed of educational bureaucrat—understandably proud of the successes of their generation in liberalising a conservative society—were correct in assessing the prescriptivism of the past to be untenable. They saw the many varieties of English—both historical and contemporaneous—and saw too the vain pomposities of those who claimed the superiority of one English over another (appropriating the term "Standard English" for their preferred English). With so much variety in English, surely any so-called rule of language had to be relative. But where these bureaucrats erred was in concluding that this relativism meant that there was no value in teaching the mechanics of language.

In ditching English teaching—or relegating it to mere textual analysis—a golden opportunity was lost to make the teaching of English language relevant and useful—not to mention scientific. Instead of replacing it with a new attitude, a new approach—one that emphasised both the fundamental importance to society of widespread communicative prowess and society's obligation to consider the long-term interests of those for whom it is a moral guardian—educational bureaucrats decided that the mechanics of the English language need no longer be taught. It was prescriptivism or nothing. They opted for nothing. The sad legacy of this decision is the impoverished writing we now encounter every day.

With the benefit of hindsight, we now see how doubly unfortunate this decision was. Little more than a decade later came the age of desktop computing, followed closely by the networked world. Word processing and email meant that we could communicate with each other—pretty well with anyone—within minutes. No more waiting by the typing pool; no more waiting on snail mail. The productivity gains possible with word processing and email put pressure on more and more of us to be the instigators of communication, and it wasn't long before every job advertisement required applicants to have expert oral and written skills. Communication—and especially communication in the form of writing—had become a significant part of everyone's working day. Everyone was expected to write emails, if not memos, letters and reports.

And then we saw just how poorly many of us wrote.

Something had to be done. Most managers know that the public's perception of their organisation can be influenced by the quality of the documents their staff produce. They know too that poor writing imposes an enormous impost on productivity, amounting to billions of dollars every year.[1] Thus began a wave of writing consultants being invited to deliver in-house training, training sometimes of a rather basic nature. Further, compulsory writing units were added to the courses of many non-humanities departments in universities, public courses in remedial writing multiplied and pressure steadily increased on governments to reintroduce the teaching of basic language skills in schools. All music, no doubt, to the ears of those passionate about language and communication.

But before we get too excited by this swing back to the study of language, it will be worthwhile to understand why the cultural warriors of the 1960s and 70s rejected the prescriptivist approach to the teaching of language. If we fail to understand their reasons, we might opt to return to a prescriptivist style of teaching (as many have started to demand). The fear is that if we do return to prescriptivism, the cycle of puzzlement, rejection and neglect will be repeated. Sometime in the future another generation will begin to doubt the usefulness of this or that rule, challenge the authority of

---

1. If every full-time worker in Australia spends just 15 minutes each working day ploughing through verbiage or seeking clarification about poorly written correspondence, the productivity forgone is about 3%. That equates to approximately $15 billion each year of lost productivity. (Employee numbers and average salaries can be found on the Australian Bureau of Statistics website: www.abs.gov.au).

teachers and, when their challenge is met with "Well, that is how it is done", come to reject the value of language teaching altogether. We will then enter another Dark Age, another period where unintentional misinformation leads to inordinate inefficiencies in commerce and industry, frayed international relations and personal misunderstandings of great cost.

But there is another way, a way sadly overlooked by the cultural warriors of the 1960s and 70s. If we accept that the principal purpose of writing is to communicate, that no-one owns the English language—much as no-one owns the internet—and that English, like all living languages, will continue to change, then it follows that our attitude towards language, and our teaching of it, must be that of *descriptivism*. In descriptivism, the language of our intended audience is what should determine the language we adopt, not the language posited by prescriptivists as correct or standard. And this is an attitude that has obvious practical benefits. For it is simply *self-defeating* to write intending to communicate with someone—as we typically do—and yet deliberately use language that they will find unfamiliar or distracting. It is also disrespectful to those who have a rightful expectation to gain from what we have written. And yet writing driven from blind adherence to a set of supposedly absolute and inviolable rules of language—rules that one's readers might find odd, distracting or purposeless—could be self-defeating. What good is a perfectly punctuated sentence of flawless syntax—as judged by a prescriptivist—if it fails in its primary purpose: to communicate to its intended audience?

The early chapters of this book examine some of the reasons why the teaching of the mechanics of the English language went into decline in the latter half of the twentieth century, unravel the logical errors behind the claim that there is correct and incorrect usage, and propose a new attitude towards language and the teaching of language. As we will see, we do not need the putative verities of prescriptivism to be able to write well, and good writing *can* be taught. But that teaching needs to be conducted under the umbrella of our moral right to write as we please. For if there is no correct language, no-one has legitimate authority to force us to write in any particular way. The apparent tension between these two approaches—teaching writing skills on the one hand and respecting moral freedom on the other—will be discussed in the final chapters of the book. We also consider whether the quality of writing can be measured—the appearance in word processing software of various readability scores boasts that it can—and what English teaching might look like if the suggestions in this book are put into practice.

The emphasis throughout is on how writers can best inform their readers. The practical advice—drawn together in chapter 5—concentrates more on principles than practices. Principles are transportable from one language to another; practices are not. Some practices are not even transportable from one flavour of a language (say, Australian English) to another flavour of that same language (such as American English). We will discuss, for example, the meaning and importance of clarity and economy, but not the everyday use of the possessive apostrophe or the serial comma. Clarity and economy will help you inform your readers whatever language, or flavour of language, you adopt. And that is likely to be so in a thousand years time. On the contrary, the way apostrophes and commas are currently used varies between languages and, if the past is any guide, those ways will be unrecognisable in a thousand years. To repeat: this book is about principles. If you want to learn about current practices, you are better off consulting an authoritative, up-to-date style guide for whatever language, or flavour of language, you need information about. You might, for instance, consult *The Chicago Manual of Style* for advice on current American English, *New Hart's Rules* for advice on current British English, or *Style Manual for Authors, Editors and Printers* for advice on current Australian English.

\*

The impetus to write this book came from three directions. First, an indecency should not go unchallenged. In the same breath that firebrand pedants bemoan the falling standards in schools they call those who cannot write as well as themselves "appallingly ignorant" (to quote arch-pedant Lynne Truss). This is a case of having your cake and eating it. Rather than belittling those who, through no fault of their own, had a seemingly impoverished education, a decent response would be one of understanding and sympathy. What if the shoe was on the other foot? What if, through no fault of her own, Truss had been denied a good education in arithmetic? I suspect she would be indignant if her inept attempts to do, say, long division were declared "appallingly ignorant".

Second, there is something morally perverse in insisting that a person should write in a particular way. Writing is a form of expression, as is painting and composing. There are no firebrand pedants insisting that painters paint in a particular way or that composers compose in a particular way. Why then are there language pedants? Don't we have a moral right to write as we please, just as we have a moral right to paint as we please and compose as we please? Yes, my writing might, on occasion, be self-defeating—some of my audience might fail to understand me—but isn't that a risk that I am entitled to consider and decide to take or not take?

Third, the continuing epidemic of language neurosis needs to be eradicated. Many of us are anxious about how our speech or writing will be perceived. But this anxiety is largely misplaced. We can introduce into schools the study of grammar as a descriptive science, but this will only help future generations. It won't help those whose school days are over and who feel intellectually bullied and belittled by language pedants. In almost every adult class I teach are folk desperate not to be seen as bogans. They fear their writing will make them appear less educated than they are. I am constantly asked what is the correct way of saying this or of punctuating that. Some—alas only some—are relieved to hear that there is no such thing as correctness when it comes to language use. Asking if a piece of writing is correct is on par with asking if honesty is green. It is what philosophers call a *category mistake*.

But this is not generally understood: hence the oxygen given to pedants to megaphone their shameless superiority and spread language neurosis far and wide. The old disease of female hysteria was eradicated when it was realised that it wasn't a disease at all. Perhaps this book will, in some small way, likewise help to eradicate a neurosis: *language neurosis*.

\*

*A note on referencing*: sources of substantial relevance are cited in the text and listed in the bibliography. Less substantial sources, and additional commentary on the major sources, are provided in footnotes (as is passing commentary).

\*

My special thanks to John Wilson, who read my supposedly final draft and pointed out numerous errors. Thanks is also owed to Caroline Petherick and Scharlaine Cairns.

# 1: The inevitable revolution

The two decades following the Second World War were, for many, decades of stifling conservatism. There were codes for this and standards for that. We were forever berated with "What will the neighbours think?"; our entrée knife—if we could afford a multi-course meal—had always to be to the right of the knife that would be used for the main course; men were expected to walk on the kerb-side of the footpath when accompanying a woman; women felt as though they had to change their surname to their fiancé's once they were married; men had to give up their seat on the train to a woman; and on it went.

But the rule-bound conservatism of the time coincided with increasing participation in secondary and tertiary education. As a result, more and more people started to ask why. Why should men always give up their seat on the train to a woman? Does this also apply to an octogenarian male capable of walking only with the help of a walking frame? Must he stand up for a twenty-something just because she is a she?

And the questioning continued. Why must it be that:

> Blue and green
> Should never be seen
> Without a colour
> In between?

Is Van Gogh's *Irises*, painted in 1889, a flawed painting because blues and greens run into each other? Likewise Monet's *Water-Lily Pond* and *La Maison du Jardinier*? Of course not. So why did one need to worry about wearing a navy blazer over a green shirt? (Or even a green blazer over a navy shirt?) Gradually, and thankfully, this sort of sartorial straight-jacketing vanished (resurfacing in the early twenty-first century on some British television shows).

The gulf between convention and art showed up in music too. The following quotation, from a 1956 book on musical harmony, is typical of the times:

> "As soon as we attempt to make an inversion of [a dominant eleventh chord] we find it necessary, *for aesthetic reasons*, to omit both root and third. This gives us a Secondary 7th chord and should be treated as such.
>
> "The root position, however, may be used in either of the forms shown ... The 9th may be either major or minor. The 3rd is *always* omitted."[1]

Students being taught musical composition according to such advice were becoming increasingly aware of the music of the previous 50 or so years, music that simply did not follow these so-called *rules* of harmony. Could the author of that book have been unaware of the by-then well-known pentatonic music of Claude Debussy or of the harmonically anarchic and yet outstanding music of Igor Stravinsky, music that paid no heed to these so-called rules of harmony? These rules may have encapsulated the aesthetics of Mozart's time, but they certainly did not encapsulate the aesthetics of baby-boomers.

The conservative truths of the 1950s—about manners, art and music—began to crumble. They lacked logic, appeared mostly a matter of prejudice or didn't match well-accepted current practices. The same weaknesses were spotted in what was being taught about language. Too much of what was taught was rightly seen as prejudice, or as downright incorrect. There was bound to be a revolution in the teaching of English. And there was.

---

1. J. A. Steele, *Advanced Harmony for Students*, Allan & Co., Melbourne, 1956, p. 6. Emphasis added.

## Too much of what was taught was blatant prejudice

Some of the authorities to whom twentieth-century language teachers deferred did a poor job at hiding their own prejudices, thereby helping to generate a view that so-called good writing really was just a matter of personal style and taste. Here are some recommendations from one of the grand masters of the English language, Eric Partridge, from a book first published in 1942 and still in print today. The personal preferences, the prejudices, indeed the simmering snobbery, is unmistakable:

- "**productivity** is a horrible word; use *output*."[2]
- "**reminiscent of** for *indicative of* or *redolent of* is feeble and incorrect."
- "**gent**, 'a gentleman', is an illiteracy except when it applies to such a man as might be expected to use the word."
- "**inevitable** has come to have an unfavourable sense."
- "**out loud** ... is stylistically inferior to *aloud*."
- "**Xmas** ... is intolerable in the pronunciation, *Exmas*."
- "**exposé** ... is a Gallicism—and unnecessary".

*Horrible, feeble, unfavourable, inferior, intolerable*? Where is the science, the logic, to back up the personal preference that so obviously lies behind such views? Surely schools are meant to teach facts, not the prejudices of some one person or those of their class. It is a fair question to ask why the prejudices of Eric Partridge are worth more than those of the common man on the Clapham omnibus. Careful readers—as teachers and curriculum developers need to be—are likely to be put off by the prejudices and downright snobbishness that pepper, and ultimately flaw, Partridge's book.

---

2. This, and the other examples in this bulleted set, are taken from Eric Partridge, *Usage & Abusage*, 3rd edn, Penguin, Australia, 2008.

They are also likely to be put off by its title: *Usage & Abusage*. It is very much loaded with pejorative intent. If I use a hammer to knock down a brick wall rather than for its customary purpose of joining wood with nails, am I *abusing* the hammer? Or *abusing* the craft of woodworking? No. So why is it that I am abusing the language if I use a word in a new way (as poets, novelists and teenagers have been doing forever)? If a surgeon devises a new instrument to make a particular type of surgery less difficult, is the surgeon *abusing* the practice of surgery? Obviously not. And yet when I use an old word in a new way, or invent a new word, or use a "stylistically inferior" expression, I am, supposedly, abusing the language. So here is another reason why the new breed of educational bureaucrats might have been tempted to cast out the teaching of grammar. Novelty is not necessarily abuse. Moreover, to disparage novelty is to attempt to repress creativity, a defining and thus irrepressible characteristic of *Homo sapiens*.

Another widely respected authority on the English language is H. W. Fowler. Fowler's advice is mostly intelligent and he is more inclined than most of his ilk to defer to common usage and idiom. But, like Partridge, Fowler's advice is sometimes couched in the subjective, expressing mere opinion and stylistic preference:

- "**and/or** [is an] ugly device ..."[3]
- "**oddment**. Though the word itself is established and useful, its formation is anomalous ... and should not be imitated."
- "**memorandum** ... The commercial abbreviation memo ... is best left unspoken."
- "**napkin** should be preferred to serviette."
- "**exposé** is an unwanted gallicism."

---

3. This, and the other examples in this bulleted set, are taken from H. W. Fowler, *A Dictionary of Modern English Usage*, 2nd edn, OUP, New York, 1965. The book was first published in 1926.

In their well-regarded book *The Elements of Style*, Strunk and White are also guilty of prejudice against common usage:
- "**Fix** ... Bear in mind that this verb is from *figere*: 'to make firm', 'to place definitely'. These are the preferred meanings of the words."[4]
- "**Hopefully** ... has been distorted and is now widely used to mean 'I hope' or 'It is to be hoped'. Such use is not merely wrong, it is silly."
- "**Like** ... has widely been used by the illiterate; lately it has been taken up by the knowing and the well-informed, who find it catchy or liberating, and who use it as though they were slumming."
- "**Noun used as verb** ... Not all are bad, but all are suspect."
- "**Personalize**. A pretentious word often carrying bad advice."
- "**Prestigious**. Often an adjective of last resort. It is in the dictionary, but that doesn't mean you have to use it."

I am not suggesting that Fowler, Partridge, Strunk and White are best ignored. Much of what they have to say about grammar, language use and the subtleties of meaning is perceptive, intelligent and superbly written. But they weaken their overall authority by their outbursts of linguistic snobbery, a common vice of the times. When a novice reader encounters blatant snobbery on one page and wise advice on another, how are they to tell whether the wise advice is not also snobbery?

Many words in British English in the early-twentieth century — and earlier — were used as class markers. Nancy Mitford's book *Noblesse Oblige*[5] has been credited with popularising the fact that U-language (the language of the British upper class) was often markedly and deliberately

---

4. This, and the other examples in this bulleted set, are taken from W. Strunk & E. B. White, *The Elements of Style*, 3rd edn, Pearson Education, Needham Heights, 2000. The book was first published in 1959.

different to non-U-language (the language of the rest). Thus you could, apparently, tell a person's breeding—or their pretentiousness—by the words they used. For example, upper-class folk would say *spectacles, mad, sofa, lavatory, napkin, ill* and *scent*, while the remainder would say *glasses, mental, couch, toilet, serviette, sick* and *perfume* respectively. This sort of snobbery leaked into schools, even those that had no pretensions of educating the upper classes. But it did so in an insidious way: a purely descriptive distinction was turned into a prescriptive distinction. Rather than simply being taught the fact that, in Britain, different classes adopt different vocabulary, many were taught that one vocabulary was correct and the other incorrect. No money for guessing correctly which vocabulary was deemed correct. Thus many of us were taught that it was wrong to say or write *serviette*, but correct to say or write *napkin*. We were not allowed to ask the teacher if we could go to the *toilet*. We had to ask if we could go to the *lavatory*. John Betjeman—well before he was made poet laureate of the United Kingdom—lampooned this sort of snobbery in his delightful poem *How to Get On in Society*:[6]

> Phone for the fish knives, Norman
> As cook is a little unnerved;
> You kiddies have crumpled the serviettes
> And I must have things daintily served.

> Are the requisites all in the toilet?
> The frills round the cutlets can wait
> Till the girl has replenished the cruets
> And switched on the logs in the grate.

---

5. N. Mitford, *Noblesse Oblige: An Enquiry into the Identifiable Characteristics of the English Aristocracy*, Hamish Hamilton, London, 1956. Mitford was largely drawing on the earlier work of Alan Ross, but the popularity of her work cemented Mitford in the public's mind as the originator of the U and non-U distinction.

6. "How to Get On in Society", from *Collected Poems* by John Betjeman © 1955, 1958, 1962, 1964, 1968, 1970, 1979, 1981, 1982, 2001. Reproduced by permission of John Murray (Publishers).

> It's ever so close in the lounge dear,
> But the vestibule's comfy for tea
> "And Howard is riding on horseback
> So do come and take some with me.
>
> Now here is a fork for your pastries
> And do use the couch for your feet;
> I know that I wanted to ask you—
> Is trifle sufficient for sweet?
>
> Milk and then just as it comes dear?
> I'm afraid the preserve's full of stones;
> Beg pardon, I'm soiling the doileys
> With afternoon tea-cakes and scones.

Many of the same schools that fussed over supposedly correct vocabulary also fussed over supposedly correct pronunciation. So it had to be *con'troversy* (with the accent on the second syllable) rather than *'controversy* (with the accent on the first syllable), and *paper* had to sound like *pepper*:

> 'Red pepper or black pepper, sir', asked the shopkeeper.
>
> 'Don't be ridiculous,' snapped the old man. 'I mean lavatory pepper.'[7]

Kept out of the classroom, class-based language might have been shrugged off as an amusing national foible. But when it started to be taught—or more importantly, when its teaching finally came to be seen for what it was: snobbery and baseless imposition—it was bound to add fuel to the fire that was to revolutionise the teaching of English.

Indeed, the snobbery of yesteryear has not entirely died out. On hearing that the words *youse* and *brang* have made it into the *Macquarie Dictionary,* many people today express animated disgust, before dismissing the dictionary as thereby second-rate. On questioning, many are unable to explain their disgust, or attribute it to "uneducated speech". These are words, some say, that you would never use if you wanted to

---

7. J. Cooper, *Class*, Eyre Methuen, London, 1979, p. 235.

create a favourable impression. *Fuck* is a word you mostly wouldn't use to create a favourable impression, but it is in most dictionaries (the *Macquarie* included). Only a handful of those I've questioned about *youse* and *brang* suggested that *fuck* should also be excluded from dictionaries. But to suggest that dictionaries should exclude words based, not on currency, but on class or on impression in polite company is about as snobbish, and as silly, as insisting that fish should only be eaten with a fish knife.

The derision of supposed low speak—so-called *uneducated* speech—is difficult to understand, given that no-one can master all there is to know about the world and the universe. Are those not educated in the mysteries of quantum mechanics to be ridiculed because they know nothing of entanglement or supersymmetry? Likewise those who know nothing of the poetry of Philip Larkin or the paintings of Francis Bacon? No. Lack of an education in physics, poetry and art is no cause for derision. And yet a lack of education in the English language is considered by many to be worthy of derision and a reason to belittle. We have just come out of the Dark Ages of English Language Teaching, that period during which the mechanics of the English language were not taught in any depth in schools. Surely that, in large part, is why some, through no fault of their own, did not get an education in the mechanics of the English language. And surely that is a reason to sympathise, not ridicule. But then again, class has always played a role in language. The higher classes have never thought much of those supposedly beneath them, even to the point of attempting to build a grammar wall between the two:

> "an upper-class revulsion at the thought of being contaminated with middle-class vulgarity was a strong motive for the eighteenth-century codification of grammar." (Hitchings 2011, p. 87)

Poets and novelists have forever tinkered with the language. Shakespeare, for instance, introduced nearly two thousand words to the language. Should only poets and novelists be given licence to do as they please with the language but not Mr

Common or Ms Average? Why do we accept Shakespeare's *dwindle, frugal, lonely* and *obscene* but not our neighbour's *youse* and *brang*? And it's not just poets and novelists who have enriched the language. Many words and expressions that pass unremarked in contemporary English first sprang from the mouths of the uneducated: *fall guy, gobble, high roller, hunch, peckish, racket*, to mention a few.[8] Perhaps these words were frowned on when they first appeared, which invites the question: Were, say, 90% of English speakers to acknowledge the legitimacy of *youse* — as we all now do with *hunch* and *peckish* — and many were to use it in their writing and speech, would those who now find *youse* revolting still do so?

## Too much of what was taught was simply wrong

The blatant prejudice peddled as advice in many of the commentaries on language that their teachers referred to was unpalatable to the cultural warriors of the 1960s and 70s. These warriors were not just pushing the boundaries of egalitarianism, liberalism and cultural innovation; they were questioning everything, including all the assumptions and presumptions that glued together the arid conservatism of the 1950s. That questioning extended to what was being taught in the classroom and lecture theatre, and it didn't take an Einsteinian mind to see that much of what was being taught in English lessons was simply wrong.

### Verbs are doing words. Really?

When I ask my students what a *verb* is, those who think they know invariably answer "a doing word". I am disappointed as much by the answer as by the number who have no idea what the answer is. I too was taught that a verb is a doing word, but it didn't take much reflection to realise that this couldn't possibly be right. For we were also taught that every complete

---

8. These words can be found in Eric Partridge's *A Dictionary of the Underworld*, Bonanza, New York, 1961.

sentence must contain at least one verb. Now if every complete sentence must have at least one verb, and a verb is a doing word, then what are we to make of the following obviously complete sentence?

The house is red.

*The* is certainly not a doing word. (It is an article.) *House* is not a doing word. (It is a noun: the name of a thing.) *Red* is not a doing word. (It is an adjective: an attribute of a thing.) We are left with *is*. This, too, is not a doing word, but by the rule that every complete sentence must have a verb, it should be a verb. And indeed it is a verb: a type of verb called a *stative verb*.

Schoolteachers should have taught that verbs are words that represent actions or states. These are called *dynamic* and *stative* verbs respectively. We might *do* running and jumping. But we don't *do* is or is-ing. *Is* is an indication of a state of being. It is a stative verb. Indeed, *am, is, are, was* and *were* are all forms of the verb *to be*, and they are the most frequently used verbs in English. Here are four more stative verbs, none with even a whiff of action: *has, know, own* and *like*.

Most verbs are doing words (or dynamic verbs), but the most frequently used verbs in written and spoken English are the stative verbs. For teachers to have defined verbs in a way that excludes the most frequently used verbs is inexplicable.[9]

*i before e except after c. Really?*

One of the very first so-called rules of language many of us were taught is *i before e except after c*. But it doesn't take a post–primary school familiarity with English to discover that there are dozens of exceptions to the exception: *neither, either, beige, vein, deign, feign,* and so on and so on. Indeed, there are so many exceptions to the exception that one has to wonder if it's worth teaching a so-called rule or simply admitting that rote learning is the only way to master English spelling.

---

9. There are also *auxiliary verbs*. In most cases, these are words that work together with other verbs (or participles) to form compound tenses.

## *a* before a consonant, *an* before a vowel. Really?

Here is another so-called rule that many schoolteachers misleadingly passed on to their pupils. Some teachers sensed that there were allowable exceptions, but simply noted them as exceptions without actually teaching the principle that brought them back into the fold. For example, they would allow, as an exception:

> She deserves an honourable mention

even though the *an* precedes a consonant, not a vowel. Words beginning with *h* were an allowed exception, but teachers were less certain about sentences like:

> Thank you for purchasing an ST-102 refrigerator.

Some teachers gave it a tick; others did not.

How many vowels are there in the English language? Five, most would say: *a, e, i, o* and *u*. But that was a trick question. There are five vowels in the English alphabet, but 20 vowel sounds (Crystal 2006, p. 57). What schoolteachers should have taught is that, in conventional English, we place *an* before a word that begins with a *vowel sound* (Peters 2007, p. 1). That is why it is idiomatic English to write (and say) *Thank you for purchasing an ST-102 refrigerator*. The first sound in the pronunciation of the *S* in *ST-102* is ɛ—to use the symbol for that sound from the International Phonetic Alphabet—just like the first sound in pronouncing *enemy* or *LBW*. This is a vowel sound, even though the *S* is an alphabetic consonant. But note the following variation:

> Thank you for purchasing *a* Stevenson ST-102 refrigerator.

The first sound you make in pronouncing *Stevenson* is not a vowel sound, and thus the article *a* is appropriate.

Teachers who made exceptions for *h* words—as in *She deserves an honourable mention*—were not really helping their students, for there are some words beginning with *h* that are preceded by *a*. Here is a sentence with two words beginning with *h* and where each takes a different article:

There is *a* how-to-do clinic in *an* hours time.

Likewise for certain words beginning with *u* and *o*:

This might well be *a* United Nations project but they have *an* unbelievable failure rate.

That was *an* onerous expense; thank heavens it is *a* one-off.

There would never have been a need to teach exceptions had teachers taught the simple usage-matching formula in the first place: *a* before consonant sounds and *an* before vowel sounds. By that formula, the exceptions disappear (unlike the confusion that still haunts the tentative writer).

## The purpose of punctuation is to help the reader breathe. Really?

Many still labour under what must be one of the silliest so-called facts of many an English classroom: that the purpose of punctuation is to help the reader with their breathing. For a start, the human body knows when to breathe. It doesn't need assistance from a schoolteacher or writer. (If it did, *Homo sapiens* would never have evolved because, obviously, we haven't always had punctuation.) Second, not all punctuation marks can possibly be equal in requiring breath. Would one take a breath at each comma in *The flag is red, blue, white and green*? (And would American readers take an extra breath after *white* given their penchant for the serial comma?) That would make reading heavy going indeed, and recitation would quickly drive listeners to distraction. So a comma must serve some purpose other than as a marker for taking a breath. Moreover, breathing is rhythmical and yet sentences vary in length. So not even a full stop gives us cause to breathe. Otherwise we would pause after reading a short sentence and wait for our lungs to expire. Thus *The cat sat. It sat on the mat. It licked. It hissed. And then it slept.* would take five breaths to read (four more than most of us would actually take). And what of sentences that might require more time to read than the time between consecutive breaths? Do we look for the full stop before we start reading a sentence, estimate how quickly we will need to read it to fit it into one breath and only then start reading? Clearly, the notion that punctuation is related to breathing is absurd.

We see the true purpose of punctuation if we imagine writing that is devoid of it. Consider the following sentence:

Mary said Alan is not very smart.

In the absence of some system of punctuation, it might be impossible to tell whether Mary is judging the intelligence of Alan or Alan is judging the intelligence of Mary. The context might help but, if the context has not been made obvious, the sentence is ambiguous. And there lies the source of punctuation: the need to disambiguate, to make clear which of two or more possible meanings is the intended meaning. For if there is some system for marking a string of words as a dependent clause rather than as part of an independent clause, we could clearly tell, in the example at hand, whether Mary is judging Alan or Alan is judging Mary:

Mary said Alan is not very smart [Mary is judging Alan: *said Alan* is part of an independent clause]

Mary / said Alan / is not very smart [Alan is judging Mary: *said Alan* is now a dependent clause]

Today we use a comma (,) to isolate a dependent clause; fifteen hundred years ago we may have used ⸌ (a *punctus flexus*; see Parkes 1993, p. 306).

Consider another example, written all in capital letters as were many European languages before the advent of the printing press:

WE WERE ALSO ANGRY BECAUSE THE BOAT ARRIVED LATE THE MEAT WAS PUTRID

In this example, two sentences are blended together, but it is impossible to tell which is which. Was the meat putrid because the boat arrived late? Or was the writer angry because the boat arrived late? The need to disambiguate led to marks to indicate the end of a sentence. Today we use the full stop (.); in the ninth century CE, a *distinctio* (·) was widely used (Parkes 1993, p. 31).

The need to disambiguate ancient texts became stronger as copies became more widespread and more people learnt to read. Religious authorities in particular were keen to ensure that the way their sacred texts were interpreted was in line with their teaching. But the meaning of ancient texts could prove difficult, in part because they were copied in *scriptio continua*, that is, without spaces between words. This much-discussed phrase from Virgil's *Aenid* makes the problem posed by *scriptio continua* clear:

COLLECTAMEXILIOPUBEM

It could be read as COLLECTAM EX ILIO PUBEM ("a people gathered from Troy") or COLLECTAM EXILIO PUBEM ("a people gathered for exile"). In other words, is EX a word on its own, or joined to ILIO? Eventually the practice of placing an *interpunct* (a raised full stop) between words arose. This could be considered the advent of punctuation. But notice that the practice was to help disambiguation: separating one interpretation from another. It had nothing to do with breathing.[10]

Some students who happily escaped the classroom nonsense that punctuation is tied to breathing were pumped instead with the equally silly claim that punctuation is related to pausing. We are, supposedly, to pause more for a semicolon than a comma, more for a colon than a semicolon and more for a full stop than a colon. There is a faint glint of truth in this

---

10. The practice of inserting interpuncts had disappeared from European texts by the end of the first century CE. *Scriptio continua* returned, along with all the difficulties of interpretation attendant upon it. It was not until the eighth century CE that word separation reappeared, thanks largely to the work of Irish scribes. Their preferred technique was not to use an interpunct, but a space, as is our practice today.

claim, but one not strong enough to warrant its teaching. For a start, punctuation arose when recitation, not silent reading, was the primary means of cultural transmission. Indeed, silent reading was considered unusual until the late Middle Ages. Scribes and members of religious orders might read, but the general population (the overwhelming proportion of whom were illiterate) did not. Rather, texts were recited to them, typically by those in holy orders.

But recitation is fraught with danger. Consider again the sentence *Mary said Alan is not very smart*. A reciter can make it clear who is judging whom by the judicious use or avoidance of a pause. If the meaning to be conveyed is that Alan judged Mary, then the reciter could add a pause after Mary and another after Alan:

Mary / said Alan / is not very smart.

On the other hand, if the meaning to be conveyed is that Mary judged Alan, the reciter recites without pauses.

To help the reciter remember (or know) that this is how the sentence is to be interpreted, a mark could be placed in the text where a pause is required. This would be a punctuation mark. But note that the punctuation is being used to disambiguate, that is, to give an otherwise ambiguous sentence a precise meaning. It is a sign to a reciter to pause. Years later, when silent reading became acceptable, pausing was no longer necessary. The punctuation marks simply guided the silent reader towards one particular interpretation of that sentence.

A reciter might help an audience disambiguate by adopting pauses of different lengths for different punctuation marks. But somehow this practical guide to meaningful *recitation* was transformed into a schoolroom prescription to adopt such pauses while engaging in *silent reading*. Why anyone should have to pause while they read to themselves has never been supported by science. Did it improve comprehension? Did it improve long-term recall? Clearly not. And yet generations of schoolchildren had the necessity of the practice beaten into them. Some still do it well into adulthood, no doubt doubling or trebling the time it takes them to read anything. We might pause at the end of a sentence if it was abstruse or set in train other thoughts. But that's a matter of practicality, not necessity.

## Too much of what was taught was illogical

Before we explore this topic, we need to be clear that there are types of illogicality. One type is a type we simply have to put up with, namely, where there seems no rhyme or reason why something is the way it is: it just is. Life itself very likely falls into this category. And so does much of what passes for idiomatic language usage. Why is the plural of *dog dogs* while the plural of *goose* is *geese*? And what does the *o* in *won't*—a contraction of *will not*—signify? One might trace the history of a word, but that is unlikely to yield anything solid: perhaps nothing more than an unpredictable influence. Perhaps the *s* in *island* can be explained, to a degree, by the influence of the Norman Conquest and the want to curry favour with the powers that be. But why did the Anglo-Saxon word *iland* undergo a spelling change when so many other Anglo-Saxon words did not? This sense of illogicality is a good defence against pedants who complain that so much new usage is illogical. A new usage might seem illogical, but so too is much of what we accept as so-called proper English.

Three other senses of *illogical* are the subject of interest in this section. These senses come into play when a claim is put forward as to why we should speak or write in such-and-such a way that is:

- based on arguments that are clearly fallacious (such as *and* and *but* cannot start sentences because these words are conjunctions)
- wrongly claimed to be foreign to common usage (such as the claim that split infinitives are foreign to English usage)
- contrary to purpose (such as singular nouns that end in *s* express possession with only an apostrophe, and not an apostrophe *s*).

## Poor old *and* and *but*

Consider the so-called rule that states that a sentence must never start with an *and* or a *but* (extended by some teachers to include *for*, *nor*, *so*, *or* and *yet*). This rule seems to be the one most remembered from primary-school days. Many adults still abide by it despite its frequent breach in common usage over many centuries, and by writers great and small:

[1] "And long upon these terms I held my city, till this he 'gan besiege me ..."[11]

[2] "But wherefore do not you a mightier way/ Make war upon this bloody tyrant Time?"[12]

[3] "But, indeed, the dictum that truth always triumphs over persecution, is one of those pleasant falsehoods which men repeat after one another until they pass into commonplaces ..."[13]

[4] "But *-or* is tending to displace *-er* for all purposes."[14]

[5] "But what was the point of any of them?"[15]

[6] "And how was I to think of Veronica now? Adrian loved her but he had killed himself. How is that explicable? ... And though subsequent years might alter this view, until some of us give up on it altogether, when love first strikes, there's nothing like it, is there? ... But Adrian didn't agree."[16]

Are we to say Shakespeare (quotes 1 and 2 above) was a poor writer? Or the brilliant Victorian philosopher John Stuart Mill (quote 3)? Or lauded language guru H. W. Fowler (quote

---

11. W. Shakespeare, *A Lover's Complaint*.
12. W. Shakespeare, *The Sonnets*, 16.
13. J. S. Mill, *On Liberty*, Longmans, Green, 1865, p. 16. (First published in 1859.)
14. H. W. Fowler, *A Dictionary of Modern English Usage*, 2nd edn, OUP, New York, 1965, p. 674.
15. H. Jacobsen, *The Finkler Question*, Bloomsbury, London, 2010, p. 154.
16. J. Barnes, *The Sense of an Ending*, Vintage, London, 2011.

4)? Or that Howard Jacobson should not have been awarded the 2010 Man Booker Prize for the work from which quote 5 is taken? Likewise Julian Barnes, the 2011 Man Booker Prize who, on page 32 of his winning novel (of which quote 6 is an excerpt) starts a sentence with *and* twice and with *but* three times. How could such writers be deemed poor writers? How could Jacobsen and Barnes have won prestigious prizes for their writing?

When prescriptivists insist that a rule has force despite widespread contrary usage, they will often insist that the rule is based on logic. That language should be based on logic is rather an odd concept. One doesn't hear prescriptivists objecting to the blatant illogicality of *i before e except after c*. Rather, logic is invoked only when it suits particular cases, as when it is argued that since *and* is a coordinating conjunction, and therefore joins things, there must be something before it.

That may be so, but a sentence before a sentence-opening *and* is something before it. Why can't an *and* link to a previous sentence? It would be odd to start the first sentence of a new section in a document with *and* because then there is nothing obvious to link to (unless it was clear that the sentence was leading on from the heading[17]). We allow, at the start of a sentence, *pronouns* that link to a noun in the previous sentence, as in "Melanoma is a particularly serious form of skin cancer. It kills 2400 Australians every year". What is the *it* linked to? A noun in the previous sentence. If a pronoun can link to a previous sentence, why can't a coordinating conjunction?

But the case against starting a sentence with a coordinating conjunction fails for a more fundamental reason. There are many words that, when placed at the start of a sentence, mean the same as *and* and yet are considered grammatically acceptable opening words. *Furthermore* and *moreover* are two examples. Consider the following two sentences:

---

17. For example, "And health too is important" could legitimately run on from a heading that read "Money, power and respect".

> The drug inflamed the pancreas, reducing the supply of insulin. Furthermore, the liver went into shock.

> The drug inflamed the pancreas, reducing the supply of insulin. Moreover, the liver went into shock.

If these are fine (and they are), then what could be wrong with:

> The drug inflamed the pancreas, reducing the supply of insulin. And the liver went into shock.

Like *and*, *but* has been used for centuries to start sentences. Moreover, *but* at the start of a sentence can be equivalent in meaning to *however*:

> This can be explained if greenhouse gases acted as an insulator. However, modelling has shown that the required pressure would have been implausibly high.

> This can be explained if greenhouse gases acted as an insulator. But modelling has shown that the required pressure would have been implausibly high.

Despite the equivalence in meaning, prescriptivists accept the former but rail against the latter.

Indeed *but* at the start of a sentence provides emphatic force that writers can put to good use:

> It is a beautiful country, with long white beaches and cute furry animals. But it is full of xenophobes.

Many a language scholar can find nothing wrong with beginning a sentence with a coordinating conjunction:

> "That it is a solecism to begin a sentence with *and* is a faintly lingering superstition." (Fowler 1965, p. 29)

> "The belief that the conjunction *and* should never begin a sentence is out of step with modern usage. *And* is a legitimate opener; it can be a way of reinforcing the sentence before, or emphasising the words that follow ..." (*The Penguin Working Words*, 1993, p. 34)

"Contrary to a very widespread belief, there is no rule against beginning a sentence with *and* … Often it is the most appropriate word to begin with, as it links what is to follow with what has gone before …"
(Wood 1962, p. 18)

To sum up: the ban on starting a sentence with an *and* or *but* has never matched common usage, is downright illogical in failing to extend to words that are their synonyms, and is rejected by many language scholars.

## Prepositions at the end of sentences

In somewhat simple terms, a preposition is a word (or string of words) that introduces, or is closely related to, a noun, pronoun or noun phrase that is providing more information about some other noun, pronoun or verb. Consider the following sentence:

The liquid in the test tube is very hot.

In this example, *in* is a preposition. It introduces a noun phrase (*the test tube*) to create a further phrase (a prepositional phrase: *in the test tube*) that provides more information about another noun (*liquid*). Put another way, how are the two nouns related? One is *in* the other. In the sentence "He yelled at the pigeons", *at* is a preposition. It introduces a noun phrase (*at the pigeons*) that provides more information about a verb (*yell*).

The seventeenth-century poet, playwright and literary critic John Dryden (1631–1700) is credited with initiating the belief that a sentence should never end in a preposition. Thus it would be unacceptable, to Dryden, to write:

Who did you talk to?

Dryden would have insisted that the sentence be written:

To whom were you talking?

Likewise Dryden would have demanded *That was the school to which he went* over *That was the school he went to*.

However, placing prepositions at the end of sentences had been common in English for a very long time (and is still common). And it has been used by writers of repute:

"Such bitter business as the day would quake to look on".[18]

"Prepositions follow sometimes the nouns they are coupled with."[19]

"... what a fine conformity would it starch us all into?"[20]

Indeed, there are numerous idiomatic English expressions where a preposition must end the sentence, such as *What are you complaining for?*, *You had better get that cough seen to* and *He's impossible to reason with*.

Dryden was especially sure of his instincts on this matter, even going so far as to rewrite (and re-order) large chunks of one of Shakespeare's early plays (*Troilus and Cressida*). It was not only stranded prepositions that irked Dryden. In the preface to his version of the play, Dryden claims that:

"many of [Shakespeare's] words, and more of his phrases, are scarce intelligible. And of those which we understand, some are ungrammatical, others coarse; and his whole style is so pestered with figurative expressions, that it is as affected as it is obscure ... Yet, after all, because the play was Shakespeare's, and that there appeared in some places of it the admirable genius of the author, I undertook to remove that heap of rubbish under which many excellent thoughts lay wholly buried ... I need not say that I have refined his language, which before was obsolete."[21]

Not exactly a temperate review. But what was Dryden's reason for insisting that idiomatic English should be rid of stranded prepositions? His argument appears to be little more than this: you can't end a sentence in Latin with a preposition—

---

18. W. Shakespeare, *Hamlet*, from the soliloquy at the end of act 3, scene 2.
19. B. Johnson, *The English Grammar* (quoted in H. W. Fowler, op. cit. p. 474).
20. J. Milton, *Areopagitica*, part III.
21. W. Scott ed., *The Works of John Dryden*, vol. 6, 1808, pp. 239–50.

it is grammatically impossible—hence you should not do so in English. But English is not a Latin-based language. It may have borrowed thousands of Latin words, but English is primarily a Germanic language. English has also borrowed many words from Greek, but we do not try to enforce Greek syntax on English. And why make English more like Latin rather than Latin more like English. Is Latin somehow superior? (Its relegation to the dead-language basket suggests otherwise.) It is surprising that Dryden and the other Latin-loving pundits didn't insist that the English alphabet change to mirror the Latin alphabet—by dropping three characters.

Many in the seventeenth and eighteenth century did consider Latin, if not superior, then stylistically, and hence socially, preferable. Moreover, it had become a sort of *lingua franca*, enabling poets and scholars from many nations to understand each other. John Milton wrote poetry in Latin; Isaac Newton wrote scientific treatises in Latin; Francis Bacon philosophised in Latin. Thus the passing of knowledge from generation to generation was largely done using Latin.

But is that a strong reason for insisting that the syntax of English should follow that of Latin? The world today is awash with English. It is the contemporary *lingua franca*. Stephen Hawking writes science in English, Carol Ann Duffy writes poetry in English, Peter Singer writes philosophy in English and on it goes. Are we to say, then, that because of the current predominance of English in scholarly and artistic works, French syntax (and indeed the syntax of *every* other language) should be modified to reflect English syntax? Of course not.

There is simply no logic in banning stranded prepositions and the ban has been rejected by many language scholars over many years:

> "There is no rule forbidding the use of a preposition at the end of a sentence. Sometimes it is the only possible place for it: e.g. 'Where has this bus come from?', 'Who is that letter for?', 'My little girl has no one to play with'." (Wood 1962, p. 182)

"The traditional caveat of yesteryear against ending sentences with prepositions is ... a pedantic and unnecessary restriction ... The 'rule' prohibiting terminal prepositions was an ill-founded superstition." (*Chicago Manual of Style* 2003, p. 188f.)

"One of the most ... illogical 'rules' of English grammar is the traditional prohibition on ending a sentence with a preposition ... The basis for this rule was Latin grammar ... However, English grammar is not Latin grammar: in English a preposition can come after a noun or pronoun, and this flexibility is in fact part of the character and strength of the language." (Khan1985, p. 456)

"Those who lay down the universal principle that final prepositions are inelegant are unconsciously trying to deprive the English language of a valuable idiomatic resource, which has been used freely by all our greatest writers except those whose instinct for English idiom has been overpowered by notions of correctness derived from Latin standards. The legitimacy of the prepositional ending ... must be uncompromisingly maintained." (Fowler 1965, p. 474)

To sum up: the ban on ending a sentence with a preposition has never matched common usage, is downright illogical in contending that English must match some other language (especially one that is not even an ancestor of English) and is rejected by many language scholars.

## Splitting infinitives

"I loathe split infinitives." (Humphrys 2004, p. 241)

Most English infinitives are made up of two words: *to* + a verb: *to run, to skip, to love* and so on. To split an infinitive is to place one or more words between the *to* and the verb. Some examples:

to *happily* play

to *better* equip oneself

"to *boldly* go where no man has gone before"

These examples would have been frowned upon by many an English teacher, for it is wrong, they were sure, to split an infinitive. Reasons were rarely given, and they are scarce in the commentaries on English. One reason that has been put forward is that splitting infinitives is rare in English and thus non-idiomatic. In 1864, Henry Alford wrote:

> "But surely, this is a practice entirely unknown to English speakers and writers. It seems to me that we ever regard the *to* of the infinitive as inseparable from its verb. And, when we have already a choice between two forms of expression, 'scientifically to illustrate' and 'to illustrate scientifically', there seems no good reason for flying in the face of common usage". (Alford 1864, p. 171)

Alford's argument has been challenged by modern language scholars:

> "split infinitives were used for centuries before they became the *bête noire* of nineteenth-century grammarians." (Peters 2007, p. 754)

> "There is precedent from the fourteenth century down for interposing an adverb between *to* and the infinitive it governs."[22]

> "The split infinitive is found at least as early as the thirteenth century. It occurs a couple of times in Chaucer, rather more often in the writings of John Wyclif, and a huge amount in the fifteenth-century works of Reginald Peacock [and then becoming uncommon] until the later stages of the eighteenth century, when it began to appear in the writings of even the most punctilious authors, such as Samuel Johnson." (Hitchings 2011, p. 12)

---

22. W. Strunk & E. B. White 2000, p. 58. Despite granting it a long history in English, Strunk and White go on to say that "the construction should be avoided unless the writer wishes to place unusual stress on the adverb". No reason is given as to why this restriction should be imposed on what is common usage.

Here are some examples:

"Root pity in thy heart, that when it grows
Thy pity may deserve to pitied be."[23]

"Who dared to nobly stem tyrannic pride."[24]

Anyway, why should we shoehorn contemporary English into the mould that defined (or may have defined) nineteenth-century English? Such an argument assumes that language should never be allowed to change. But the English language has been in constant flux (as we'll see in the next chapter) and no-one has any authority over how it changes. Consider, for instance, the possessive apostrophe. It was once not part of the English language (taking off only in the eighteenth century). So its use, when it began, could not have been idiomatic. One has to wonder whether Alford and his ilk would have argued against using the possessive apostrophe—a useful clarifying mark in some situations—on the grounds that it was not idiomatic at the time (as it is now).

Another reason sometimes given for why you should not split an infinitive is that it is indecorous, and indecorous because it goes against the syntax of Latin:

> "... some people view split infinitives as a social indecorum. The rule forbidding split infinitives comes from a time when Latin was the universal language of the world. All scholarly, respectable writing was done in Latin ... In Latin, infinitives appear as a single word." (Moriaty 1996, p. 253)

The argument is that since you cannot split an infinitive in Latin—as all infinitive forms are single words—you should not split an infinitive in English. For instance, *to love* is *amare* in Latin: just one word. It makes no sense to put another word inside *amare*—it would destroy the meaning of the sentence—so we shouldn't put another word inside an English infinitive. Once again, we have to ask why Latin should be the gold

---

23. W. Shakespeare, *Sonnet 142*, lines 11 and 12.
24. R. Burns, *The Cotter's Saturday Night*, stanza 21.

standard for other languages. Latin is Latin and English is English. The fact that English is the predominant language of the world today is no reason why other languages—French, Swahili or whatever—should force their syntax to match that of English. Likewise, the fact that Latin was the predominant language of the world three hundred years ago is no reason why we should force the syntax of English to match it.

Indeed, if Latin were the gold standard—so that what cannot be done in Latin should not be allowed in English—then we would have to disallow much more than split infinitives:

> "... in Latin there is no definite or indefinite article – 'a girl' is *puella* and 'the threads' is *fimbriae*. No one would suggest that we cannot say 'a clever girl' or 'the broken threads'. Yet isn't this a split nominative? Is it not as much of a crime as a split infinitive?" (Hitchings 2011, p. 12)

As with conjunctions at the start of sentences and stranded prepositions, the so-called rule against splitting infinitives has been rejected by many language scholars over many years:

> "Reactions to the split infinitive still beg the question as to what is wrong with it. The answers to that question vary from 'It's ungrammatical' to 'It's inelegant'. The first comment has no basis, as we've seen. The second is often subjective ..."(Peters 2007, p. 754)

> "Although from about 1850 to 1925 many grammarians stated otherwise, it is now widely acknowledged that adverbs sometimes justifiably separate the *to* from the principal verb ... Recasting a sentence just to eliminate a split infinitive or avoid splitting the infinitive can alter the nuance or meaning ..." (*Chicago Manual of Style* 2003, pp. 175 and 187)

> "There is no rule that an infinitive must never be split." (Wood 1962, p. 219)

Indeed, sometimes it is impossible to make clear what you want to say without splitting an infinitive, as in:

They failed to completely understand the problem.

To move the adjective *completely* so as to avoid splitting the infinitive *to understand* is likely to change the meaning of the sentence, as in:

They failed completely to understand the problem.

To sum up: the ban on splitting infinitives has never matched common usage, is rejected by many language scholars, sometimes cannot be avoided without clouding meaning, and has no logic on its side.

## Possessive apostrophes: useful marks defeated by illogical teaching

> "[Punctuation's] primary purpose is to resolve structural uncertainties in a text, and to signal nuances of semantic significance which might otherwise not be conveyed at all, or would at best be much more difficult for a reader to figure out." (Parkes 1993, p. 1)

If only this entirely rational sentiment had always driven the teaching of English punctuation. Take the humble possessive apostrophe. The teaching of its supposedly correct use has baffled many a student. Many of us were taught that to indicate the possessive of a singular noun we place an apostrophe and an *s* on the end of the word (as in *student's homework*). So far so good. But then we were taught that if the singular noun ends in *s* (*atlas*, for example), only an apostrophe is to be added (*atlas'*). *Why?* many were to ask. This was never clearly explained.

The teaching of this curious *s*-exception rule has waxed and waned. Early in the twentieth century the rule was moribund:

> "It was *formerly customary*, when a word ended in -*s*, to write its possessive with an apostrophe but no additional *s* ... In verse, and in poetic and reverential contexts, this custom is retained, and the number of syllables is the same as in the subjective case, e.g. *Achilles'* has three not four syllables, *Jesus'* two not three. But elsewhere we now usually add the *s* and the syllable [as in] *Pythagoras's doctrines*." (Fowler 1965, p. 466, emphasis added.)

So, with the exception of poetic and reverential contexts, the *possessive s*-exception was dead in Fowler's time. Its apparent revival is a mystery, given that it does not appear to be a reflection of some new, strong convention. (Perhaps credit for the revival is owed to the spell-checker in the near-ubiquitous Microsoft Word, which invites us to disinter the exception.) Leaving that issue aside, it is curious that Fowler should tie punctuation practice to the wholly subjective notion of reverence. If your sympathies lie with Priam, Hector and the residents of Troy, I doubt that you would revere Achilles. And many feel no special reverence towards Jesus. Must a Catholic write *Jesus' teaching* and an atheist write *Jesus's teaching*? Perhaps it's the majority view of reverence that matters. But why should reverence be the yardstick? Why not majority detestation? Why not gender? Isn't it equally illogical to claim that if a person's name ends in *s* and they are female, we apply an apostrophe only, whereas if they are a male, we apply an apostrophe and an *s*, thus it is *Tess' books* but *James's books*.

Other commentators seem equally incapable of providing useful guidance on the use of the possessive apostrophe with singular nouns. Some give up altogether:

> "singular words which end in *s* … can show possession by ending ' or '*s*." (Shrives 2011, p. 5)

Others suggest that it is the sound of the ending of a word that determines whether an apostrophe on its own is warranted:

> "The possessive of words ending in an *s* or *z* sound can either have the normal '*s* ending or simply take the apostrophe without the *s* … Except where it sounds awkward or ugly the full '*s* ending is preferred." (Murray-Smith 1987, p. 27)

But this is all about pronunciation (and aesthetics). Why should punctuation be determined by pronunciation? Punctuation is to help readers see *on the page* what meaning the author intends. Readers should not have to know how the author pronounces words in order to work out the author's meaning.

Fowler too appears to link correct punctuation to pronunciation. In the quote given on page 43, he implies that if we wrote *Jesus's*, readers would take three syllables to pronounce it and this would, supposedly, be unidiomatic. But English is only a weakly phonetic language. We do not pronounce every letter in every word. Words with silent letters are abundant: *night, weight, debt* and so on. And there are many words with consecutive *s*'s where each *s* is not enunciated. For example, we don't pronounce *pass* in two syllables, or *assist* in three. So the fact that *Jesus's* has two *s*'s in it doesn't mean that each needs to be, or even will be, pronounced. It might be retorted that there is an apostrophe between the two *s*'s in *Jesus's* and that this changes things. But why should an apostrophe cause one syllable to be broken into two? Do we pronounce *it's* and *its* differently, the first with two syllables the second with one? Likewise *cant* and *can't*?

So the practice recommended by Fowler, Murray-Smith and many teachers past and present is illogical. This illogicality is compounded by the fact that it contradicts the primary purpose of possessive apostrophes. For if we place only an apostrophe after singular nouns that end in *s* — as we do with all regular plural nouns — we would write *scissors' weight* whether we were talking about one pair of scissors or many pairs of scissors. Likewise, we would write *species' distribution* whether we were talking about the distribution of one species or of a number of species. Similarly, we would write *Halls' book* whether we were talking about the book written by someone whose surname was *Halls* or a book written by two people whose surname was *Hall*. Thus the *s*-exception rule that many teachers taught (and some still do) is contrary to the very purpose of possessive apostrophes: to help readers see whether the modifying noun is intended to be singular or plural.

Another silliness taught in some classrooms is that we can only use 's to show possession by the higher animals. For lower animals the *of* form must be used instead (Quirk et al. 1972, p. 201). Thus we can write *the horses's neck* but not *the slug's length*. In the latter case we would have to write *the length of the slug*. Horses are higher animals; slugs are not. From where did this madness come?

Of course, there is much illogicality in English. We accept an illogical usage if deviating from it would be unidiomatic, distract our readers and fail in its purpose of communicating. We continue to write *I have a problem* even though it appears to break the subject–verb agreement rules. (We would all be saying *I has a problem* if logic were to be our sole guide.) Likewise we continue to write *seizure* even though it breaks the *i before e except after c* rule. So perhaps, we should accept the so-called rule that if a singular noun ends in *s* it takes just the possessive apostrophe after it and not an apostrophe and an *s*.

Earlier we distinguished four types of illogicality. The illogicality discussed in the previous paragraph—the illogicality inherent in the lack of rhyme or reason—is minor compared to the illogicality of being *contrary to purpose*. One might accept that necessity forces on us a usage of some sort. We need to communicate, to do so we need to agree on some usage, a particular usage gains favour, and there we have it. No rhyme or reason other than that some usage was needed (or found especially useful). Some other usage might have reigned but it didn't. The fact that a full stop rather than, say, a solidus now marks the end of a sentence is a point of historical rather than logical interest. But it is a different and more notable matter when the teaching of a usage contradicts the very purpose that established the usage in the first place. The placement of the apostrophe of possession was meant to help us distinguish singular from plural. But, as we've just noted, many of us were taught to use the apostrophe of possession in a way that made that distinction impossible in some cases. This sort of illogicality stands out naked among the lesser illogicalities that bedevil languages. It was noted by many a cultural warrior of the 1960s and 70s and it added fuel to the symbolic fire that was about to burn down the English-language classroom.

## The old school crumbles

The remaking of Western culture that took place in the 1960s and 70s was carried along by many currents. One such current was a gathering suspicion of authority and of those who claimed to be authorities. That suspicion had its outlet in many ways: anti-war moratoriums, student sit-ins, subversive publications. Youngsters refused to attend for national service. Students demanded that the political assumptions of apparently scientific subjects (such as economics) be taught. Women began to demand an equality they had been denied—and denied on flimsy and deceptive grounds. Dissent was everywhere and change became inevitable.

The rebellion was most furious in the universities. And it was the universities that would provide the next generation of academics and bureaucrats who would be responsible for primary and secondary school education. Thus the restless questioning that led to the cultural revolution of the 1960s and 70s—Why are we fighting a war in Vietnam? Why is the political basis of economics not being taught? Why do women get less pay for the same work?—would inevitably be at the core of new thinking about education.

The spirit of the times was the rejection of authority, especially authority that appeared to have no logical foundation. The pre-rebellion culture was one of unquestioning respect for teachers. They were considered authorities, and the textbooks they set were written by people who were likewise considered authorities. But what was being taught by English teachers—and what was written in many grammar books— began to be seen by many to have no logical foundation. It was not only the smartest kids in the classroom who could see the snobbery in much of what was being taught as correct writing, who could see the irrationality in the superstitious avoidance of *and* at the start of sentences and who could find words and idioms that broke the so-called rules of spelling and grammar (rules which were even broken by teachers themselves in the classroom, such was the gulf between rules and idiomatic usage). Most students did. So it would be inevitable that those students who went on to become teachers of student teachers, or bureaucrats in state education departments, would have an unkindly attitude towards the teaching of the English language. Teachers have a primary obligation to teach facts. That is the unshakeable axiom upon which all education rests. *Force = mass × acceleration*. That is taught in secondary school physics. It is a fact. So let's keep teaching it. Never start a sentence with *and* or *but*. That is taught in secondary school English. It is not a fact. So let's stop teaching it.

As English curricula continued to be critically analysed, it became clear that much of what had been taught as correct grammar simply wasn't. It was merely the convention of the times. And the merely conventional would get no respect from the cultural warriors of the 1960s and 70s. The short-back-and-sides had been the conventional haircut of men in the 1950s. Out it went. Changing one's surname on marriage if one was a female was conventional in the 1950s. Out it went. Most things purely conventional were ditched. And that included the traditional English language syllabus. Thus began the recent Dark Ages of English Language teaching.

I have much sympathy with the cultural warriors of the 1960s and 70s. The world is definitely a better place for their anger and their efforts. But I am also passionate about language and communication. I see every day the crawling convolutions of engineers, scientists, managers and bureaucrats as they struggle to convey even the simplest of ideas on paper. The point of this book is to show that, in ditching the teaching of the mechanics of the English language, the cultural warriors of the 1960s and 70s abandoned—or simply failed to see—a golden opportunity to make the teaching of language both vocationally relevant and based on science. Instead, curricula were developed that gave today's engineers, scientists, managers and bureaucrats—indeed anyone who needs to write—little in the way of useful knowledge. The mere study of texts does not a good writer make.

But the answer is not to return to the prescriptivism of the past. Some contemporary authors of language handbooks seem to want to do just that. In a 2003 publication, Australian editor and language teacher Deb Doyle writes:

"In non-fiction, it's preferable not to commence a sentence with a coordinating conjunction."[25]

"it is preferable not to end a sentence with a preposition"

"... it's preferable not to split the infinitive ..."

Why? Preferable to whom? Where is the logic? There is a touch of Eric Partridge in this style of teaching.

John Humphrys (2004, p. 241) is in the same camp:

"... it is better not to end sentences with [prepositions]."

"Mostly there is no reason to split infinitives."

Better? On what grounds? *No reason*? Well, does that mean I can't do it? There's *no reason* to start a sentence with *quarks* either, but I'll do it if I want to. When it comes to reasons, Humphrys offers nothing more than "I loathe [such-and-such]".

We risk another backlash against language teaching if we revert to basing our grammatical principles on the personal preferences of those seen as pundits. Surely there has to be a reason why we should adopt a particular practice if it is not already so well-entrenched that readers are expecting it. As we'll see, sometimes there is, but mostly there is not. Throughout this book we will progressively draw out the fact that some language use can be rationally, scientifically judged to be better than others. But most language use is discretionary. We are free to be as creative with it as we like (just as we are fee to paint as we like and compose music as we like). The sneering, belittling pontifications of the pedants and the language snobs cannot take this away from us. It is our moral right.

---

25. D. Doyle, *Grey Areas and Gremlins*, self-published, 2003, p. 57. See pp. 67 and 43 for the quotations that follow this one.

# 2: The myth of correctness

"Language is a city, to the building of which every human being brought a stone."[1]

Can any particular use of language be sensibly labelled *correct* or *incorrect*? To answer this question we need to be clear about the meaning of *correct*. There are only two definitions of the adjective *correct* to be found in two well-respected dictionaries, the *Oxford English Dictionary* and the *Macquarie Dictionary*. The first is this:

"correct *adj.*: In accordance with fact, truth, or reason: right." (Oxford)

"correct – *adjective* 6. conforming to fact or truth; free of error, accurate." (Macquarie)

Thus "2 + 3 = 5" is correct, but "Water boils at 50 °C at sea level" is incorrect.

Both dictionaries give a second definition of *correct* (identically worded):

"In accordance with an acknowledged or accepted standard; proper."

According to this definition, it would be correct for a male to remove his hat before entering a church and incorrect for a woman not to curtsey when introduced to the British monarch.

Like *incorrect*, the word *wrong* is also used to express disapproval. In certain contexts, the two words are synonymous. The *Oxford English Dictionary* and the *Macquarie*

---

1. Ralph Waldo Emerson, "Quotation and Originality" in *Letters and Social Aims*, Houghton, Mifflin and Company, Boston, 1884.

*Dictionary* both give a number of meanings, two of which almost exactly mirror, in the negation, the two definitions of *correct* discussed above:

"wrong *adjective* 2. deviating from truth or fact; erroneous; ... 4. not in accordance with a code, convention or set of rules; not proper."

We will use the terms *correct* and *incorrect* throughout this book, but our conclusions will apply equally to claims that language use can be *wrong*.

In many contemporary grammar books, and blogs on language scattered around the web, we find the words *incorrect* and *wrong* liberally assigned to various ways of writing. It is clear, then, that many people think that language use can be correct or incorrect. But the meaning they intend for these words is never made clear. As we have seen, there are two senses of *correct* when it is used as an adjective: *conforming to truth* and *conforming to a standard*. It is pertinent, then, to ask which sense these grammarians and pundits have in mind when they express their disapproval of some form of writing.

Given the strident fulminations of many prescriptivists—such as members of the Apostrophe Protection Society, who scrape offending apostrophes from shopkeepers' windows after dark—it is undoubtedly the first sense of correctness they have in mind: in accordance with fact, truth, or reason. For them language use can be correct or incorrect no less than a mathematical equation can be correct or incorrect—or so it seems—and it rankles them when they see supposedly incorrect usage. Perhaps the best known of all contemporary prescriptivists is Lynne Truss. Judging by the staggering sales of her punctuation manifesto, *Eats, Shoots & Leaves: The Zero Tolerance Approach to Punctuation*, punctuation neurosis must be widespread among English speakers. More than 1.7 million copies of the book have been sold, and no doubt many purchasers share Truss's belief—espoused with vacillating conviction—that the rules of punctuation are transcendental absolutes, epistemological neighbours of the axioms of Euclid and of Descartes's famous *cogito ergo sum*. This somewhat common assessment of Truss's views might be a little unfair. She does say in her book that her goal is to:

> "... usefully combine a descriptive and prescriptive approach [to punctuation] ... Somewhere between these positions is where I want us to end up: staunch because we understand the advantages of being staunch; flexible because we understand the rational and historical necessity of being flexible." (Truss 2003, p. 26f.)

Nonetheless, her own firebrand language gives powder to the charge that deep-down Truss is really a dyed-in-the-wool prescriptivist. She talks of "plummeting punctuation standards", of "ignorance and indifference", of "illiterate mistakes" and "appalling ignorance", all in the first four pages of her book. Later she writes "My own position is simple: in some matters of punctuation there are simple rights and wrongs [and] I want apostrophes where they should be". The charge of prescriptivism is looking more and more well-grounded. And note the subtitle to her book: *The Zero Tolerance Approach to Punctuation*. The allusion is to the practice in some countries of not tolerating some minor crimes. *Zero tolerance* means that punishment is meted out without the benefit of a judge's discretion. Does Truss really think that misplacing an apostrophe is on par with a legal (or even moral) transgression? Does she want Mr and Ms Malaprop to be issued with on-the-spot fines or even given a mandatory jail sentence?

John Humphrys is another stickler who thinks that the misuse of language should be brought to the attention of the authorities:

> "How can people speak and write this sort of rubbish? How can they be so indifferent to the way their words sound? How can broadcasters transmit them and newspapers print them? How is it that the purveyors of the equivalent of junk food are not hauled up before the linguistic equivalent of the Food Standards Agency and forced to forfeit their licence to speak." (Humphrys 2004, p. 3f.)

Like Truss, Humphrys is not adverse to shrill pontifications, declaring some writing to be "ugly", "so obviously wrong", "horrible" and "profoundly irritating" (to quote just some of his ungracious put-downs).

In passing we should note that the pedants' philosophy doesn't always match practice—the *walking* match the *talking*. The philosophy of prescriptivism is that there are laws or rules that should not be breached, but prescriptivists can be just as sloppy in their own writings as those they criticise. In a paper exploring why readers detect fewer errors in a text when they are reading for content rather than for language, Joseph Williams gives numerous examples of where so-called language pundits—W. H. Fowler, E. B. White and Jacques Barzun—write in ways that contradict their own commandments (Williams 1980).

Truss's much-discussed book might, perhaps, have been born in a marketing boardroom divorced from any serious educative impulse. And Humphrys's semi-jocular tone suggests that he is not altogether comfortable with his own beliefs.[2] Still, the idea that there is a set of inviolable laws that govern, or should govern, the expression of the English language is widespread, and anecdotal evidence suggests that it is the most common view. Newspapers still publish letters from readers fulminating over this or that linguistic trend, and talkback radio hosts take calls from adults concerned about some new speech habit that their children have adopted (with the invariable lament, in both cases, over falling standards). No wonder internet discussion forums for writers are littered with anxious requests for help on aspects of correct usage: "Is it correct to hyphenate e-mail?", "Is it correct to capitalise the first word in a bulleted list item?", "Do I put one space or two between sentences?" and so on and so on. It is difficult to

---

2. Adding fuel to the suspicion that Humphrys's book is not meant to be a serious contribution to the language debate is his sloppy scholarship. Here is one clanger of many: *battle,* Humphrys declares, is a noun not a verb. A quick look at the *Oxford English Dictionary* would have enlightened him to the fact that it has been both since Middle English.

imagine the passion being as intense if the concern was only for some convention or standard.

## Prescriptivism and descriptivism

"... prescriptivism is the view that one variety of language has an inherently higher value than others, and that this ought to be imposed on the whole of the speech community ... Adherents to this variety are said to speak or write 'correctly'; deviations from it are said to be 'incorrect'." (Crystal 1987, p. 2)

This chapter will explore the notion that a particular language usage can be correct or incorrect. To help us position certain views on linguistic correctness, we will draw a distinction between laws, rules and conventions. The distinction is somewhat forced, but it will serve our purposes. To many believers in linguistic correctness, there are some principles that must be followed come what may. Such a principle is what I'll call a *law*. It is conceived as an inviolable, knowable imperative. A law of grammar is no less a law than a law discovered by a scientist. To a believer in grammatical laws, the prescription that one must, for example, match a verb with its subject in number is no less compelling than the statement that water boils at 100 °C at sea level. By *rule* I mean a prescription that, although not in the same class as a law of physics, should be followed come what may lest we are made worse off. A believer in linguistic rules might accept that possessive apostrophes are human inventions—unlike boiling points—but insist that their value is so great that their protection is worth fighting for. Lastly, a *convention* is just the description of a common practice. It is, if written down, a codification of the way things are generally done. (Later I'll coalesce rules and conventions and then split the amalgam into *artificial* and *natural* conventions, but that's a complication we can avoid for the moment.)

Let's start our investigation of linguistic correctness by considering the first definition of *correct* noted above: "in accordance with fact, truth, or reason: right". This is the notion of correctness at the root of what I'll call *strong prescriptivism*. A strong prescriptivist believes that there are inviolable laws of language use that should never be broken. These laws are true—they are statements of fact or reason—and it is only right that they are followed. In contrast, *weak prescriptivism* is the view that language can at best be governed by rules not laws. Although essentially the product of human invention, language rules are still worth treating as inviolable—in other words, still worth fighting for—because without them we would be worse off in some way (such as our ability to communicate would be severely diminished). Like a strong prescriptivist, a weak prescriptivist vows to continue to advocate certain practices regardless of common usage. On the other side is *descriptivism*, the view that the so-called laws or rules of language are nothing more than flexible conventions, waxing and waning as they have always done, and failure to adjust our own practices accordingly can lead to communication problems. Unlike prescriptivists, descriptivists won't hold on to a language use come what may. They will bend in whatever direction common usage takes them. Their blood would not boil with Truss-like intensity if, for example, the non-possessive genitive apostrophe in *two weeks' notice* fell by the wayside.

Another notable distinction between prescriptivists and descriptivists is the former's fetish for the English that they were taught at school. No prescriptivist is clamouring for a return to the language of Keats, Shakespeare or Chaucer. Nor are they proposing language reform. Rather, in declaring some usage or other to be sloppy or ungrammatical, it is the language use *of their time* that prescriptivists use as their yardstick. This suggests that prescriptivists are mere conservatives at heart rather than defenders of the language (as they are apt to portray themselves). They want to preserve things as they were when they were learning the language, and refuse to entertain any idea of reversion or change—even if a reversion or change might improve the language or be a legitimate expression of natural creativity.

Strong prescriptivism seems to be the view of most people (not just firebrand pedants like Truss and Humphrys). Thus it is worth beginning an analysis of what it means for language use to be correct or incorrect from the perspective of strong prescriptivism. That is, let's assume that there are inviolable laws of language, laws that should no more be broken than the laws of arithmetic. We'll mount two attacks on this view, first by examining what the diversity of the English language suggests and then by challenging the epistemological credentials of the so-called laws of language.

## Change and difference: our restless language

> "I have no sympathy with the criticism which would treat English as a dead language ... Purism, whether in grammar or in vocabulary, almost always means ignorance. Language was made before grammar, not grammar before language."[3]

> "It is in no sense wrong for human language to change, any more than it is wrong for humpback whales to alter their songs over years." (Aitchison 2001, p. 249)

The English language shows much historical variation—it's not what it once was—and much contemporary variation (different groups of current English speakers use English differently). Both forms of variation pose challenges for prescriptivists.

Language use changes for many reasons. Some meanings become fashionable after dropping from the lips of celebrities (such as *cool* in the sense of *up to date* and *with it*); others drop out of favour for being seen as stale (such as *hot* to mean *up to date* and *with it*) or by being nudged out by a new fad. The influence of particular professions can lead to semantic changes and widely accepted neologisms. For example, the

---

3. M. Ray, quoting Thomas Hardy in *Thomas Hardy Remembered*, Ashgate, Farnham, 2007.

influence of information technology is probably behind the recent change in meaning of *acronym* from a shortened form pronounced as a word (such as *scuba*) to any shortened form (such as ABC and USA). Social pressure too can lead to language change. The widespread, although not ubiquitous, elimination of gender-specific language since the 1970s was largely the result of the influence of the feminist movement. Other rights movements have had success in influencing how language will be used in written documents. For example, the movement to enshrine in law the right of citizens to be able to understand the obligations governments impose on them has had success in the US. From October 2011, all public documents originating from the US public service must, by law, be written in a Plain English style.[4] There can be little doubt that this requirement will influence writing styles in general (if only in the US).

The flux that permeates language has given us not only variation along any one branch of evolutionary English—Old English, Middle English, Early Modern English, and so on—but has given us different branches: British English, American English, Australian English and so on. We thus have *diachronous* and *synchronous* variation (that is, historical and contemporary variation respectively).

## Historical variation

History is a good place from which to attack the authoritarianism that fuels the obsession with linguistic correctness, for history shows that the English language we know today is vastly different from the English language of the past. Let's begin with pronunciation. Sometimes it seems that, like tuberculosis and polio, the issue of correct pronunciation has become a concern of the past. But every so often an outraged pedant manages to find a forum through which to infect the insecure with unnecessary worry. In letters to editors we still see television newsreaders chided for pronouncing *h* as *haitch* rather than *aitch* and public

---

4. See *Plain Writing Act 2010*.

figures mocked for taking five syllables to enunciate *temporarily* rather than four. In 2012, *The Age* newspaper in Melbourne published letters criticising the country's prime minister for pronouncing *communities* as *communidies*, and others for pronouncing *pursue* as *pershoo*. Behind these singular complaints is the more general one that standards of pronunciation (like everything else) are in decline, the implication being that some earlier standard was correct or more worthy of adoption. But the great unanswered question has always been *How far back do we go?* Why do pedants go back only as far as their own schooling? What makes the pronunciation of, say, the 1950s especially worth adopting over the pronunciation of earlier times? What makes it correct and others incorrect?

Throughout the 1,600 or so years of the existence of a distinctly English language, standard or received pronunciation has been in flux (as has the pronunciation of every English dialect). The fifteenth century saw what linguists call the Great Vowel Shift, a change that affected nearly all the long vowel sounds in the language (Burchfield 1985, p. 23f.). For instance, *mood* gained its present pronunciation over *mode*, as did *house*, previously pronounced to rhyme with *loose*. In Chaucer's time, *wife* was pronounced *weef*, but by Shakespeare's time it had become *wayf*. In nineteenth-century England, the accepted pronunciation of the words *off*, *cross*, *cloth* and *lost* was *orff*, *crors*, *clorth* and *lorst* respectively, pronunciations we certainly don't hear today (Burchfield 1985, p. 41).

The overwhelming problem for strong prescriptivists is to show why we should adopt the standard applying at one time over the standard applying at another time? Why *wife* and not *whiff*, *wayf* or *weef*? Why *off* but not *orff*? Few prescriptivists even try to provide a justification.

The same flux plays with spellings. Chaucer's *Canterbury Tales* is difficult for the modern reader largely because spellings are now so different. Are we to say that Chaucer spelt incorrectly? And the flux continued well beyond Chaucer. For example, before the sixteenth century, *reign*, *island* and *debt* were spelt (or spelled) *rein*, *iland* and *det* respectively. Were scholars in the fifteenth century poor spellers when they wrote *rein*, *iland* and *det*? Or are we now misspelling the words when we write *reign*, *island* and *debt*? Are contemporary Australian and British writers misspelling *authorise* and *moralise* because Shakespeare wrote *authorize* and *moralize*? Or was Shakespeare a poor speller? A strong prescriptivist today is forced to the view that Shakespeare was indeed a poor speller (although few would admit it).

The meaning of words is likewise inconstant. The principal meaning of a significant slab of English words is no longer what it was centuries, and sometimes just decades, ago. Any dictionary compiled on historical principles is fat with examples of semantic evolution. Take the word *villain*, for example. It once meant a low-born, base-minded rustic. Now it means an unprincipled or depraved scoundrel. Are we to say that the current meaning is correct and the earlier meaning incorrect? Or is it the other way round? Do strong prescriptivists really believe that the use of *villain* to mean a low-born, base-minded rustic was incorrect? And what of *girl*? Before the sixteenth century it meant a young child—of either sex. Now it means a young female. One more: *quibble*. This word once meant to pun, or to play on words. It now means to evade the point with frivolous and trifling objections.

Syntax too has undergone change. Two-hundred years ago no criticism would have been made of constructions such as:

"the writing this book was a difficult job" or "writing of this book was a difficult job".

Nowadays, such constructions would be deemed odd (and a strong prescriptivist would call them incorrect). Instead we would write "the writing of this book was a difficult job" or "writing this book was a difficult job" (Aitchison 2001, p.101).

Let's end this quick survey of historical variation with a consideration of punctuation. Again, history rains on the strong prescriptivists' parade. Consider the following, a snippet of a facsimile edition of John Dryden's translation of Virgil's *Aeneid*:

> And plowing frothy furrows in the main ;
> When lab'ring still with endless discontent,
> The Queen of Heav'n did thus her fury vent :
> 'Then am I vanquish'd? must I yield ?' said she,
> 'And must the Trojans reign in Italy ?'[5]

Dryden, you might recall, was an arch-pedant, so much so that he was overwhelmed by an urge to rewrite Shakespeare. But what are we to make of the spaces, in the quotation above, between characters and a colon, semicolon and question mark? This was no fad of Dryden's. It had a long history, stretching into the early twentieth century. Here is a representative sample of 1920s punctuation taken from "A Cooking Egg", a poem of T. S. Eliot:

> But where is the penny world I bought
> To eat with Pipit behind the screen ?
> The red-eyed scavengers are creeping
> From Kentish Town and Golder's Green ;

No-one includes such spaces nowadays, not even the great writers. So, are contemporary writers right and Dryden and Eliot wrong? Or is it the other way around? Is there a prescriptivist strong enough to publicly claim that T. S. Eliot was backward when it came to punctuation?

The use of quotation marks is another case where historical variety is evident. Before Dryden's time numerous markers were used to denote spoken passages: line breaks, dashes, italics, parentheses and differing scripts, to name a few. Our commas and colons were once indicated by points of varying height and at other times by consecutive points of varying number. Capitals only began to adorn the start of sentences in the ninth century CE. In the fourteenth century, the mark we now call a colon was often written with two diagonal hairlines

---

5. Virgil, *The Aeneid*, translated by John Dryden (1697), lines 53–57.

drawn between the points. Parentheses appeared only in the fifteenth century, as did the semicolon (Parkes 1993).

So as with pronunciation, spelling, meaning and grammar, the punctuation practices of writers of undoubtable greatness have varied across time. For prescriptivists like Truss to ridicule divergence from current orthodox practice is to assume that current orthodox practice is correct, and that those writers who punctuated differently got it wrong, despite their greatness. That is the implication of strong prescriptivism when it is yoked to a fetish for contemporary usage. The fact that the necessary conclusion—that writers of prior times were poor writers—is not widely espoused suggests that strong prescriptivists do not have the courage of their convictions (or, what is more likely, have not carefully thought through their position).

There is no reason to assume that English will not continue to change:

> "All societies are constantly changing their languages with the result that there are always co-existent forms, the one relatively new, the other relatively old; and some members of a society will be temperamentally disposed to use the new (perhaps by their youth) while others are comparably inclined to the old (perhaps by their age)." (Quirk et al. 1972, p. 31)

Change has been constant. With the democratisation of publishing born of the web, the rate of change can only increase. And this only amplifies the problem for strong prescriptivists. In 50 years time when the principal meaning of *alternate* is *alternative*, will prescriptivists still insist that it is incorrect? Will they still insist that *disinterested* really means *objective* and *impartial* when the overwhelming majority of people use it primarily to mean *uninterested* or *bored*? The life of the strong prescriptivist is sure to be a solipsistic one.

The many differences between the Old English of Anglo-Saxon times and contemporary English—differences so great that few people nowadays can read, say, *Beowulf*, the best-known text in Old English—strongly suggests that there is no feature or set of features that makes English English. The most we have is a Wittgensteinian *family resemblance* running through overlapping versions of English. But without a single set of necessary and sufficient features that define English, prescriptivism loses its best chance of a solid foundation.

## Contemporary variation

In the preceding section, we considered how English pronunciation, meaning, spelling, and punctuation have varied throughout history. Such variation poses a sticky problem for strict prescriptivists, namely those who think (a) that the rules of language use are inviolable rules akin to the laws of mathematics and science and (b) that contemporary rules are correct. Their position is made even more uncomfortable by the fact that variation can also be seen in contemporary English.[6]

Consider, first, pronunciation. For US speakers, *temporary* has four syllables and *medieval* three; but for many British and Australian speakers, the syllable count is three and four respectively. Indeed there are many words that are pronounced differently in Britain and the US, such as *comparable, secretary, laboratory, medicine, veterinary, extraordinary, gaseous, library* and *glacial*. Are British prescriptivists game enough to tell American speakers that their pronunciation is incorrect? Are American prescriptivists willing to do the same to British speakers?

Vocabulary and meaning too can vary between variants of contemporary English. In American English a *bill* is what a speaker of Australian English would call a *banknote*. Similarly, an American *drugstore* is a *chemist* in Australia. A *period* in American English is a *full stop* in most other Englishes. A *lay-by* in Australian English is a purchasing arrangement while in British English it is a part of a road where vehicles can pull up out of the stream of traffic. Likewise, a *capsicum, footpath* and

---

6. Strictly speaking it is the English of their school days that most prescriptivists consider to be correct. We consider variations between *contemporary* Englishes here, but there is no reason to doubt that variation also existed between the Englishes of the past.

*nature strip* in Australian English are called *pepper, pavement* and *verge* in British English.

There are intra-country variations too. For example, in most states of Australia, the pole that carries electricity and telephone cables is called a *power pole*; but in South Australia it is more commonly known as a *stobie pole*. Another regional variation is the name for German sausage which, depending on where you live, might be called *fritz, devon, polony* or *strasbourg*. *Flake* in Victoria is called *shark* in Western Australia, and a *potato scallop* in New South Wales is called a *potato cake* in Victoria. Finally, a *suitcase* is still called a *port* by many residents of Queensland.

What is called a *beach house* in Australia is called a *crib* in the South Island of New Zealand, but a *bach* in the North Island. A *sandwich* in the south of England is a *butty* in certain northern counties; and a *turnip* south of Hadrian's Wall is a *neep* north of the Wall. Further, gym shoes (or trainers) are variously called throughout the British Isles *plimsolls, sandshoes, pumps, gollies, daps, whiteslippers* and *gutties* (Trudgill 1999, p. 110).

There are also grammatical differences. In the south-west of England it is common to say *I did go there every day* whereas most other speakers of British English would say *I went there every day* (Finegan et al. 1992, p. 359). Double negatives are not a feature of the language of south-east England (where, for example, the preference is for *I don't want any trouble*) whereas the double-negative is preferred in most other parts of England: *I don't want no trouble* (Finegan et al. 1992, p. 87).

Grammatical differences can also be seen in other variants of English. For example, in most of Australia the past tense of *to bring* is *brought*, but many in Far North Queensland prefer *brang*. As for American English:

"Instead of *I saw it*, a New Englander might say *I see it*, a Pennsylvanian *I seen it* and a Virginian either *I seen it* or *I seed it* ..." (Quirk et al. 1972, p. 14)

There are numerous spelling differences between American English and other Englishes. Americans typically drop the *u* from words ending *-our*, so that *colour* in British English is *color* in American English. There is less letter-doubling in American English: *labeled* is preferred to *labelled*, as is *canceled* to *cancelled* and *modeled* to *modelled*. (There are some words, however, where letter-doubling occurs only in American English: *enroll* and *fulfill*, for example.) American English prefers *-ize* to *-ise* endings in such words as *organize, colonize, authorize* and so on. This was the preference in Elizabethan England, but it is not so today. In Australian and New Zealand English, these words have always had an *-ise* ending.

Finally, punctuation. Inter-country variation is less common than it is with pronunciation, vocabulary and spelling. The most notable variation is the widespread use of the serial comma in American English and its near absence in most other Englishes. A serial comma is a comma before the final *and* in a run-on list (that is, in a series of listed items). The second comma in the following sentence is a serial comma:

The flag is red, white, and blue.

In British and Australian English, the serial comma is rarely used. It is added to a sentence only if ambiguity would result without it, as in the following example:

This page of the intranet covers departmental policy, organisational charts and resource plans and purchasing templates.

A serial comma would make clear what the second and third items covered on that page of the internet are. At present it is impossible to tell.

Among the seeming chaos that is contemporary English, how conceivable is it that there should be one and only one correct English? And how conceivable is it that a small group of English speakers—the prescriptivists who favour one variant over another—would ever succeed in convincing the speakers of those variants of English they consider aberrant that they must change the way they speak and write? Strong prescriptivism is looking increasingly shaky. Its program is looking stillborn.

## Variation and relativism

Such variation as we have discussed might be put forward in support of the claim that there can't be any correctness or incorrectness when it comes to language. But strictly speaking, variation in views about a subject does not imply relativism (the view that there is no single correct position to take). Thus it could be argued that historical and contemporary variation in language use does not imply the necessary absence of correctness. Take science as a parallel. The plethora of wrong, illogical or unfalsifiable beliefs held by scientists over the last 500 or so years does not imply that there cannot be scientific truth. There obviously is, otherwise we could not have landed astronauts on the moon nor determined that the Sun causes melanoma. Nor do contemporary differences in scientific view—for example, between those who believe the universe will eventually collapse back on itself and those who believe it will continue to expand—imply that there cannot be scientific truth. The universe may very well continue to expand, or collapse, in which case one view will be correct. Perhaps if we were to discard the prejudice, illogicalities and obvious untruths in the study of correct language use there would be left a core set of truths that cannot be denied. We may not have discovered that core set yet, but that doesn't mean that we won't. There are plenty of issues unresolved in science too—the mechanism that unifies the four fundamental forces of nature, what existed before the Big Bang, what causes the human immune system to turn against itself—but that doesn't imply that they are irresolvable.

All that is true, but there are some important differences between what might pass as language-use knowledge and what is acceptable scientific knowledge. For example, when one scientific position contradicts another, it follows that both positions cannot be correct. If Ptolomy believed that the Sun revolved around the Earth and Copernicus believed that the Earth revolved around the Sun, Ptolomy and Copernicus could not both have been correct. Similarly, if one school of scientists believes that stomach ulcers are caused by stress and another school believes that they are caused by *Helicobacter pylori* bacteria, both cannot be correct. At least one school of thought must be wrong. If we apply parallel logic to language use, we would have to say that of any two competing schools of thought on language use, at least one must be wrong. Now suppose, for the sake of argument, that one such school holds that Shakespeare's language use was correct and another holds that Dickens's language use was correct. Now since Shakespeare and Dickens used language quite differently, both schools cannot be correct. But is anyone game enough — or mad enough — to contend that either of these two great writers used English *incorrectly*, that their language use was not in accordance with fact, truth, or reason? But that is the position a strong prescriptivist is forced to take.

If strong prescriptivists — that is, those who elevate the rules of language to the realm of science — were themselves true scientists of language, they would be willing to admit that even contemporary usage might be incorrect. Scepticism and challenge are welded into the DNA of scientists. Everything is open to challenge; everything is tentative. The history of science justifies this cautious, ever-tentative approach. As we learn more and more about the world and the universe, some scientific theories are overturned. For example, the Aristotelean view of gravity was challenged by the Newtonian view of gravity, which was subsequently challenged by the Einsteinian view of gravity, which is now under challenge from quantum physics. As our understanding of gravity matured, the old models were relegated to history. Scientists accept that. It is the *modus operandi* of scientific endeavour: propose, test, refine, re-propose, test, refine and so on. So if strong prescriptivists viewed language as physicists viewed the universe, there would need to be acceptance that the current view of correct language use might well be overturned by future discoveries.

But this is not a view you will find in the writings of prescriptivists. Current usage is the gold standard and any deviation is shouted down or scraped from shopkeepers' windows. There seems no willingness to accept that what we believe now about what constitutes good writing might very well be relegated to a mere footnote in the history of our species's faculty of communication.

## Language and knowledge

> "Epistemology *noun* ... the branch of philosophy which deals with the origin, nature, methods, and limits of human knowledge" [Macquarie Dictionary]

To be fair, we should admit the possibility that there are strong prescriptivists who, while claiming that language use can be correct or incorrect, are still willing to accept that even the assumed correctness of contemporary usage needs to be proved. For these folk, language variation—both diachronic and synchronic—poses no challenge. If it can be proven that some set of language prescriptions is correct—that is, in accordance with fact, truth and reason, as per the dictionary definition of *correct* we are currently exploring—then Shakespeare, Dickens and even Lynne Truss could have used the English language incorrectly. Likewise, Americans, Britons or both could be using contemporary English incorrectly. Thus there may be strong prescriptivists willing to admit that their own language use could be incorrect. But how might we prove that any particular language use is in accordance with fact, truth and reason? What might lead us to the knowledge that this particular language use is correct or incorrect? For the strong prescriptivist, the answer will be in the use being counter to some inviolable, absolute law of grammar. But this just pushes our enquiry up a level, for now we can ask how we can prove that this so-called law of grammar is in accordance with fact, truth and reason. In other words, how do we *know* that the law is true?

We can explore this in at least two ways: (a) by looking at the possible sources of knowledge and asking which, if any, could lead to grammatical knowledge (a term I'll use as shorthand for knowledge of correct language use) and (b) by looking at the mood of those sentences used to express so-called grammatical knowledge and asking whether the notion of truth or falsity can possibly be applied to it.

Consider this statement:

"INCORRECT: 'So always check your weight after doing aerobics'." (Doyle 2003, p. 57)

There is nothing special about this particular sentence, so the claim that it is incorrect is, presumably, made on the basis that it is a breach of a more general rule (or, for a strong prescriptivist, a *law* of grammar). In this case, the law would be something akin to *All sentences that begin with a coordinating conjunction are incorrect*. (Recall that Doyle wrote that "In non-fiction, it's preferable not to commence a sentence with a coordinating conjunction": see page 49.) So the logic adopted by Doyle appears to be this:

[1] All sentences that begin with a coordinating conjunction are incorrect.
[2] *So always check your weight after doing aerobics* begins with a coordinating conjunction.
[C] Therefore *So always check your weight after doing aerobics* is incorrect.

The logic is impeccable. It is a valid syllogism. The conclusion follows logically from the two premises. But there is more to proof than simple validity. An argument must also be *sound*, by which logicians mean that all the premises adduced in support of the conclusion must be *true*.

"*Proofs* are a certain sort of sound argument. After all, a proof is always understood to be a completely conclusive argument—hence it must be a valid one. And a proof is always understood to establish the truth of its conclusion. So it must proceed from true premises." (Richards 1978, p. 29)

Thus we need to show that the major premise in the argument above—premise [1], the putative grammatical law— is true. So how do we gain the *knowledge* that all sentences that begin with a coordinating conjunction are incorrect (without which we cannot claim that premise [1] is true)?

To know something is to be *justified* in believing it to be true. Truth alone is not enough. Just as validity without truth does not constitute a proof, truth without justification is not enough. It might well be true that there is life on the exoplanet Alpha Centauri Bb, but if I have no strong reasons to back up my belief that there is, I cannot be said to *know* that there is life on Alpha Centauri Bb. As British philosopher A. J. Ayer put it:

> "we do not say that people know things unless they have followed one of the accredited routes to knowledge."[7]

So what are the accredited routes to, or sources of, knowledge? Where do we get knowledge (or how do we become knowledgeable)? First, let's discount revelation as a source of grammatical knowledge. We don't look to holy books for advice on splitting infinitives, ending sentences with prepositions or starting a sentence with a coordinating conjunction. Grammar has never been included in Sunday school lessons, nor pushed from the pulpit.

We do, though, get most of our knowledge—and many of our falsehoods—through the testimony of accepted authorities: mostly teachers and lecturers. But what knowledge we do get in this way is *derivative knowledge*: knowledge derived by consulting accepted authorities. You gain knowledge from a school teacher, and the schoolteacher gained that knowledge from their lecturers and the books they studied at university. Further, the authors of those books may have cited other authors, taking what those other authors wrote on trust because of their reputation as an authority. And so on. But if we are to avoid an infinite regress of reliance on the testimony of so-called authorities, derivative knowledge must have a starting point. And that starting point is *discovery*. Something is discovered and the knowledge thus gained—in this case, *primary* knowledge—is passed on as derivative knowledge.

---

7. A. J. Ayer, *The Problem of Knowledge*, Penguin, Harmondsworth, 1956, p. 33.

So the question as to how we know that some sentence is grammatically incorrect becomes this: *On what primary knowledge is the relevant general grammatical law based?* In the example at hand, the question becomes: *What primary knowledge justifies the claim that all sentences that start with a coordinating conjunction are not in accordance with fact, truth and reason?* It is not enough to consult so-called authorities on language. We must establish the claim from first principles.

## Sources and types of knowledge

There are only two ways of gaining primary knowledge: by *a priori* means and by *a posteriori* means. *A priori* knowledge is knowledge gained by thought alone; *a posteriori* knowledge is knowledge gained by observation and experimentation.

> "Some statements we can know to be true (or false) only by observation and experiment [such as] *The planet Saturn has rings* ...[If] we are to find out whether the statement is true or false we must do some looking around the world (or get someone to do it for us). Statements like these are known as *empirical* or equally, *a posteriori* statements ... All other statements are known as *a priori* statements. They are the ones we can know to be true (or false) prior to experience." (Richards 1978, p. 154f.)

Are there other sources of knowledge? Some might think that intuition can be a source of primary knowledge, but intuition only gives us ideas (often just hunches). Those ideas still need to be tested before they can be elevated into the realm of knowledge: tested either by logic (*a priori* means), or by observation or experiment (*a posteriori* means). Most of us have had ideas or hunches that have turned out to be false. To repeat: knowledge requires justification.

Another distinction—and one that cuts across the *a priori–a posteriori* distinction—is between deductive and inductive reasoning. Reasoning is either one or the other:

> "All knowledge is acquired and all proof is achieved through either deduction or induction."[8]

Deductive reasoning begins with a general statement or a definition and concludes with a specific statement. For example:

All men are mortal.
Socrates is a man.
Therefore Socrates is mortal.

From a *general* statement about *all* men we derive a statement about a *specific* man. In the next example, we begin with a definition and again derive a statement about a specific thing (the number 17):

By definition, a prime number is a number divisible only by itself and 1.
The number 17 is divisible only by itself and 1.
Therefore 17 is a prime number.

Deductive reasoning can lead to knowledge only if the argument is valid and the premises are true (that is, if the argument is *sound*).

Inductive reasoning adopts the reverse process: inferring a general statement from specific instances. An inductive argument looks like this:

In patient $P_1$ a daily dose of 250 mg of erythromycin cured laryngitis.
In patient $P_2$ a daily dose of 250 mg of erythromycin cured laryngitis.
In patient $P_3$ a daily dose of 250 mg of erythromycin cured laryngitis.
...
In patient $P_n$ a daily dose of 250 mg of erythromycin cured laryngitis.
Therefore a daily dose of 250 mg of erythromycin can cure laryngitis.

---

8. E. P. J. Corbett & R. J. Connors, *Classical Rhetoric for the Modern Student*, Oxford University Press, New York, 4th edn, 1999, p. 60.

In one sense, inductive reasoning doesn't *prove* anything. But it can justify us in believing that something is true. Inductive knowledge is like an asymptote. Repeated verification (or failed falsification) brings us ever closer to truth even though we never can reach it. There is always some chance that a falsifying instance will be found. (Patient $P_{801}$ might receive a daily dose of 250 mg of erythromycin and not be cured of laryngitis.) So inductive reasoning does not establish truths *beyond all doubt*, but it can still give us *knowledge* as the word is commonly used. If that were disallowed, then much of what we accept as scientific knowledge would not be *knowledge*.

To sum up: knowledge is either *a priori* or *a posteriori*. Further, any reasoning which gives us knowledge is either *deductive* or *inductive*.

## a priori knowledge

In an attempt to establish what couldn't be doubted, the French philosopher René Descartes (1596–1650) came up with the famous *cogito erg sum*: I think, therefore I am.[9] Using thought alone, Descartes proved that it is impossible to doubt one's own existence, since the very act of doubting presupposes a doubter. *If I doubt, I exist.* That is a true statement the knowledge of which is gained purely by thought alone. This is an example of *a priori* knowledge. No observation of the outside world was needed to derive it.

Another example: the famous Greek mathematician Euclid (who flourished around 300 BCE) proved that there is an infinite number of prime numbers—that is, numbers divisible only by themselves and by 1, such as 2, 3, 5, 7, 11, 13 and so on. And he did so simply by thinking and applying logic. No-one has ever produced a formula or algorithm that will generate the entire sequence of prime numbers, but, by using

---

9. R. Descartes, *Discourse on Method*, 1637. The original statement was in French: *Je pense donc je suis.*

thought and logic alone, Euclid proved that there must be an infinite number of them.[10]

Could the truth (or falsity) of the claim *All sentences that begin with a coordinating conjunction are not in accordance with fact, truth or reason* be gained by thought or logic alone along the lines of Descartes and Euclid? For *a priori* deduction to succeed, it must be based on either an axiom or a definition. (An axiom is a proposition considered to be self-evident, such as *Two points in two-dimensional space can always be joined by a straight line.*) An axiom or definition is needed to halt what would otherwise be an infinite regress of subsidiary justifications. One or the other is a necessary starting point in any deduction. Euclid makes use of both: much of his geometry—the geometry still taught in schools—is based on axioms, and his proof of the infinity of prime numbers is based on a definition (of *prime number*). What axiom or definition might conceivably compel us to accept that all sentences that begin with a coordinating conjunction are not in accordance with fact, truth or reason?

For a start, we are on safe grounds in ruling out axioms as the bedrock for grammatical knowledge. If the so-called rules of grammar were axiomatic—that is self-evident truths—there would be little or no disputation among linguists and grammarians (just as there is no disputation among mathematicians as to whether the angles in a two-dimensional triangle sum to 180°). But there is disputation. Moreover, if self-evident, the teaching of grammar could then be simplified by mirroring the teaching of mathematics: axiom–deduction–fact. The fact that English-language teaching doesn't should indicate that teachers—folk who presumably know a thing or two about grammar—don't consider grammatical rules to be self-evident. That leaves us with definition. And some prescriptivists have based an argument against beginning a sentence with a coordinating conjunction on what they believe

---

10. Euclid, *Elements*, book 9, proposition 20.

to be the definition of *coordinating conjunction*. Fleshed out in the form of a deduction, the argument appears to go like this:

[1] By definition, a coordinating conjunction is a part of speech that links clauses *within* a sentence.

[2] In a sentence that begins with a coordinating conjunction, the coordinating conjunction is not linking clauses *within* a sentence.

[3] To use something in a way other than how it is defined is incorrect (that is, not in accordance with fact, truth or reason).

[C] Therefore a sentence that starts with a coordinating conjunction is incorrect (that is, not in accordance with fact, truth or reason).

This deduction can be challenged in a number of ways. For a start, premise [1] might be what strong prescriptivists have in mind, but it is not what we find in contemporary dictionaries and grammar books. Consider this definition from the *Oxford English Dictionary*:

> "coordinating conjunction *noun* A conjunction placed between words, phrases, clauses, or sentences of equal rank, e.g. *and, but, or.*"

Note that by this definition coordinating conjunctions can be placed at the start of *sentences*.

Here is another definition from a well-respected source that challenges premise [1]:

> "A conjunction connects sentences, clauses or words within a clause." (*Chicago Manual of Style* 2003, p. 254)

Premise [3] is also suspect, as the following parallel deduction should make clear:

[1] By definition, a knife is an instrument that is used for cutting things.[11]

[2] In an action where a knife is being used to spread icing on a cake, the knife is not cutting anything.

[3] To use something in a way other than how it is defined is incorrect (that is, not in accordance with fact, truth or reason).

[C] Therefore to use a knife to smooth icing on a cake is incorrect (that is, not in accordance with fact, truth or reason).

Obviously it is not unfactual, false or unreasonable to use a knife as a spatula even if *knife* is defined in dictionaries as an instrument for cutting. Similarly, a *ruler* is defined as "a strip of wood, metal, or other material with a graduated straight edge, used in drawing lines or measuring" (to borrow again from *Macquarie Dictionary*). That doesn't mean I can't use a ruler for other purposes (or that if I did it would be incorrect or unreasonable). A ruler is holding open a window in my study right now. Our *primary use* of coordinating conjunctions might be to link clauses within a sentence (just as our primary use of knives is to cut things). But why should that prevent me from using a coordinating conjunction (or knife) for other purposes?

It might be retorted that by choosing fuzzy concepts like *knife* and *ruler* we have introduced equivocation into the argument. Perhaps the best that lexicographers can do with such concepts is recognise that instances of them share at most a Wittgensteinian family resemblance. Hence a dictionary definition can give no more than *sufficient* conditions for their use and not also the *necessary* conditions. Perhaps if we had chosen concepts that can be more precisely defined—such as *bachelor* meaning an unmarried man—it would be incorrect to use them in ways other than how they are defined. If Simon is married then it would be incorrect—it would be contrary to fact, truth or reason—to state that Simon is a bachelor. But for all its promise, this line of reasoning is of no help to the prescriptivist. At best the claim that a bachelor is *necessarily* an unmarried man enables us to draw the altogether unhelpful

---

11. "*knife*: a cutting instrument consisting essentially of a thin blade (usually of steel and with a sharp edge) attached to a handle". (*Macquarie Dictionary*)

conclusion that if someone is not unmarried they are not a bachelor. Likewise, if a coordinating conjunction *necessarily* links clauses within a sentence, then *no* word at the beginning of a sentence could, by definition, be a coordinating conjunction. It might have the same spelling as a coordinating conjunction, but it must be some other part of speech altogether. Just as *cut* can be both a verb and a noun, the word *so* would have to be both a coordinating conjunction and some other part of speech. (Indeed some linguists call a conjunction at the start of a sentence a *conjunct* rather than a coordinating conjunction.[12]) It follows that there would be no point having a grammatical law that prohibits coordinating conjunctions at the start of a sentence, for no coordinating conjunction can ever appear at the start of the sentence — by definition.

It is not obvious what other definitions could be summoned to help us deduce that a sentence that starts with a coordinating conjunction is incorrect. None, it seems, have been proposed. But it should be clear that the same line of reasoning we have used above can be used against the *a priori* deduction of any so-called grammatical law. Either there is no lack of truth, fact or reason in using language outside the boundaries apparently set by a fuzzy (that is, sufficient-but-not-necessary) definition of some grammatical feature — as there is no lack of truth, fact or reason in using a ruler to prop up a window rather than to rule or measure — or a precise definition (one that specifies necessary conditions) simply rules out some feature as being of the type prescriptivists rail against. Akin to our treatment of the word *so* at the start of a sentence, we could conclude that the word *to* at the end of a sentence is either no less incorrect than using a ruler as a prop or that *to* in that position is, by definition, not a preposition. Thus *Never end a sentence with a proposition* too cannot be grounded in *a priori* deduction. And so on.

---

12. See Peters 2007, p. 168. Talking of the words *and, but, or, nor* and *yet*, Peters writes "conjunctions such as these can appear at the start of a sentence, and are then strictly speaking conjuncts".

Taking the *a priori* deductive path to grammatical knowledge would make grammar akin to mathematics and philosophy. From a handful of axioms or definitions, we would be able to derive—by logic alone—the grammatical laws. The existence of such laws would imply that certain ways of writing and speaking are, not just incorrect, but *illogical*. To start a sentence with a conjunction would be a demonstrable *failure of logic*. This is a far stronger claim than any made by strong prescriptivists. None claim that grammatical knowledge can be obtained in the same way that mathematical or philosophical knowledge is obtained. Grammar books are not awash with syllogisms and proofs. Nor do we find logicians providing grammatical advice. Given this longstanding, well-recognised gulf between logic and grammar, I suggest we can safely conclude that we cannot obtain grammatical knowledge by means of *a priori* deduction.

Perhaps *a priori* induction might prove more useful. Here we gather, by thought and logic alone, numerous instances of grammatically incorrect sentences in support of the general claim that *all* like sentences are grammatically incorrect.

For example:

> Sentence $S_1$ has a coordinating conjunction at the start and it is incorrect.
> Sentence $S_2$ has a coordinating conjunction at the start and it is incorrect.
> Sentence $S_3$ has a coordinating conjunction at the start and it is incorrect.
> ...
> Sentence $S_n$ has a coordinating conjunction at the start and it is incorrect.
> Therefore sentences with a coordinating conjunction at the start are incorrect.

But how would we tell that a particular instance—say, $S_3$—is grammatically incorrect? If we are to stay within the realm of *a priori* reasoning, we must rely on an axiom, definition or induction. For a start, it should be obvious that *"So always check your weight after doing aerobics* is incorrect" is neither axiomatic (that is, self-evident) nor true by definition. (*An unmarried man is a bachelor* is true by definition because we define *bachelor* as "an unmarried man". Clearly we do not define *incorrect* as "So always check your weight after doing aerobics".) That leaves us with induction. But induction does not establish *particular* statements. At most it establishes *general* statements based on the accumulation of particular instances. Even if we could use induction to prove that a particular sentence is grammatically incorrect, we could simply ask the same question—*How do you know it is true?*—about each of the instances presented in support of the conclusion. We have, in other words, just pushed the argument back one level without having made any ground. It should now be clear that *a priori* induction can be of no help in the discovery of grammatical laws.

We therefore conclude that grammatical knowledge—if it exists—cannot be *a priori* knowledge.

## a posteriori knowledge

The only other way to gain primary knowledge is by observation or experiment. For example, we know that nitrogen is odourless because, by observing pure samples of it, we do not detect an odour. We know that water boils at 100 °C at sea level because many people have done the experiment and got the same result. And we know, also by experiment, that the higher the altitude, the lower the boiling point (so that in, say, Kathmandu, water boils at just 95.5 °C). Most of what we know comes to us by observation and experiment, that is, by *a posteriori* means. Every scientific discovery provides us with *a posteriori* knowledge: our knowledge of medicine, of chemistry, of astronomy. Our knowledge of history and of the social sciences also comes to us by *a posteriori* means. Something is observed—an ex-prime minister's letter, or the mean value in a sample of values—on the basis of which a conclusion is drawn.

*A posteriori* knowledge can gestate as a hypothesis before observation or experiment turns it into a theory. Observation or experiment can also precede a hypothesis and further experimentation confirms the original observation thereby turning it into a theory. Theory gives birth to knowledge only when it has been repeatedly tested (by many successful verifications or failed falsifications).

A *posteriori* knowledge is gained in three ways:
- direct observation (that is, by way of our senses)
- observation-based deduction
- induction.

Direct observation enables us to assign concrete attributes to things non-inferentially (where a concrete attribute is one that can be detected with our senses). Colour is a concrete attribute. A sense, namely sight, notices that the moon looks just like many other things to which the word *white* has been applied. I can thus look at the moon and see—in a single, unmediated observation—that the moon is white. If I make the same observation many times, I can justifiably claim to *know* that the moon *is* white. (Of course, there will be some qualifications, but such is the case with most things we rightly claim as knowledge. Grass *is* green except during a prolonged drought. The angles in a triangle sum to 180° except in hyperbolic space.) Likewise, I *know* that a pot of boiling water is hot because the sensation it creates when I go near it is just like the sensation I felt when I was near numerous other things to which the word *hot* has been applied.

Is *correctness* a concrete attribute like *whiteness* and *hotness* such that, once its meaning is learnt, the learner can directly observe its presence in a sentence? To return to our sample sentence: can I read *So always check your weight after doing aerobics* and observe, with my senses, the very same attribute that I have observed in many other things to which the word *incorrect* has been applied? Recall the sense of *correct* we are exploring at present:

"Correct *adj*.: In accordance with fact, truth, or reason: right."

Our question now becomes: can I directly sense factuality, truthfulness or rationality—or its absence—in *So always check your weight after doing aerobics*? The answer is clearly no. None of the human senses enable us to perceive correctness or its opposite whatever the context (senses such as sight, taste, smell, touch, hearing, balance, temperature, movement, pain, time and so on). If that wasn't the case, then a vast number of writers—those who pay no attention to the prohibition on starting sentences with conjunctions—are either wilful delinquents or carry a physiological deficit that prevents them from enjoying one of the innate human senses. (If the latter, then it's a deficit of epidemic proportions.) Neither possibility is plausible. Indeed, a moment's reflection should make it clear that correctness is not a concrete attribute. It is an *abstract* attribute. Rather than being directly observed, its presence needs to be inferred from the presence of other attributes.

So direct observation is not a path to grammatical knowledge. What now of observation-based inference? Here we infer the presence of an abstract attribute by observing certain other attributes and bringing them together in a suitable inference. (These other attributes can be concrete or abstract, but abstract attributes need ultimately to be based on concrete ones to avoid an infinite regress.) An example of an abstract attribute is *economy*. We do not look, smell, feel, hear or taste, say, a car to determine if it is economical. Rather we look for various attributes that, when combined in a logical way, enable us to infer the presence of economy. For instance, the attributes of fuel consumption and distance travelled can be combined to give a measure of economy. I can directly measure volume and directly measure distance, mathematically combine them to derive a value for consumption and then compare the result against a definition or standard of *economical*. Like all abstract attributes, economy is a *derived* attribute. We derive its presence from the presence of other attributes. Thus we assess the correctness of the statement *This particular car is economical* by observing some attributes (fuel consumed and distance travelled) and making a definition- or standards-based inference. Likewise, a forensic scientist examines the skeleton of a corpse and derives the abstract attribute of *maleness* from the attributes of bone shape and size.

Are there some attributes of *So always check your weight after doing aerobics* that, when taken together, prove that it is incorrect (just as there are some attributes of a typical V8 SUV that, when taken together, prove that *This V8 SUV is economical* is incorrect)? First we need to know what are *relevant* attributes, for some might have no bearing on what we are seeking. For instance, the diameter of the steering wheel and the capacity of the boot are not attributes that are relevant to determining the economy or otherwise of a car. And we know this because of the *meaning* of *economical*, namely, requiring below-average fuel consumption. Likewise we know that a person's salary is an irrelevant attribute in determining if they are educated because of the meaning of *educated*: characterised by or displaying qualities of culture and learning. So does the definition of *correctness* as in accordance with fact, truth or reason tell us what attributes of a sentence determine its correctness or otherwise? Obviously some attributes are irrelevant, such as the number of words and the number of clauses. But which attributes are relevant? Alas, if you consult any dictionary, you will find nothing in any of the meanings of *factual*, *true* or *reasonable* that specifically refers to the attributes of *sentences*. *Factual* and *true* can be ignored, since *So always check your weight after doing aerobics* — being an imperative rather than a declarative sentence — cannot be factual or not factual, true or not true. As for *reasonable*, the *Macquarie Dictionary* defines it as "endowed with reason ... agreeable to reason or sound judgement ... not exceeding the limit prescribed by reason ... moderate". Nothing in that definition helps us determine what attributes to look for in a sentence in order to declare it correct or incorrect. (And, of course, pointing out the coordinating conjunction at the start of the sentence in question as the determining attribute is to merely assume what we are trying to prove.)

It might be retorted that it is not common-or-garden fact, truth or reason at issue here, but *grammatical* fact, truth or reason. A sentence might be factually correct but grammatically incorrect (such as *And London is the capital of*

*England*). Conversely, a sentence might be factually incorrect but grammatically correct (such as *Adelaide is the capital of Australia*). Thus *So always check your weight after doing aerobics* might be grammatically incorrect even if it cannot be factually incorrect. But we do not find in dictionaries special definitions of *incorrect, fact, truth* or *reason* that specifically refer to grammar (or refer to concepts that can subsequently be decomposed into sub-concepts of explicit relevance to grammar). That's not a fault of dictionaries. If no such meanings are listed, it no doubt means that *Homo sapiens* have never found a need for them. But without such definitions, how do we know what attributes of a sentence to look for to prove grammatical incorrectness? In other words, our argument holds whether the issue is factual correctness or grammatical correctness.

Thus neither direct observation nor a deduction based on direct observation will help us assess whether *So always check your weight after doing aerobics* is incorrect. We are left then with *induction* as the only potential source of *a posteriori* knowledge. Induction is the bread-and-butter work of the experimental scientist. For example, an agronomist interested in the truth or otherwise of the general statement "DDT reduces thrip damage in brassica vegetables" will look at specific instances of the effect of DDT on brassica vegetables. They will examine numerous crops treated with DDT and numerous similar crops not treated with DDT, tallying the incidence of thrip damage in each. The tallies will then be compared to see if the difference between them is statistically significant (that is, not merely the result of chance). This is the essence of scientific experimentation: collect numerous observations under varying conditions and, through numerical or statistical analysis, look for differences that are significant, differences that generate, support or falsify some hypothesis. This process leads to knowledge: either through repeated verification (after which the hypothesis is considered true) or falsification (upon which the hypothesis is declared false).

Note that induction attempts to prove *general* statements. "DDT reduces thrip damage in brassica vegetables" is the result of an inductive study. It is a claim that whatever the variety of brassica vegetable, DDT will reduce thrip damage. On the other hand, "DDT reduced thrip damage in broccoli planted in plot A5" is the result of observation-based deduction, not induction. It is a claim about a specific treatment of DDT to one of many types of brassica vegetables. Now the statement *"So always check your weight after doing aerobics* is incorrect" is a specific statement. It is a statement about just one sentence. So induction is not relevant to establishing its truth. However, just as we could correctly deduce that DDT will reduce thrip damage in my cauliflower crop from the induction-proven general statement "DDT reduces thrip damage in brassica vegetables", perhaps we could deduce the truth of *"So always check your weight after doing aerobics* is incorrect" by deducing it as an instance of a general statement that has been derived inductively. In this case, the general statement would be akin to *A sentence is incorrect if it starts with a coordinating conjunction* and the deduction would be:

[1] A sentence is incorrect if it starts with a coordinating conjunction.

[2] The sentence *So always check your weight after doing aerobics* begins with a coordinating conjunction.

[C] Therefore *So always check your weight after doing aerobics* is incorrect.

Now for premise [1] to have been derived inductively, we would need to have observed many instances of sentences that begin with a coordinating conjunction and noted that each and every one was grammatically incorrect. Our argument would look like this:

Sentence $S_1$ has a coordinating conjunction at the start and it is incorrect.
Sentence $S_2$ has a coordinating conjunction at the start and it is incorrect.

Sentence $S_3$ has a coordinating conjunction at the start and it is incorrect.

...

Sentence $S_n$ has a coordinating conjunction at the start and it is incorrect.
Therefore sentences with a coordinating conjunction at the start are incorrect.

Consider again the example of inductive reasoning that might show that erythromycin cures laryngitis (see page 72). There are independent tests that can be relied on to establish whether a cure for laryngitis has in fact occurred (such as the disappearance of symptoms). If someone asked how you know that in patient $P_3$ a daily dose of 250 mg of erythromycin cured laryngitis, you could reply that *cure* means the disappearance of symptoms and invite the challenger to examine $P_3$ for symptoms of laryngitis. But what independent test do we have to show that a particular instance of a sentence with a coordinating conjunction at the start is incorrect? Can we reply that *incorrect* means not in accordance with truth, fact or reason and invite the challenger to examine the sentence and note its lack of truth, fact or reason? But what exactly would they be looking for? If incorrectness could be observed, the observation would have to be either direct (as in the case of observing the moon to be white) or the result of an observation-based deduction (as in the case of observing a particular car to be economical). There are no other types of *a posteriori* observation. But we have just shown that neither type of observation can be of help in determining that *So always check your weight after doing aerobics* is incorrect. There are no attributes of that sentence—whether observed directly or indirectly—that compel us to the conclusion that the sentence is incorrect. And this applies to whatever conjunction-leading sentence you might care to consider. But if we cannot prove that any specific instance is incorrect, then we certainly cannot make a general claim of incorrectness based on those specific instances. A parallel: if I am blind and cannot tell what colour any particular flower is in my garden, then I am not justified in claiming that all the flowers in my garden are red. Thus *a posteriori* induction too is not a path to grammatical knowledge.

We have concentrated on one claim in this and the previous section: "*So always check your weight after doing aerobics*" is incorrect, a claim made by the prescriptivist Deb Doyle. None of the arguments we have put forward to show that that claim cannot be knowledge are specific to it. Replace the embedded sentence with any other that shows a construction that prescriptivists frown upon, and the arguments against its claim to knowledge will still apply. For instance, "*Who were you speaking to?* is incorrect" would be claimed by someone who finds fault with prepositions placed at the end of sentences. Now we can't establish the truth of that claim by *a priori* means: it is neither axiomatic nor based on a definition (and if it was, the definition would either be fuzzy enough to be non-prohibitive or precise enough to make the railed-against practice logically impossible). Nor can we establish the truth of that claim by *a posteriori* means: there are no sentential attributes that enable us to observe incorrectness, either directly or inferentially. There are no other sources of knowledge bar the *a priori* and the *a posteriori*. Thus we conclude that grammatical knowledge is an oxymoron. There can be no such thing.

\*

Before proceeding, a word should be said about the language nativists, those such as Noam Chomsky and Steven Pinker who posit a language instinct that generates a universal grammar. If this is the case, it might seem as if the rules of grammar are innate and what is innate should be knowable. We will discuss universal grammar in some detail in the next chapter, but it should be clear that whatever grammar is universal (if any), it can't be the grammar that we are taught at school. What is innate is, by definition, what we are born with, but no-one is born with the knowledge of how to use hyphens in compound adjectives or how to avoid dangling participles. If all grammar were innate, we wouldn't need to be taught it. (Eating is innate and we don't need to be taught how to eat.) And if grammar were innate, we would all be excellent writers. That is clearly not the case. In the discussion that follows, the term *grammar* will be used to refer to those aspects of language use that can only be taught, not to some innate Chomskyan template from which all language can, supposedly, be generated.

## Grammatical truth and category mistakes

The so-called laws of grammar that are stamped into us at school do not, then, come from divine revelation, intuition, innate awareness, logic, observation or experimentation. They are the product of neither *a priori* reasoning nor *a posteriori* investigation. Thus they are not proper objects of knowledge. They are, in effect, undiscoverable. Thus it makes no sense to talk of grammatical *knowledge*, for it makes no sense to say that we know something if that something is undiscoverable. Thus it would not be rational to say that we *know* that a sentence with a coordinating conjunction at its head, or one containing a split infinitive, is incorrect.

To know that something is true is to be justified in believing it.[13] To be justified in believing something is to be able to cite strong reasons for believing it. I am not justified in believing that the world will end on 24 October because I have no strong reasons for believing that it will. No matters of logic compel me to believe it (thus there are no *a priori* reasons to believe), nor does any observation or experiment (thus there are no *a posteriori* reasons). I might believe it, but I have no grounds to claim that I *know* it. However, reasons could well present themselves to me that the world will in fact end on 24 October. (I might be made aware of the approach of a devastating meteor.) *Now* it makes sense to say that my belief may well be true. But nothing that might present itself to me — no logic, no observation, no experiment — could turn a mere belief that it is

---

13. Despite a few paradoxical edge cases, philosophers mostly agree that knowledge is justified true belief.

wrong to split infinitives into knowledge that it is wrong to split infinitives.

If *correct* means "in accordance with fact, truth, or reason", it is impossible—logically impossible—to call a piece of writing incorrect. Facts and truths are the objects of knowledge, and the only doors to knowledge—*a priori* and *a posteriori* investigation—are shut on matters grammatical. No pure reasoning, observation or experiment can decide whether any putative grammatical law is true or not. Thus it makes as much sense to ask "Is it true that *We expect to more than double our profit next year* is incorrect" as to ask "What is the colour of honesty?" or "What is the circumference of wisdom?" To do so is to invoke what the philosopher Gilbert Ryle called a *category mistake*: applying terms to things where they cannot logically apply:

"[A category mistake represents facts] as if they belonged to one logical type or category (or range of types or categories), when they actually belong to another."[14]

Correctness belongs to the category of things that we can know; grammar cannot be placed in that category; thus correctness does not apply to grammar.

## Truth and mood

We have just seen that the only sources of knowledge open to us—*a priori* means and *a posteriori* means—are not available to the so-called laws of grammar. The same point can be made by analysing the type of sentence used to express so-called grammatical knowledge.

Sentences can be classified in four ways, each way being called the *mood* of a sentence (Finegan et al. 1992, pp. 121–3):

- declarative

  The sentence makes a statement, as in *The water is cold*; *The Sun revolves around the Earth*; *The angles in a two-dimensional triangle sum to 180°*.

---

14. G. Ryle, *The Concept of Mind*, Hutchinson, London, 1949, p. 17.

- interrogative
  The sentence asks a question, as in *What time is it?*; *Have you brought the presents?*
- imperative
  The sentence commands someone to do something, as in *Keep off the grass*; *Adopt the surname of their fiancé upon marriage*; *Never split an infinitive.*
- exclamative
  The sentence makes an exclamation, that is, conveys emotive force, as in *She is so cool!*; *What a film!*

For a sentence to add to the body of knowledge, it must be capable of being true or false. Exclamative sentences obviously cannot be true or false. They are merely expressions of emotion. (They are not even statements about one's feelings, as in *In my opinion she is really cool*, which could be true or false.) Interrogatives likewise cannot be true or false. If I ask you *What is the time?* it makes no sense to retort that that is false (or even true). So interrogatives, like exclamatives, make no contribution to the body of knowledge. But declaratives obviously do. If you say *The water is cold*, I could test the water and confirm or falsify your observation. Likewise, I could repeat the experiments of Copernicus and a hundred other astronomers and prove that the sentence *The Sun revolves around the Earth* is false. Declaratives are the quintessential dressing of that body of statements we call knowledge.

Can an imperative sentence be added to the body of knowledge? Let's start by noting that there are two types of imperative: *categorical* and *conditional*. A categorical imperative is of the form *Do y*. Some examples: *Do not walk on the grass, Click OK, Never start a sentence with a coordinating conjunction.* A conditional imperative is of the form *If x, do y*. Some examples: *If you want to become a physicist, you must study mathematics at university* and *If you want to avoid defeat in this chess game, do not move your rook.*

Now whatever one's view of the value or importance of any particular imperative, it should be clear—as most philosophers have pointed out—that *categorical imperatives* cannot be true or false:

"commands cannot be true or false"[15]

"imperatives are unverifiable"[16]

Just as it makes no sense to ask whether an interrogative— *What's the time?*, for example—is true or false, it makes no sense to ask whether a categorical imperative is true or false. A rational response to *Do not walk on the grass* is *Why?* or *OK*, not *Is that true?* Likewise *Click OK*. Under what conceivable circumstances might it be rational to ask whether *Click OK* is true?.

Notice now that the so-called laws of grammar are commands, that is, they are expressed in the imperative mood. *Never start a sentence with a conjunction* is just another way of saying *Do not start a sentence with a conjunction*, the imperative nature of which is now obvious. Likewise *Always start a sentence with a capital letter*, which can also be expressed as *You must start a sentence with a capital letter*. Note too that they are expressed as *categorical* imperatives. They do not express any condition—an *if* clause—that might limit the application of the command. They are of the *do-regardless* variety of imperative.

We can now draw an important conclusion:

[1] Sentences in the imperative mood expressed categorically (that is, commands) cannot be true or false.

[2] The laws of grammar, as presented by a strong prescriptivist, are categorical imperatives (that is commands).

[C] Therefore the laws of grammar, as presented by a strong prescriptivist, cannot be true or false.

This is a sound syllogism. Not only is it logically valid; its premises are also true. Thus the so-called laws of grammar are

---

15. R. M. Hare, "Some Alleged Differences between Imperatives and Indicatives", *Mind*, vol. 76, no. 303, July 1967, p. 325.
16. E. L. Beardsley, "Imperative Sentences in Relation to Indicatives", *The Philosophical Review*, vol. 53, no. 2, March 1944, p. 179.

neither objects of knowledge nor capable of being true or false.

Only one avenue is left to the strong prescriptivist: accept that the laws of grammar cannot be true or false but argue that they can nonetheless be derived from statements that can be true or false. But this can easily be dismissed. If there is a categorical imperative among the statements that form the premises from which a law of grammar can be derived, then we can push the argument back a step and ask from which true sentences is this supporting imperative derived. Obviously this process cannot go on forever. But might it be possible to derive a categorical imperative from a set of true non-imperative sentences (that is, declaratives)? But now we are faced with the justly famous Hume's Guillotine:

> "In every system of morality, which I have hitherto met with, I have always remarked, that the author proceeds for some time in the ordinary ways of reasoning, and establishes the being of a God, or makes observations concerning human affairs; when all of a sudden I am surprised to find, that instead of the usual copulations of propositions, is, and is not, I meet with no proposition that is not connected with an ought, or an ought not. This change is imperceptible; but is however, of the last consequence. For as this ought, or ought not, expresses some new relation or affirmation, 'tis necessary that it should be observed and explained; and at the same time that a reason should be given; for what seems altogether inconceivable, how this new relation can be a deduction from others, which are entirely different from it. But as authors do not commonly use this precaution, I shall presume to recommend it to the readers; and am persuaded, that this small attention would subvert all the vulgar systems of morality, and let us see, that the distinction of vice and virtue is not founded merely on the relations of objects, nor is perceived by reason."[17]

---

17. D. Hume, *A Treatise of Human Nature*, John Noon, London, 1739, p. 335.

Hume's view—widely accepted by philosophers—is that it is impossible to derive an imperative statement (a statement that tells us that we should do such-and-such) solely from one or more declarative statements (statements that describe or purport to describe facts). As Oxford University philosopher Richard Hare puts it:

> "No imperative conclusion can be validly drawn from a set of premises which does not contain at least one imperative."[18]

Thus, being an imperative, no set of declarative statements can succeed in deducing *Never start a sentence with a conjunction*. By extension, no law of grammar can be derived solely from declarative statements.

Thus in insisting that the laws of grammar are categorical imperatives, strong prescriptivists are neither imparting knowledge nor giving us statements about language that could be true or false. There are no accredited routes to so-called grammatical knowledge, the so-called laws of grammar are not of a grammatical mood that enables them to be true or false, and it is logically impossible to derive such laws from other statements without invoking an infinite regress. Strong prescriptivism is looking increasingly untenable.

But what if we consider the so-called laws of grammar as *conditional* imperatives? Might not truth or falsity (and knowledge) be then allowed back into the discussion, even if only in support of weak prescriptivism?

A conditional imperative is of the form *If x, do (or don't do) y*. We gave two examples earlier: *If you want to become a physicist, you must study mathematics at university* and *If you want to avoid defeat in this chess game, do not move your rook*. Unlike categorical imperatives, conditional imperatives can be true or false. If someone could become a physicist without studying tertiary mathematics, the first conditional imperative would be false. Similarly, if moving one's rook in that particular game of chess

---

18. R. M. Hare, *The Language of Morals*, Oxford University Press, Oxford, 1952, p. 28.

led quickly to your opponent claiming checkmate, the conditional imperative would be true.

If we can't say *Never split an infinitive* and claim that it is a truth—as we've just shown—perhaps we can say *If x is the case, never split an infinitive*. But what might *x* be? This is a difficult question, for *x* must be some condition that will *compel* us to do whatever action is specified in the consequent clause. In other words, it must have considerable persuasive force. If it didn't, prescriptivism could not claim any of the intellectual credentials it now claims.

Perhaps prescriptivists have in mind for *x* something like *If you want to be understood*. Thus arguments of the following structure might be proposed:

[1] If you want to be understood, you must avoid *y*.

[2] Sentence *z* contains *y*.

[C] Therefore, in *z* you must avoid *y*.

An example might be where *y* is *a split infinitive* and *z* is *He failed to completely understand the issue* (where the split infinitive is "to completely understand"). But no competent English speaker could reasonably claim not to understand *He failed to completely understand the issue*. Similarly, no competent English speaker could fail to understand *Who were you talking to?* or *And James also won a scholarship* or *Queue here if you have 12 items or less*. And yet each breaks a supposed rule of grammar dear to many prescriptivists: *Never end a sentence with a preposition, Never start a sentence with a conjunction,* and *Modify plural nouns with* fewer *and singular nouns with* less.

Indeed, it doesn't matter how heterodox your language is, you can still be understood *providing that you explain to your audience what you mean by your usage*. For example, if you explain at the start of a document that the word *or* should be read as the inclusive Boolean *or* rather than as the idiomatic exclusive *or*, then you can realistically expect that your readers will understand what you have written.[19] Thus any claim that grammatical rules provide a necessary foundation for *understanding* is clearly false.

What else might prescriptivists have in mind for x, the antecedent in their conditional imperatives? Could it be:

- If you want to exhibit clarity of thought …
- If you want to mirror Standard English …
- If you don't want to be mistaken for someone from an unsophisticated background or with limited education …

But the so-called rules of grammar we have just discussed do not introduce an otherwise elusive clarity of thought. The sentences *He failed to completely understand the issue*, *Who were you talking to?*, *And James also won a scholarship* and *Queue here if you have 12 items or less* do not exhibit ambiguity or vagueness. Rather, their meaning should be quite clear to anyone with a basic understanding of English. As for Standard English, who has the authority to declare any variant of English "standard" (with the implication that all other English speakers should modify their English to match it)? Do Londoners have a right to tell Lancastrians that their English is non-standard and that they ought to modify it accordingly? Do the English have a right to tell the Americans that their spellings and punctuation are non-standard and thus they should pull themselves into line? (We'll revisit this issue in the next chapter.) Finally, revealing social class has never been considered the primary purpose of grammatical rules. The primary purpose of a car is transportation, but a secondary purpose might be to flaunt one's wealth. Likewise, there might be word- and accent-snobbery, but this springs from attitudes that have little to do with the primary purpose to which language is put (namely, to communicate). Wouldn't it be downright hollow-headed to reject someone's scientific discovery or poetic masterpiece simply because the language used in it was not that of an Oxford don or Park Lane hostess? Thus to insist that the

---

19. There is nothing new in this. Technical writers have for years included a *Documentation Conventions* page in user manuals and work instructions the purpose of which is to tell readers how to interpret various typographical cues: bold for literals, inverted commas around error messages, mono-spaced font for text to be entered, small capitals for key names, and so on.

primary purpose of following grammatical rules is to avoid appearing unsophisticated or uneducated is to relegate grammar to Mitfordesque etiquette. So not one of the suggested antecedents in *If x is the case, never split an infinitive* appears at all compelling.

Perhaps there are other antecedents that warrant consideration. But the onus is on the prescriptivist to provide a *compelling* condition for why any so-called rule of grammar demands our attention. On the face of it, a condition stronger or more relevant than *If you want to be understood* would seem to miss the whole point of inter-personal language: to enable speakers or correspondents to understand one another. What higher purpose could public language serve? And yet, as we've just seen, that purpose does not commit us to some of the rules held dear by prescriptivists.

*

This is a good moment to reflect on the distinction between the purpose of language and the purpose to which language is put. A chair has a purpose. It was designed to enable us to sit comfortably. A knife has a purpose. It was designed to enable us to cut things. And the purpose of a chair and knife strongly correlates with the purpose to which they are primarily put. In other words, the purpose of a chair is for sitting and that is also primarily what we use chairs for, despite the fact that we occasionally use them for other purposes.

Now consider a tree trunk I find washed up on a beach. Not being designed for anything in particular — or, more simply, not being designed — it has no intrinsic purpose. It just is. But I could put it to use. I could, for example, hew a seat out of it. So now, even though the trunk has no intrinsic purpose, there is a purpose to which I put it.

Like the tree trunk, language does not have a purpose. It was not designed by anyone or anything for any particular use. Like life itself, language is the accidental spawn of deterministic forces. Some products of these forces — of our blind, mechanistic universe — give the possessor no special advantage. They either vanish (such as body hair) or linger harmlessly (such as the human appendix). Others give the possessor advantage. Take sight, for example. A seemingly random clumping of neurons eventually gave rise to the faculty of sight. We use sight to great advantage. But sight has no purpose. It was not designed as a chair or knife are designed. It simply came about—like the tree trunk on the beach. And having come about, we put it to many uses. In other words, it has no purpose, but we put it to many purposes. Likewise language. A wonderful capacity for symbolic representation evolved, with no divine cultivation or teleological magnetism. But once we got it, we found advantageous purposes to which it could be put, most notably, thinking, speaking and writing. Indeed, the primary purpose to which we put language is to *communicate*—with ourselves and with others. We use language to collect and order our thoughts and to give permanence to our memories. And we use language to communicate with others: friends, employers, shopkeepers and so on. In chapter 4, we will use this simple fact—that the primary purpose to which we put language is to communicate—to hammer a few more nails into the coffin of prescriptivism.

\*

We should not be surprised that the so-called laws of language do not have the same epistemological credentials as the laws of science and mathematics. Language use is not like a mechanistic system, where everything and every action is governed by deterministic laws. It is not like the solar system, or the climate system, or the homeostatic system. Instead, it is the creation of our species (and possibly a handful of others). We might not have created the faculty of language, but having been blessed with it—no doubt through some benign genetic mutation—we have largely done with it what we pleased.

Nor should we be surprised by the number and variety of languages. If language is evolutionary, then we would expect to see speciation (just as there is speciation in the animal world). Languages might not be as varied as, say beetles—of which there are over 350,000 species—but there is still plenty of variation.[20] We have simple languages, we have complex; we have inflected languages, we have tonal; we have some in which articles precede nouns and others in which nouns precede articles. If the strong prescriptivists were correct, we would have to explain why there should be 6000 or so sets of absolute and inviolable laws of languages, one for each of the world's languages. (For surely languages other than English must have absolute and inviolable rules too. Aren't Roumanian and Chinese prescriptivists entitled to the same assumptions about their language as English-language prescriptivists?) Imagining 6000 or so sets of absolute and inviolable laws of language is about as difficult as imagining 200 or so different sets of the laws of physics, one for each of the world's countries. This is not just difficult; it contradicts what we understand a law of nature to be. Laws of nature apply universally, regardless of country. For example, the law of universal gravitation is the same in Poland as in Peru; Ohm's Law applies equally in Zambia and in Korea. So if the laws of language are laws of nature akin to the laws of physics, we should expect those laws to be the same in each and every country. Obviously they are not. This strongly suggests that the laws of language are not the product of a deterministic universe, but are created by the users of that language. They are, at most, natural conventions.

## Correctness and standards

> "The shape of our language is not rigid; in questions of usage we have no lawgiver whose word is final." (Strunk & White 2000, p. 39)

---

20. Sadly, half the world's 6000 or so languages are likely to become extinct over the next century. See *Dying Words: Endangered Languages and What They Have to Tell Us* by Nicholas Evans (John Wiley & Sons, Richmond, 2009).

Having disposed of the relevance to language of the first dictionary definition of *correct* noted at the start of this chapter—namely, *in accordance with fact, truth, or reason*—let's now consider the second definition:

> "In accordance with an acknowledged or accepted standard; proper."

Using an earlier example, we can imagine this definition being put to use in this way:

> [1] For a practice to be correct, it must be in accordance with an acknowledged or accepted standard.
>
> [2] If a practice is not in accordance with an acknowledged or accepted standard, it is incorrect.
>
> [3] The practice of beginning a sentence with a coordinating conjunction is not in accordance with an acknowledged or accepted standard.
>
> [4] *So always check your weight after aerobics* begins with a coordinating conjunction.
>
> [C] Therefore *So always check your weight after aerobics* is incorrect.

This argument is valid: the conclusion logically follows from the premises. However, we need to consider whether the argument is also sound. In other words, are the premises true. We could challenge premise [3], as we did earlier in this chapter, but a better place to start is with the first premise—the definition of *correct*—for if this premise is found wanting, *all* forms of this argument necessarily fail. The definition prompts three questions: what does it mean in practice, is it workable (by which we mean is it free of perplexing or contradictory implications) and does it advance the case for prescriptivism?

Let's begin unravelling the definition by considering the meaning of *standard*, the pivotal word in it:

> "standard *noun* anything taken by general consent as a basis of comparison; an approved model" (*Macquarie Dictionary*)

From this definition, it is possible to discern two types of standard: *explicit* and *implicit*. Explicit standards are invented, often formalised and sometimes legislated. There is an acknowledged or accepted body that creates or maintains them. For example, there is an explicit standard governing the game of chess and a body authorised to maintain it (authorised, perhaps, by the considered decisions of elected representatives from numerous chess-players' associations worldwide). This body is the World Chess Federation (also known as FIDE, which stands for *Fédération Internationale des Échecs*). Chess players agree to play by this standard—that is, according to the rules of chess—and will modify how they play the game should FIDE change the standard (that is, change the rules).

Explicit standards abound.[21] For example, there is an explicit standard governing each computer programming language. The C++ Standards Committee maintains the standard for programming in C++ and programmers typically follow this standard. (If they don't, their programs might not always run as expected.) Language use is sometimes governed by an explicit standard. Simplified Technical English (STE) is a stripped-down variant of English widely used in the aerospace and aviation industries. In STE, writers have at their disposal only a limited vocabulary and limited set of writing rules. For example, a writer can only use *about* if they mean "concerned with", not if they mean "around" or "approximately". Hence the wording of the sentence *The bolt should be about 5 cm long* would be a breach of the STE standard, a standard officially maintained by the Aerospace and Defence Industries Association of Europe. One final example of an explicit standard is a country's weights-and-measures system. Some countries maintain an imperial system, others a metric system, and a hybrid system is in place in the USA. A body usually oversees the system and might even have legislative authority to bring charges for breaches of the standard. In Australia that

---

21. The International Organization for Standardization alone has published over 19,500 standards. See www.iso.org/iso/home/about.htm.

body is the National Measurement Institute; in the US it is the National Institute of Standards and Technology.

The examples we have so far considered are examples of *formal* explicit standards. These are typically made public so that those who wish to follow them—chess players and programmers, for example—know what they must do if they want to be compliant. Explicit standards can also be *informal*. For example, a group of children might invent a game and agree among themselves that it will be played in such-and-such a way. They have created some rules and thereby created an explicit standard. But it is not a formal standard in the sense of it being promulgated beyond the group and widely adopted.

There are also *implicit* standards. These lie behind behaviours that, although not directed by an explicit standard, are done widely enough to be considered routine and even expected. We talk of it being *standard* practice to shake hands when meeting a new acquaintance, or waving when farewelling someone, or buying a present for one's partner on their birthday and so on. There are no authoritative bodies that direct us to do these things. If we feel compelled to do them, the compulsion is private. We might do it out of politeness, a desire to fit in or a wish not to be seen as a curmudgeon. But if we fail, say, to shake the hand of someone we are being introduced to, we are considered to be acting in a *non-standard* way. We have gone against a custom.

We can simplify our investigation of whether language use can be correct or incorrect by considering whether it is directed by an explicit standard or is the expression of an implicit standard. If language use follows an explicit standard, there must be some body that has authority over the standard, some body authorised to set or maintain usage (just as FIDE has the authority to set and maintain the rules that comprise the standard to be adopted by chess players). But there is no such body for the English language.[22] The so-called rules of English

---

[22]. We are excluding here controlled versions of English such as Simplified Technical English.

are not set and controlled by anyone. (Indeed any suggestion that they should be is unlikely to gain favour throughout the English-speaking world. Where might the authority derive to force an English-speaking country to give up its variant of English in favour of some other variant, or some artificial variant concocted by a committee?) If there is no body that has authority over the use of the English language then we must conclude that its use—in so far as it has more than just private currency—follows *implicit* standards, with one such standard for each variant of English (American English, Yorkshire English, Australian English and so on).

There have been occasions in the history of the English language where a certain usage has been set down, and in ways that some might think carry authority. At the time the printing press was introduced into England, there was great linguistic diversity in the country. Folk in one part of England could have immense trouble understanding folk from another part. William Caxton printed many books in English, including the very first (in 1471). In *Eneydos*, one of his last works, Caxton tells the story of some merchants sailing down the River Thames and stopping on the Kent side to buy food. One merchant asked for a serving of *eggys* and was told that his French could not be understood. The merchant was not French and became angry at not being understood. All was resolved when another merchant explained that his colleague wanted *eyren*, a word understood in that part of England.[23] Caxton had to make many decisions about word-use throughout the 30 years he published. Was he to print *eggs* as *egges* (common in the north of England) or as *eyren* (common in the south). Caxton admitted to preferring the language of "a clerke and a noble gentylman". But whatever his preference, the fact that some spellings made it into print at the expense of others would have given those spellings a special prestige and improved their chances of becoming widespread and

---

23. This story is taken from the British Library's website. See http://www.bl.uk/treasures/caxton/english.html. Viewed 13 March 2011.

eventually standard. But none of this suggests that Caxton had any special authority to decide what words would be kept alive. He made a decision—apparently based on his own preferences—and as a result some words (and no doubt some idioms and grammatical forms) were given prominence at the expense of others. But there is nothing special about the words, idioms and syntax he chose to make us think that they are correct and all others incorrect.

It is sometimes said that dictionaries are an authoritative source of information, at least with regards to spellings and meanings. Just as there is a book titled *The Official Rules of Chess*, a dictionary might be perceived as *The Official Rules of Spelling and Meaning*. Looked at this way, it might seem reasonable to call a spelling mistake incorrect if it flouts what is in *The Official Rules of Spelling and Meaning*, just as we might call a chess move incorrect if it flouts what is in *The Official Rules of Chess*. But there is a significant difference between the chess standard and a dictionary. FIDE, the publisher of *The Official Rules of Chess*, has been given authority to set the rules of chess. Lexicographers—the compilers of dictionaries—have not been granted authority to set spellings and meanings. It makes no sense to ask whether the rules of chess as set by FIDE are correct, for FIDE is allowed to set the rules as it pleases. But it does make sense to ask whether the spellings and meanings one finds in a dictionary are correct. And here *correct* is being used in the sense we first discussed in this chapter: in accordance with fact, truth or reason. For dictionaries are meant to record the way words are spelt and the meanings users of a language give to those words. Their entries can be checked to see if they really do reflect actual usage. In other words, dictionaries are not authoritative in their own right. A particular dictionary might be considered authoritative only in the sense that it has a well-deserved reputation for accuracy and comprehensiveness. Thus many believe that the *Oxford English Dictionary* is more authoritative than *Collins English Dictionary*. But the *Oxford English Dictionary* has no authority to set spellings and meanings. It just does a very good job at recording them.

## Can natural conventions be incorrect?

Given that language use is not directed by an explicit standard but follows (or sets) an implicit standard, the definition of *correct* we are here exploring can be recast as:

> In accordance with an acknowledged or accepted implicit standard; proper.

We noted earlier that standards arise "by general consent" (see page 98). Note now the definition of *convention*:

> "convention *noun* a rule, method, or practice established by general consent or usage" (*Macquarie Dictionary*)

Since an implicit standard is obviously a convention, we can recast our definition of *correct* in terms of conventions.

Before we do so, we should note that conventions are either *artificial* or *natural*. Artificial conventions are practices that result from following *explicit* standards. Explicit standards are concocted to serve a special purpose. They do not arise naturally. Thus the conventions that result from people following them are artificial. Moving a bishop diagonally in chess is conventional. It matches a general practice. Moreover, that general practice happens to follow what is set out in an explicit standard. There is nothing natural about chess. It did not arise out of any force of nature. It is a game *Homo sapiens* invented. In other words, it is an artificial construct. On the other hand, natural conventions are not concocted, but arise unaided. They are not the product of a standard. Rather it is the adoption of a practice that makes it a standard. A natural convention is the practice of waving to farewell someone. Another is a natural language, such as English.[24]

How is it that a natural language develops unaided? This is a difficult question. The origins of any language will always be a matter for speculation. No doubt *Homo sapiens* communicated in some form or other prior to the ascent of language, perhaps with shrugs, screams and pointing fingers.

---

24. One artificial language is Esperanto.

But at some point must have come the realisation that sounds—and later symbols—can be representative. They can *stand for* a thing, action or attribute. And then must have come another equally important realisation: a sound or symbol can conjure a *precise* meaning more so than can a shrug or a scream. Shrugs and screams might procure members of a tribe some of the benefits of collaboration, trust and trade. But these benefits would multiply many times over once members could precisely specify what they needed, what they had and what they could trade.

Gestures, sounds and symbols are, however, of little use unless there is shared understanding between sender and receiver. (What good is a sound I utter to you if you do not know what I intend by it?) Any such understanding is likely to arise only after much interpretative effort. We can imagine one member of a tribe deciding to use a particular sound to represent, say, a dog. Through repeated associations, another member comes to understand what that sound is representing (much as a linguist eventually comes to understand what the speakers of a newly discovered tribe are saying). The two members begin to use the sound when communicating with each other. Soon others work out—again through repeated association—what is going on and begin to imitate them. The usefulness of such vocalised representation becomes apparent to more and more of the tribe and suddenly there is an explosion of new representative sounds—that is, *words*—each giving new precision to intra-tribe communication. Some words will live healthy lives and be assimilated into the entire tribe, others will stay limited to sub-groups, and others will wither. Words that are adopted by the entire tribe become its language, and the way those words are used become its language conventions.

Unlike the conventions of, say, chess—which are governed by a body that has been granted authority to set the rules of the game—the conventions of a natural language are not set by anyone. Perhaps in the early days of a tribe, what was allowable language use might have been vested in the tribe's chief. But as tribes grow from small gatherings into large states, the limits of language use can no longer be controlled by any one person. No-one, in other words, owns or controls the language. It has turned into a self-governing, self-evolving, self-organising set of natural conventions. That is the state of all the world's dominant natural languages.

Even if we ignore our speculations about how language might arise, it should be clear from our earlier discussion of historical and contemporary language variation that rules of language have followed usage, not the other way round. Nowhere in history do we find a set of continually revised explicit standards, with each revision forcing on language users some new practices. Instead, standards come from usage, not usage from standards. That is what we would expect if language is a natural convention.

The idea that language is purely conventional and exists solely to meet the needs of its speakers is in no way new. In the late nineteenth century, the American linguist William Whitney wrote that:

> "[Language is] the work of those whose wants it subserves; it is in their sole keeping and control; it has been by them adapted to their circumstances and wants, and is still everywhere undergoing at their hands such adaptation." (Whitney 1867, p. 48)

Given that language use follows an implicit standard and whatever follows an implicit standard is a natural convention, we can recast our definition of *correct* to read:

> In accordance with an acknowledged or accepted natural convention; proper.

Natural conventions are not defined by any person or body, but are implied in the way things are *generally done*. Men generally shake hands in Australia when being introduced. It is common. That's what makes it conventional. It is not something that is explicitly stipulated. That's what makes it a *natural* convention. Likewise, we wave when we are farewelling someone. We are not compelled to, but we do it because this is how farewells are generally done (and we have no wish to be seen as unfriendly by not waving). So how are things generally done in the case of language use? The way things are generally done, commonly done, is usually called *common usage*. And common usage is usage that is acknowledged and accepted, otherwise it wouldn't be common. So our definition of *correct* can be rewritten as:

> In accordance with common usage; proper.

The first thing to ask is whether this definition itself matches common usage. If common usage is taken to mean *majority* usage, then the definition doesn't meet common usage. In other words, the definition of *correct* would itself be incorrect. We can see this by noting that the majority usage of a word is what matches its *primary* definition. In a dictionary, this is the definition listed first for the word, with less widely used meanings listed second, third and so on all the way down to obsolete and archaic. But the dictionary definition we are trying to make sense of now—"in accordance with an acknowledged or accepted standard", from which we derived our language-specific version: in accordance with majority usage—is not the first definition given in many dictionaries. In the *Macquarie Dictionary*, for example, the first definition given is the one explored first in this chapter: in accordance with fact, truth or reason. This must then be the definition that accords with majority usage, and all others must be incorrect. Thus the second definition, as we've interpreted it, rules itself out as a legitimate definition, as it doesn't match majority usage. It would also rule out as incorrect the secondary, tertiary and other definitions of *any* word. Since we do allow secondary and tertiary definitions of words—dictionaries are full of them—correctness cannot be limited to majority use.

Perhaps we should interpret *common usage* to mean usage that is *accepted by most users* of the language. In this case it is not majority *usage* but majority *acceptance* that would determine correctness. Thus our definition becomes:

> In accordance with what is accepted by the majority; proper.

Thus incorrect usage would be usage not accepted by the majority. But from where should we draw the majority? *All* speakers of the language, regardless of where they live? That would mean that usage widely accepted in one variant of English could be deemed incorrect. Take, for example, the word *youse*. It is widely used in Irish English as the second-person plural pronoun but frowned upon by many in other English-speaking countries. Should the majority of English speakers worldwide find the use of the word unacceptable, are we to tell the Irish that their use of it is incorrect? Likewise, should the majority of English speakers worldwide find *prepone* unacceptable, are we to tell English-speaking Indians that their widespread use of that word (as an antonym of *postpone*) is incorrect? I suspect not. Insisting that the Irish or the Indians change their language would be an undiplomatic incursion on sovereign culture justly riposted with "No-one owns the English language, so mind your own business".

Perhaps, then, we should limit majority acceptance to acceptance within the borders of countries. Thus if *youse* happened to be acceptable to the majority of Irish speakers, its use in Ireland would be correct; if unacceptable to the majority of Australian speakers, its use in Australia would be incorrect. So the usage of a word—or idiom, syntax, pronunciation or punctuation—could be correct in one country but incorrect in another. (In passing we should note that few prescriptivists would accept this degree of relativism.)

We can extend this application of *correct* to variants or subgroups even further. Recall that for a language to be correct it must be in accordance with an accepted implicit standard, an implicit standard is a natural convention and a convention is a practice established by general consent or usage (see page 103). Now the *Macquarie Dictionary* tells us that *general* means:

"relating to, affecting, including, or participated in by all members of a class or group ... common to many or most of a community."

The two parts of this definition appear to be in conflict. Is it *all* members? Or *many or most*? Other dictionaries take the latter position. For example, *The Shorter Oxford English Dictionary* defines *general* as "pertaining to all, or most, of the parts of a whole". This is more in keeping with common usage. To say "In general, Americans are better off than they were 10 years ago" does not rule out the possibility that some are not.

Thus the only consent or usage needed to make a convention correct is the consent or usage of *many or most* of a group. Moreover, a *group* is defined as "a number of persons or things ranged or considered together as being related in some way". And mere membership of a group is sufficient to indicate that you are related in some way to the others in the group. You have membership in common.

So our definition of *correct* becomes:

> In accordance with a practice accepted by many or most members of a group; proper.

The summary on page 109 shows how this definition logically follows from the dictionary definition of *correct* as "in accordance with an acknowledged or accepted standard".

Observe that our derived definition does not require a group to have a certain minimum number of members. This implies that there can be intra-country standards as well as country-wide standards. Thus if two states or counties within a country use language differently they each have their own standards, that is, their own general practices, and the fact that they do use language as they do indicates that those general practices must be accepted. (Why use language in ways you don't accept?) Thus a resident of Birmingham would be no less correct in saying *Lindy is stood at the window* than a resident of Oxford who prefers *Lindy is standing at the window* to express the same thing. And if a South Australian calls a pole a *stobie pole* and a Tasmanian calls it a *power pole*, both would be correct. And why stop at states and counties? Groups within states might have their own generally accepted practices. For example, it is generally accepted in the aeronautical engineering profession that *safety* can be used as a verb (as in *Now safety the valve lock*). Thus using *safety* as a verb cannot, on the definition we are considering, be incorrect. Many or most members of the

## Dissecting the meaning of correct

**correct** = in accordance with an acknowledged or accepted standard

*standard* = anything (for example, a practice) taken by general consent as a basis of comparison

(A criterion for comparing correct with incorrect obviously provides a basis of comparison.)

∴ **correct** = in accordance with an acknowledged or accepted practice undertaken by general consent

*general* = relating to many or most members of a group

*general consent* = accepted by many or most members of a group

*group* = a number of persons ranged or considered together as being related in some way

∴ **correct** = in accordance with a practice accepted by many or most members of a group

profession — being a group — accept that usage as standard usage. Finally, suppose that a majority of under-21s prefer *John and me went to the cinema* rather than the more common *John and I went to the cinema*? Within that group, the *John and me* version is generally accepted (otherwise it wouldn't be used). It is a standard that is followed, so it must be correct.

Recall that the dictionary definition of *group* — "a number of persons or things ranged or considered together as being related in some way" — does not require a group to have a certain minimum number of members (although it implies that there must be a least two). It follows that even two people could form a group. Let's imagine that two people — say a husband and wife — routinely avoid eating yellow vegetables (which they believe to be carcinogenic). This is a convention, a general practice, accepted by the group. Thus what these two do with respect to vegetable-eating is correct. And if one of them ate yellow vegetables, that would be a breach of an accepted standard and thus incorrect.

The point of this line of reasoning should now be clear. We would not call the eating of yellow vegetables *incorrect* even if both parties had accepted the yellow-vegetable-avoidance standard. Perhaps it was backsliding, a temporary revolt or mere forgetfulness. Whatever it was, common usage would not declare it incorrect. And yet this conclusion is forced on us by the definition of *correct* we are trying to make sense of. By parallel reasoning, we should not call *John and I went to the cinema* incorrect if it was written by a 20-year-old at a time when most 20-year-olds preferred *John and me went to the cinema*. Nor should we accuse a resident of Birmingham of writing incorrectly if they wrote *Lindy is standing at the window*.

These examples fit on a spectrum ranging from the smallest group possible (a husband and wife with their vegetable-eating standard) to the largest actual group (all English speakers in the case of the English-language standard). Routine behaviours, conventions and standards apply at all points along that spectrum, that is, regardless of group size. Now if it makes little sense to say that breaching an accepted standard in a group of two is incorrect, how can we say that breaching a standard accepted by a group of any size is incorrect? To draw the line at any particular group size would be arbitrary and thus unhelpful. And it's no use deferring to the standards of any *particular* group. Doing so would go well beyond the dictionary definition of *correct*. It also invites the question of how could we determine—without introducing circularity into the argument—that the standards of this chosen group were correct. (Group *x*'s standards are correct because, according to the definition of *correct*, group *x*'s standards are correct.) It appears, then, that the dictionary definition of *correct* we are considering is looking increasingly muddled.

This suspicion is reinforced by the fact that there are, and have been, many widely accepted natural conventions the breach of which could not conceivably be incorrect. Before the 1960s, there was a strong natural convention in Australia—and in much of the Western world—that saw women adopt their fiancé's surname after marriage. That was the convention at the time: widely accepted, indeed expected. But those women who refused to adopt their fiancé's surname didn't do something that might conceivably be considered *incorrect*. They simply did something that, at the time, was unconventional (and even laudable). Similarly, there was once a strong convention that a woman didn't engage in paid employment but maintained a household for her husband and family. Was it *incorrect* for women to work outside the home? (And were those employers who offered them a job equally complicit?) Likewise, it was not that long ago that a widely accepted natural convention saw most people in Western countries attend church every week. Were the atheists who refused to do so doing something incorrect? Similarly, it was once conventional for men to wear black-tie at dinner. Were those who decided to don lounge suits instead doing something incorrect? Hardly. Hence any definition that ties correctness to following a natural convention—and, by extension, incorrectness to the flouting of a natural convention—appears far too general. It strips the word of its strongly pejorative connotation. To call behaviour *incorrect* implies that it should be discouraged. But why should a woman be discouraged from keeping her own surname after marriage just because the majority happen to change their name? Why should I be discouraged from wearing a lounge suit to dinner just because the majority of my contemporaries prefer black-tie?

Attempts to improve language pose another problem for anyone who wants to tie correctness to majority acceptance (however *majority* is defined). Suppose I decide to indicate grammatical possession by adding *'s* to all singular nouns irrespective of spelling, as in *The species's distribution was unexpected*. I might break a strong natural convention, but I'm also avoiding an ambiguity present in common usage. For if I write *The species' distribution was unexpected*, as one commonly sees it, it is not clear whether I'm talking about one species or many species. But it would be somewhat odd to call my unconventional practice incorrect if it avoids ambiguity and thereby improves clarity. Must every improvement necessarily be incorrect? Was the placement of spaces between words at first incorrect, only to become correct when the majority accepted the immense value of the practice? Must all punctuation have been incorrect when it was first introduced? Given the strong pejorative connotation of *incorrect*—that the behaviour to which it is applied should be discouraged—it is difficult to accept that a practice could be incorrect if it is beneficial. Why discourage what is obviously good? A parallel: should doctors have refused to allow anaesthetics into the operating theatre—despite the obvious benefits—on the grounds that the current convention at the time was to operate without using anaesthetics? So a definition that labels all unconventional practices incorrect clearly doesn't match common usage.

Tying correctness to following a natural convention also strips the word of its connotation of universality. A practice only becomes a convention when a critical mass of people adopts it. So at time $t_1$ a practice might not be conventional and at time $t_2$ it has become conventional. Perhaps little more than a day separates the two, the day on which one extra person adopts the practice and the balance dips to the other side. Thus a person who had adopted the practice before $t_2$ could be acting incorrectly one day but correctly the next. This sort of relativism swims against a strong connotation of *correct* and *incorrect*: the connotation of universality. An act might be *unlawful* one day but *lawful* the next—laws being at the discretion of parliaments—but to claim that an act can be *incorrect* one day and *correct* the next (or vice versa) strikes a dissonant chord. This no doubt explains why tying correctness to conventionality does not encapsulate the *primary* meaning of *correct*.[25]

It might be retorted that we have misunderstood the meaning of *incorrect*. The *Oxford English Dictionary* defines it as "not in conformity with a recognised standard" and it is possible to interpret this in two ways:

- not in conformity with a recognised standard *that exists*
- not in conformity with any recognised standard, *existing or otherwise*.

Our argument that the dictionary definition of *correct* implies that a practice can be incorrect one day but correct the next assumes the second interpretation, namely, that a practice can be incorrect in the absence of a standard. And this interpretation does lead to some odd conclusions. For example, it implies that collecting orange peel is incorrect. It is not in accordance with an acknowledged or accepted standard precisely because there is no standard governing the collection of fruit peel. So am I to be discouraged from collecting orange peel if that is my inclination? To argue so would be odd. Indeed, this interpretation of *incorrect* implies that *every* novel action must be incorrect. For a novel action, by definition, cannot accord with an acknowledged or accepted standard (whether explicit or implicit). Thus all novel

---

25. The universality connotation of *incorrect* could well be entwined with its pejorative connotation. To call an action incorrect is to suggest that it shouldn't be done. This invites a comparison with morality, and moral rules are widely perceived as applying universally: if I shouldn't do something, then no-one else should either.

action must be discouraged. Change must cease and creativity suppressed, whatever the field. Thus every change we have seen to the English language over its long history—the introduction of spaces between words, single full stops at the end of sentences, possessive apostrophes and so on—would have initially been incorrect and should have been discouraged.

The only way to avoid these odd conclusions is to reinterpret the dictionary definition of *incorrect* to make it apply only when standards already exist (as per the first definition above). But this interpretation has its own problems. We would now have to allow *three* classes of judgement about an action: it is *correct* (that is, it follows a standard), *incorrect* (it flouts a standard) or *neither correct nor incorrect* (it is not covered by a standard). Thus to call an action *not correct* is not necessarily to disapprove of it. It might or might not be covered by a standard. In that case we should be able to say *Collecting orange peel is not correct* confident that our audience will note the ambiguity and not immediately assume that collecting orange peel is to be discouraged. But this is clearly *not* how it would be interpreted. To call something *not correct* is to strongly imply that it should not be done. There is no pejoratively neutral meaning of *not correct*. Moreover, this interpretation is at odds with the universality connotation of *incorrect*. A practice could be not correct one day and correct the next (or vice versa). It could even be not correct one day and incorrect the next (or vice versa). Thus our interpretation of the dictionary definition of *incorrect* as not in conformity with an *existing* standard does not match common usage. It is at odds with our general understanding of the concept of incorrectness (just as a definition of *animal* that implied that some plants were animals would be at odds with our general understanding of the concept of animal). Thus it can be discarded.

We are left with an interpretation of *incorrect*—not in conformity with a recognised standard, existing or otherwise—that invites the criticisms we made of it earlier: it declares many breaches of natural conventions incorrect when they clearly are not, it thwarts the universality connotation of the word and declares any novel action to be incorrect and thus to be discouraged. Obviously this interpretation needs to be discarded too. But that exhausts all ways of interpreting *incorrect*, for either a standard exists or it doesn't. There are no other possibilities.

This forces us to reject the second dictionary definition of *correct*, namely, in accordance with an acknowledged or accepted standard. For clearly it is not a cohesive or even informative definition. Its sieve is too tightly woven to capture only what is incorrect. That, together with the illogical implications that follow from it, suggest that its use must be fuzzy, inconsistent and poorly thought-out. It may be in dictionaries more as a sop to the prescriptivist lurking in many of us than as the wording of a clear and distinct idea.

We have hitherto ignored the word that dictionaries tack on to the end of their definitions of *correct*, namely, *proper*. What does it mean for something to be proper? Sadly the dictionaries are of little help here. The *Macquarie Dictionary* lists 15 definitions of *proper*, and yet its definition of *correct* as "proper" does not indicate which meaning of *proper* it is referring to. The situation is similar with the *The Shorter Oxford English Dictionary*. If we are not told which meaning of *proper* is relevant to language use, how can these dictionary definitions be authoritative?

Moreover, in the absence of such guidance, both dictionaries can be criticised for offering repetitive or circular definitions. For example, as a definition of *proper* the *Macquarie Dictionary* offers "conforming to established standards". This could make the second dictionary definition of *correct* equivalent to "In accordance with an acknowledged or accepted standard; conforming to established standards", which unhelpfully states the one thing twice. *The Shorter Oxford English Dictionary* defines *correct* as "proper" and then offers, as one definition of *proper* "accurate, exact, correct". This is a circular definition, defining correctness in terms of correctness. Again, this is not especially helpful. If lexicographers cannot tell us precisely how correct language is proper (and, presumably, incorrect language is improper), then our assumption must be that the connection between the two concepts is at best nebulous. Thus no-one in the debate over whether language use can be correct or incorrect is likely to advance their cause by relying on the meaning of *proper*.

\*

There is another way we can show that language use cannot be correct or incorrect. Consider any usage that a prescriptivist might call incorrect. For example, suppose *nite* is declared to be an incorrect spelling of *night*. What, then, are we make of this passage from a Charles Dickens novel:

> "God forbid as I, that ha' known, and had'n experience o' these men aw my life—I, that ha' ett'n an' droonken wi' 'em, an' seet'n wi' 'em, and toil'n wi' 'em, and oov'n 'em, should fail fur to stan by 'em wi' the truth, let 'em ha' doon to me what they may!"[26]

It would be odd to accuse Dickens of *incorrect* spelling in this passage. The spellings might not match those adopted elsewhere in the novel (or taught in the schools of nineteenth-century England). But that is what Dickens intended. Now if it was not *incorrect* of Dickens to intentionally introduce so many non-standard spellings, why is my equally intentional non-standard spelling of *night* as *nite* incorrect? One might retort that Dickens was trying to achieve some special effect. Well, yes; but so might I. I might, for example, be actively involved in a campaign to reform English spellings, inspired perhaps by Harry Lindgren or George Bernard Shaw. Surely correctness cannot apply to some writers but not others. If it could, we would have to strip the word of it universality connotation. We would also have to address the thorny issue of why some authors are allowed artistic licence and others are not.

But what if I intended to spell *night* according to its conventional spelling and spelt it as *nite* instead? Doesn't this

---

26. C. Dickens, *Hard Times*, Chapman & Hall, London, 1911, p. 164.

change matters? Can't writing *nite* while intending to be conventional be called incorrect? The short answer is: no. Suppose I didn't intend to over-cook the asparagus, but I did. Was my cooking *incorrect*? No. That would be another example of a category mistake. So why must my *nite* be incorrect if I intended to write *night*? I wanted to cook the asparagus lightly/ spell *night* as it is commonly spelt, but I failed. If it's not incorrect in the first case, why is it incorrect in the second? At most I have made a *mistake*, and to be mistaken is not necessarily to be incorrect. *Mistaken* carries none of the pejorative energy of *incorrect*. To say *I mistook Peter for Paul* is not to imply that I behaved incorrectly. Another example: suppose I intend to wear black-tie to a dinner of The Oxford Society (where black-tie is the longstanding unwritten conventional dress code). Suppose further that I wrongly think that black-tie just means wearing a tie that is uniformly black. I arrive at the dinner wearing jeans and a black tie. It would, I suggest, be unduly stretching the meaning of words to call my dress that evening *incorrect*. I have simply made a mistake.

If unintentional language mistakes could be labelled incorrect, we would have to allow that a particular instance of language use could be both correct and incorrect. To see this, suppose that Mary and Paul both write "Mat the cat sat on the". If Mary knew that the sentence didn't follow conventional English syntax and Paul thought it did, we would have to say, of the very same sentence, that it is both incorrect (Paul's version) and not incorrect (Mary's version). That is an impossible position to maintain. But if we allow *intention* into the argument as a mitigating condition—as we must if we are not to criticise Dickens for his spelling—then that is the position we would be forced to adopt. Since that position is clearly untenable—it involves a logical contradiction—so too is the claim that unintentional language mistakes are incorrect.

To sum up: if I *intentionally* use unconventional English, what I have done is not incorrect. (That is the Dickens defence.) If I *unintentionally* use unconventional English, the most that can be said is that I have made a mistake. Whatever error there might be is with me, not with what I have written. I intended to write conventionally but failed to do so. And there lies another difference between prescriptivists and descriptivists: a prescriptivist would criticise what I have written; a descriptivist would criticise me.

Earlier we noted that *incorrect* and *wrong* are sometimes strong synonyms. There is one meaning of the word *wrong* that makes it appropriate to apply to a mistake, so perhaps mistakes can be incorrect. The meaning in question is this:

> "not in accordance with needs or expectations: *to take the wrong road; the wrong way to hold a golf club*". (*Macquarie Dictionary*)

This is not the first meaning given, but the fifth, and it carries none of the pejorative connotation of *incorrect*. Indeed the two words overlap in meaning only in a few contexts. In other words, they are not strong synonyms. I might execute a correct move in chess—one that doesn't break any rule of the game—but it turns out to be a wrong move in that it doesn't give me the advantage I hoped it would. Similarly, becoming a compositor might have been a wrong career move—as the profession is now moribund—but there was nothing incorrect in my decision, some years back when the profession was flourishing, to do so. Thus in this sense of *wrong*, it seems quite innocuous to call my *nite* spelling wrong. It didn't meet my needs, just as that chess move or career choice didn't. My need, and what I expected myself to do, was to use your language. But I made a mistake. I chose a wrong spelling. Or better still, I wrongly chose a spelling I didn't want. But what I did was not incorrect.

*

The definition of *correct* we have been considering in the second half of this chapter is clearly at odds with prescriptivism. It requires us to accept that two inconsistent uses can both be correct—and no prescriptivist is likely to accept that. Rather, a prescriptivist is certain to declare that *John and me went to the cinema* is incorrect despite its general use among some class or group of people. Indeed, a true prescriptivist would not even countenance the definition of *correct* we have been considering. For them, some language use is correct *come what may*. Numbers are not important. It wouldn't matter to them if 99% of English users omitted the apostrophe in *two weeks' notice*. It would still be incorrect. But the definition of *correct* we have been considering is all about numbers. Once a certain critical mass of people start using language in a particular way, an accepted standard has been created. And that is all that is necessary for that use to be declared correct or incorrect. In other words, there is no *inherent* quality or attribute that makes a particular use correct. It is just a matter of the number of people who have adopted it.

\*

We have considered the only definitions of the adjective *correct* provided in two respected dictionaries: *Oxford English Dictionary* and *Macquarie Dictionary*. The first definition ties correctness to fact, truth or reason. This definition would, if applied to the so-called laws of language, make them subject to the same rigorous challenges that can be put to the laws of mathematics and science: verification or falsification. For them to be knowledge, their truth must be ascertainable. We found, however, that the truth of grammatical laws cannot be ascertained. There are simply no accredited epistemological paths open to us to verify or falsify them. Hence they must be beyond the scope of that particular definition of *correct*. (This should also be clear from the non-declarative mood in which they are expressed, for only sentences expressed in the declarative mood can be true or false.) The second definition ties correctness to being in accordance with some acknowledged or accepted standard. In the case of language, this definition is equivalent to being in accordance with a natural convention. But breaches of natural conventions are not typically considered incorrect. At most they are unconventional or mere mistakes. Moreover, the definition carries implications that are clearly untenable: either novel behaviour is incorrect or some behaviour is not correct but nonetheless warrants no disapprobation. The definition, then, is clearly at odds with how the concept of correctness is generally understood. It is thus too deformed or too fragile to be of any use in the debate about whether language use can be correct or incorrect.

To sum up: neither dictionary definition of *correct* provides justification for calling language use correct or incorrect. Prescriptivism is tenable only if language use can be correct or incorrect. Therefore prescriptivism is untenable.

## Beyond dictionaries

We began this chapter by examining dictionary definitions of *correct*. Prescriptivists won't complain about this approach, as they are forever chiding others for using words in ways not sanctioned by dictionaries (or at least their favourite dictionary). But can dictionaries always be relied on to prove points and solve arguments? Surely the answer must be no, as some dictionary definitions are certainly dubious. This is usually not the fault of lexicographers. With a few notable exceptions in the field of dictionary publishing[27], lexicographers record *actual* usage, and actual usage is often coloured by people's *beliefs*. And dubious beliefs can lead to dubious definitions.

For example, the *Oxford English Dictionary* defines *mind* as "the seat of consciousness". If the Oxford lexicographers have done their work, then that definition must have some currency, some common usage. But does that mean that there really is a mind, some thing seemingly separate from the non-conscious parts of a human? Science has begun to doubt this. That same dictionary defines *God* as "the one object of supreme adoration; the Creator and Ruler of the Universe" and no doubt many people use the word in that sense. But that does not mean that there is such a God. The *Macquarie Dictionary* defines *wrong* as *not in accordance with a code,*

---

27. One notable exception is *The American Heritage Dictionary of the English Language*, well known for combining prescription with description. In other words, it tells readers not just how words are used, but how they should be used. Preferred usage is decided by a panel, some members of which have no background in linguistics or lexicography.

*convention or set of rules*. In many societies there is a strong convention against lying and another against harming innocent people. Imagine that it is Dusseldorf in 1942. A Gestapo officer knocks on your door and asks if you are harbouring Jews in your attic. If you are, there is no way you can answer without being both wrong and not wrong. Since that is not possible, it follows that the *Macquarie Dictionary* has not given us a workable definition of *wrong*.

Dictionaries can offer a good starting place for discussion and argument, but they are not necessarily the best stopping place. If we could rely on dictionary definitions for our knowledge, we wouldn't need philosophers, and much argumentation would be futile. Lexicography is meant to be a descriptive science. Lexicographers investigate how people use words and then record their findings in dictionaries. They pass no judgement on whether a common meaning has philosophical merit.

But it should be patently clear to anyone who pays attention to arguments in journals and newspapers that words are often slippery creatures. Many carry multiple denotations, connotation can sometimes crowd out denotation, and sometimes the concepts are simply too nebulous to be the pivot in any useful argument. *Race, intelligence* and *justice* are just a few grains on a beach of words that common usage—as recorded in dictionaries—is unlikely to define with any precision useful in settling disputation. So even if there are people who use *correct* to mean in accordance with an acknowledged or accepted standard, it doesn't necessarily follow that there is correctness in that sense. One needs also to think about the concept, unravel its complexities and assess whether those users really understand what they are saying. That is what we have done in this chapter. And what we've found is that this definition of *correct* is hopelessly muddled.

The fact that dictionaries are not infallible guides to clear thinking does not mean that our approach in this chapter— dissecting dictionary definitions—is misguided. If we are to avoid straw-men debates, we must use concepts that have currency. Dictionaries attempt to pin down those concepts and their meanings. That is their primary purpose. Thus they make the best starting point in any debate. To encounter generally accepted concepts that are poorly thought out is part and parcel of human enquiry. The history of thinking — whatever the discipline — is littered with concepts thought valuable but subsequently found wanting. Think of *aether*, *phlogiston* and *forms* (the latter of the Platonic variety). Dictionaries will try to make sense of such concepts. And they may well fail. But analysis must start somewhere. And if it can't start with common meanings, as sketched out in dictionaries, where can it start? It would be pointless starting with the interpretations of eccentrics whose private definitions are alien to all but an insignificant few. Thus the invaluable role of dictionaries — warts and all — in attempts to clarify our ideas and resolve our disputations.

# 3: Prescriptivists fight back

"Tongues, like governments, have a natural tendency to degenerate."[1]

"Coin brassy words at will, debase the coinage;
We are in an if-you-cannot-lick-them-join age,
A slovenliness provides its own excuse age,
Where usage overnight condones misusage.
Farewell, farewell to my beloved language,
Once English, now a vile orangutanguage"[2]

To many lovers of language, the arguments of the previous chapter are likely to be unsatisfying. The cold, unemotional tools of philosophical dissection will be seen as blind to all that is valuable in language. Surely language is one of our most important assets, on par with opposable thumbs and a large skull. Without language, life would resemble a Hobbesian dystopia, devoid of the cultural, technical and scientific riches we now enjoy and depend upon. None of these riches would be ours without the transmissibility and permanence that language affords our discoveries. Language is thus fundamental to our wellbeing. With it we have been able to accumulate discoveries and turn them into knowledge that benefits us all. We live happier lives than Neanderthals because we have uncovered the laws of mechanics that enable us to live in solid structures protected from the harsh elements. We live longer and less painful lives because we have discovered how pathogens infect us and how such infections can be combated. Without the

---

1. S. Johnson, *A Dictionary of the English Language*, 1755, preface, para. 91.
2. O. Nash, "Laments For a Dying Language", *The New Yorker*, April 23, 1960, p. 43.

accumulation of discoveries passed from one to another by language, we would still be living in caves, disease-ravaged and dead by thirty. So how can it be that what enables us to conceptualise and then uncover fundamental laws of nature is not itself governed by fundamental laws? Surely logic and philosophy have missed something in declaring that the rules of language use are outside the scope of knowledge, being neither true nor false but mere human-created conventions.

A parallel from moral philosophy might add fuel to the prescriptivists' passion for inviolable, stone-set language. Moral precepts, like grammatical rules, are also imperatives. *Never lie. Do not steal from others. Harm no-one. Help those in greater need than oneself. Never commit murder.* These are considered by most people to be moral obligations. But they are all expressed as commands, that is, in the imperative mood. By the reasoning of the previous chapter, they can be neither true nor false. Nor can they be derived from statements that can be true or false. They are outside the realm of knowledge. Thus we have no more reason to be punctilious in matters of morals than we have in matters of language. And yet a life not governed my morality would indeed be a Hobbesian dystopia: it would be "solitary, poor, nasty, brutish and short".[3] Morality lies at the heart of civilised life. It is what gives law its justification. It's what makes it possible to get on with life without continually looking over a shoulder and walking over a cliff. Surely, then, any philosophical analysis that concludes that the laws of morality are an illusion must harbour a flaw; so too must any analysis that concludes that the laws of grammar are an illusion.

However, the utility of a system—in other words, its usefulness—is quite independent of the truth or otherwise of the claims made within it. *No Standing* is a statement that is neither true nor false, but its presence on a roadside sign might be especially useful in reducing accidents. *Do not lie* is a statement that is neither true nor false, but its widespread

---

3. T. Hobbes, *The Leviathan*, 1651, chapter 13, paragraph 9.

adoption helps cement the trust we need to build a cooperative and harmonious society. *Place a hyphen in a two-word compound adjective* is also neither true nor false, but it is a useful practice to adopt if we want to avoid writing ambiguously. Usefulness and truth are distinct and unrelated concepts. Neither implies the other. The true statement *I have five toes on my left foot* has no useful, no practical application. *Do not lie* has useful, practical application even though it is neither true nor false. So we cannot argue that since language cannot be true or false, it must be useless or unimportant. (Wouldn't it be contradictory to use language to prove the uselessness or unimportance of language? Only with the hubris of post-modernism would one attempt such a thing.)

In this chapter we consider some further arguments that prescriptivists have put forward for wanting to grant certain language uses privilege over others. None of the arguments assume that laws, or rules, of language use are true or false, but most do assume that language use can be correct or incorrect. Fortunately we can counter these arguments without needing to discern (or concoct) a definition of *correct* that does a better job than the dictionary definitions discussed in the previous chapter.

## Some usage is unnecessary

Many prescriptivists contend that unnecessary usage is incorrect usage. A contemporary example: prescriptivists such as Lynne Truss rail against the apostrophe in *CD's for sale* because it is unnecessary.[4] It *is* unnecessary, assuming—as seems to be the case—that by *unnecessary* is meant "adding nothing to the meaning". But so much in accepted English is unnecessary in that sense. For example, the colon one usually sees at the end of a stem sentence introducing a set-off list could

---

4. The apostrophe used to indicate a plural is often called, somewhat snidely, the *greengrocer's apostrophe*. Of course, in *the CD's capacity is 600 Mb*, the apostrophe would be quite acceptable, for possession, not plurality, is intended.

be discarded without any loss of meaning. So too could the comma before quoted speech and the serial comma much loved of Americans (and of Oxford University Press: thus its other name, the *Oxford comma*). The second comma in *The flag is red, white, and blue* is a serial comma, and it is quite unnecessary. It adds nothing to the meaning of the sentence. By the reasoning of prescriptivists, the use of these punctuation practices would be incorrect (at least in the contexts mentioned).[5]

Pedants decry the practice of omitting the apostrophe of elision (a practice becoming increasingly common in messages sent from smartphones and tablets). An example: *Dont forget to pick up the mail*. But how necessary is the apostrophe of elision? *Dont forget to pick up the mail* is not ambiguous, vague or meaningless. No competent English speaker will fail to understand it, so what purpose does the apostrophe serve? It does indicate something: that at least one letter has been omitted. But is that information useful? Is it important? Does it contribute to the communicative potency of the word?

Note too that the apostrophe of elision is used inconsistently. We don't write *D'r* to indicate that letters have been omitted from *doctor*. So why must we write *don't* to indicate that a letter has been dropped from *do not*? There are numerous words formed by concatenating other words and then omitting some letters. These are called *portmanteau* words. For example, *Eurasia* is a concatenation of *Europe* and *Asia*, but no-one sees the need to add the apostrophe of elision to indicate that some letters have been omitted. Likewise *Oxbridge, avionics* and *smog*. If we don't write *Eur'asia, Ox'bridge, avi'onics* and *sm'og*, why do we write *can't, don't and won't*?

In fact, the apostrophe of elision is unnecessary in all contractions of the form *can't, don't, won't* and so on. As with *Dont forget to pick up the mail*, the meaning of *I cant wait any longer* and *She wont be coming* is crystal clear. In other words, the apostrophe in *can't* (and in *won't*) contributes nothing to

---

5. The serial comma might be useful when an item being listed contains a conjunction (as discussed on page 65).

the meaning. Some claim that the apostrophe avoids ambiguity in those cases where there is a similarly spelt word (as with *cant* and *wont*). But this overlooks the fact that we can—and more often than not do—rely on syntactic context to determine which meaning is intended. For example, the syntax of *I cut my finger* makes it clear that *cut* is being used as a verb. However, in *I have a cut on my finger*, it is clear that *cut* is being used as a noun. (The article announces the imminent arrival of a noun.) The word *cut* does not need to be altered in some way to make its part of speech clear in each case. Similarly, the meaning of *cant* is clear from the syntax alone in both *I cant vote yet* and *I'm tired of all their cant*. The apostrophe is simply unnecessary, despite the pedants' insistence that it is required.

But wouldn't the apostrophe be helpful if the syntactic context of a word was not apparent until the reader had got well into the sentence? We can imagine this happening with the word *its*. An exception in English that confuses many writers is that most possessive pronouns omit the possessive apostrophe when indicating possession.[6] So while we write *The cat's whiskers are long*, when we replace *The cat's* with the equivalent possessive pronoun, we write *Its whiskers are long*. Note the omission of the apostrophe. Without some way of marking the difference between a possessive *its* and an *its* that is meant to be read as *it is*, readers could get lost in a sentence. Consider the following sentence:

Its crying all night—and often for most of the morning—is keeping me awake.

The meaning will not be clear until after the parenthetic phrase. Initially, some readers will interpret *crying* as a noun (reading *its* as a possessive pronoun) and others as a present participle (reading *its* as a contraction of *it is*). Thus some readers will not be able to make immediate sense of the sentence. But this problem is not insurmountable. One solution—and the most

---

6. What contributes to the confusion is that this practice too is inconsistent. We write *Its whiskers are orange* but *Is this anyone's hat?* Both pronouns—*its* and *anyone's*—are being used possessively but are treated differently.

logical, as it removes a confusing inconsistency—is to use a possessive apostrophe in *all* possessive pronouns (and thus write *It's whiskers are long*). Another is to allow the apostrophe of elision in cases where its omission would otherwise confuse readers. Finally, writers could avoid using *its* to mean *it is* if there is any chance of this type of ambiguity. It is not as if the contracted version—any contracted version—is *necessary*.

To sum up: if all unnecessary usage is to be jettisoned from English, then much of what is now considered conventional English—even *good* English—would also need to be jettisoned. The conservatism that drives much of the prescriptivist approach to language is hardly likely to accept that.

## Some usage is necessary

"The reason to stand up for punctuation is that without it there is no reliable way of communicating meaning."
(Truss 2003, p. 20)

This rather sweeping claim by punctuation pundit Lynne Truss is somewhat dubious, and for a number of reasons. First, we saw in the last section that some widely accepted contemporary punctuation is unnecessary (such as the apostrophe of elision and, in most cases, the serial comma). Hence communication would not be rendered unreliable if these marks were to be ditched. No competent English speaker would fail to understand *Dont forget to pick up the mail* or *The flag is red, white and blue*. Second, Truss seems blind to the fact that English punctuation has had an evolutionary history. Punctuation marks have come and gone, and some are fairly recent. Take the apostrophe of possession for example (as in *John's book*), a punctuation mark that has been part of English for just 200 or so years. It would be pulling a long bow to claim that before then communication had been unreliable. Did Isaac Newton have trouble communicating reliably for the want of the possessive apostrophe? Was Restoration and Augustan literature flawed for its apparently scant punctuation? The possessive apostrophe might be useful—though it has its problems, as we'll see shortly—but it is certainly not *necessary*.

But perhaps *some* punctuation is necessary. Truss gives an example that might appear to prove the point (Truss 2003, p. 9):

"A woman, without her man, is nothing.

"A woman: without her, man is nothing."

Clearly the internal punctuation in these examples—the commas and the colon—carries some of the meaning. But this does not mean that the internal punctuation is necessary. For both meanings can be expressed *without* such punctuation:

A woman is nothing without her man.

A man is nothing without a woman.

English syntax is so flexible that there is always more than one way to write something. So the only useful advice we can gain from Truss's examples is that if your preferred way of writing something would render it ambiguous, then you may need to do something about it. And one thing you could do is consider applying some form of punctuation, for punctuation in certain places can be useful. It offers stylistic flexibility and efficiency of expression. But usefulness and necessity are different things.

The same argument can be applied in the case of supposedly necessary hyphenation. Consider the following sentence:

We need an airborne particle detector.

As it is written it is not clear whether the sentence is referring to an airborne detector of particles or a detector of airborne particles. In other words, does the sentence contain a compound adjective or a compound noun. We could use hyphenation to make this clear:

We need an airborne-particle detector. [The need is for a detector of airborne particles.]

We need an airborne particle-detector. [The need is for an airborne detector of particles.]

But the hyphenation is only necessary if you choose to write the sentence using compound structures. You could make the meaning just as clear by writing *We need a detector of airborne particles* or *We need an airborne detector of particles*. The issue is one of style, not necessity.

Even if some punctuation is necessary—a mark to indicate the end of a sentence, perhaps—it is punctuation that is important, not the particular punctuation mark. Numerous marks have been used throughout the history of English punctuation to indicate the end of a sentence. There is nothing special about the full stop (other than the fact that it is now the current convention). To return to Truss's examples: as long as there is some mark doing the work now done by the colon (say a caret: ^), and some mark doing the work now done by the comma (say a tilde: ~), we could still make clear the intended meanings of those sentences without restructuring them (provided, of course, that the practice was known to our readers). Could not the caret replace the colon, and the tilde the comma, some time in the future? That is certainly a logical possibility. Could they not be used now, perhaps by a creative writer (preferably one who has alerted readers beforehand of the marks' special uses)? Indeed, we see punctuation marks in flux right now. For example, the open hyphen is increasingly being used to mark out parenthetic material. This is a case of transitional punctuation. Pedants may not like it, but no meaning is lost or obscured by the practice, as the following examples show:

> The refugees—most of whom have come from Iraq—are to be flown to Nauru. [waning]
>
> The refugees - most of whom have come from Iraq - are to be flown to Nauru. [waxing]

The practice may distract some people while it settles down (or dies out), but it is probably no more distracting than the practice of omitting a space before a semicolon and a colon (a practice that went on to become the current convention). Indeed, even the apostrophe of possession that Truss seems obsessed with would have distracted many folk when it first appeared two centuries ago.

Finally, let's revisit Truss's claim that "without [punctuation] there is no reliable way of communicating meaning". It is pertinent to ask whether her own punctuation prescriptions pass the test of being a reliable means of communicating meaning. Take, for example, her insistence that an apostrophe is used whenever the noun is expressing the genitive case (that is, where the noun modifies another noun). Why the genitive case needs to be explicitly marked in English is a moot point. In some languages, such as Latin, case is important. It determines a word's inflection. But case is largely irrelevant to the construction of English syntax and many of us only remember case for its relevance in other languages. Speaking of case, Fowler makes the following telling point:

> "grammarians are often accused, and indeed are often guilty, of fogging the minds of English children with terms and notions that are essential to the understanding of Greek and Latin syntax, but have no bearing on English." (Fowler 1965, p. 77)

Truss demands the genitive apostrophe be used even when it contributes nothing to the meaning, as in *two weeks' notice* (Truss 2003, p. 3). Many others think likewise. Consider this passage from the website of the surprisingly serious Apostrophe Protection Society:

> "When considering the use of an apostrophe, possession involves *of* and *for*. Consider a notice outside a golf club: *Captain's parking space*. The captain doesn't own the space; it is a parking space *for* the captain."[7]

Let's ignore the confused thinking that allows possession to be involved even when there is no possession and note instead that this recommendation will *not* guarantee reliable communication. Indeed, it encourages ambiguity, the very antithesis of reliable communication. For example, consider *my brother's presents*. If the genitive apostrophe is required when the context is either *of* or *for*, then this phrase could be read as *the*

---

7. See www.apostrophe.org.uk/page4.html. Viewed 16 August 2014.

*presents of my brother* (possessive genitive) or *the presents for my brother* (non-possessive genitive). This example might appear to show that the current trend towards omitting the genitive apostrophe when possession is not obvious has merit. However, without the apostrophe in non-possessive cases we will not always be able to distinguish singular from plural. For example, does *my brothers presents* mean presents for the only brother I have or presents for all my brothers?

So, contrary to Truss's claim, the genitive apostrophe does not offer a *reliable* way of communicating. Its use when the context is either possessive (*of*) or non-possessive (*for*) means that we cannot immediately distinguish which context is intended. But if we use the apostrophe only for true possession, then we will not be able to immediately distinguish singular from plural in non-possessive cases. The English apostrophe is, alas, a confusing beast. Clearly, its introduction was ill-thought-out.

We have concentrated on punctuation in this section, but the brief history of the evolution of English given in the previous chapter should make it clear that, with English changing so much over the last 1600 or so years, it is difficult to assign necessity to any aspect of it (including spelling and syntax). If we could once have got by without full stops at the end of sentences, then it is difficult to see how anything more complex than a full stop must be necessary for English to function as a language.

## Some usage is inconsistent

Language sticklers are also fond of pointing out inconsistences in usage they do not approve of. But any argument from inconsistency presupposes that there is an acceptable solution to a more fundamental issue, namely, why must usage *A* be consistent with usage *B* rather than usage *B* be consistent with usage *A*. Of course, any argument that can settle that issue can't itself be based on consistency, and this implies that any argument from inconsistency necessarily fails. Still, let's play along with the argument for the sake of argument. First, note that many examples of inconsistent usage can be found if you compare, say, American English with British English or with Australian English. Are those who demand consistent usage going to insist that Americans speak and write like the British, or alternatively that the British should speak and write like Americans? That is likely to be a battle lost before it has begun.

Even if they limit their pedantry to one particular variant of English, prescriptivists will have to contend with the almost anarchical state of accepted, idiomatic English. Consider the quite common use of the pronouns *their, them* and *they* as a substitute for a singular noun, as in the following examples:

> Each person has a right to their own opinion.
>
> The author must submit two copies of their paper to the editors.
>
> Because the team arrived late, they were turned away.

Many prescriptivists object to this usage because it is inconsistent with the so-called *principle of agreement*. This principle declares that a singular noun should be matched with a singular verb and singular pronoun, and a plural noun should be matched with a plural verb and plural pronoun. However, in the first example given above we have:

> each person [*singular noun*] has [*singular verb*] a right to their [*commonly a plural pronoun*] own opinion

The problem for the prescriptivists is the pronoun. If the principle of agreement were to be applied consistently, the sentence would, in their opinion, need to be written as:

> Each person has a right to his or her own opinion, or
>
> People have a right to their opinion.

However, the marrying of singular nouns with seemingly plural pronouns has a very long history (going back at least to the sixteenth century). It was common in Shakespeare's day:

> "There's not a man I meet but doth salute me/As if I were their well-acquainted friend".[8]

And it is common today:

> "If a scientist claimed they had discovered how the UFOs around Saturn got there ..."[9]

And it was fine enough for many notable writers over the centuries, none of whom were chastised for their poor grammar: Philip Sydney, Henry Fielding, William Thackeray, John Ruskin and Phillip Larkin to name a few. It was, and still is, common, idiomatic usage. Indeed, many dictionaries these days accept the Shakespearean practice of allowing plural pronouns to be paired with singular nouns, especially when referring to people. Indeed, this is not so much a question of allowing singular to be paired with plural as acknowledging that certain pronouns can be both singular and plural:

> "The word *they* (with its counterparts *them*, *their*, and *themselves*) as a singular pronoun to refer to a person of unspecified sex has been used since at least the 16th century. In the late 20th century, as the traditional use of *he* to refer to a person of either sex came under scrutiny on the grounds of sexism, this use of *they* became more common. It is now generally accepted ...". (*Oxford English Dictionary*)

In other words, *they*, *them* and *their* are not purely plural pronouns, as pedants insist. They can be plural or singular, just as the pronoun *you* can be plural or singular:

> "If *you* are not quiet, *you* will all have detention." [plural *you*]

> "Bob, can *you* pass me the salt please." [singular *you*]

In pointing out that a particular usage is inconsistent with the principle of agreement—or any other principle, for that matter—prescriptivists conveniently overlook the fact that

---

8. *A Comedy of Errors*, Act IV, Scene 3. This is but one of a number of such usages in Shakespeare's oeuvre, which suggests that it was quite deliberate and not a singular grammatical aberration.
9. *New Scientist*, 15 December 2007, p. 14.

English is littered with inconsistences: rules qualified by odd yet accepted exceptions, *i* before *e* except after *c* being one of the first we learn at school. There are, of course, exceptions to this exception: *either, neither, seizure*, etc. There are even exceptions to the principle of agreement when it comes to subjects and verbs. In the following examples, singular subjects—*I* and *you*—are happily matched with a plural verb (*have*):

I have a problem.

You have scabies.

There is no furore in the prescriptivists' camp over these usages, no insistence that they be written *I has a problem* and *You has scabies*. Why prescriptivists allow some exceptions to the subject–verb agreement rules but not others is a mystery.

Sometimes prescriptivists see a breach of the subject–verb agreement rules when there isn't one. Clive James is undoubtedly a fine poet, essayist and entertainer, but his self-avowed sticklerism can sometimes come back to bite him. Consider "Windows is shutting down", a poem he published in *The Guardian* on 27 April 2005:

> Windows is shutting down, and grammar are
> On their last leg. So what am we to do?
> A letter of complaint go just so far,
> Proving the only one in step are you.
>
> Better, perhaps, to simply let it goes.
> A sentence have to be screwed pretty bad
> Before they gets to where you doesnt knows
> The meaning what it must of meant to had.
>
> The meteor have hit. Extinction spread,
> But evolution do not stop for that.
> A mutant languages rise from the dead
> And all them rules is suddenly old hat.
>
> Too bad for we, us what has had so long
> The best seat from the only game in town.
> But there it am, and whom can say its wrong?
> Those are the break. Windows is shutting down.

There's humour in ridicule, and in exaggeration—mostly. Of course, the style of language James parodies is not widespread. So no parent should be alarmed by the imagery evoked by the poem. No-one is writing like this *en masse*. It is just James's playful imagination.

But there is a particular oddity about this poem that works against James. There is one sentence in it—and it is repeated— that is perfectly respectable, unlike every other sentence in it: *Windows is shutting down*. The internal logic of the poem suggests that James thinks that this sentence too is ungrammatical, that it should be, perhaps, *Windows are shutting down*. For doesn't a plural noun (*windows*) need a plural verb (*are*) if it is not to breach the principle of agreement (just as the singular noun *grammar* in the first line needs the singular verb *is*)?

If that was James's thinking, then he is wide of the mark and the poem becomes little more than a cheap shot. The fact that a noun ends in *s* doesn't necessarily indicate that it is a plural noun and thus needing to be paired with a plural verb. In the poem, James is referring to the *Windows* operating system, and the sentence in question appears on the screen of many Windows-based computers when the computer is being shut down. *Windows is shutting down* means that the operating system (singular) that goes by the name *Windows* (a proper noun) is shutting down. *Windows* is, in fact, a singular proper noun—referring to a single operating system—and thus takes the singular verb *is*, not the plural verb *are*. Would James prefer *James are writing another book* on the basis that a proper noun (*James*) ends in *s* and thus should be treated as a plural? Or *The town of Willows are to the east of Rockhampton*. I suspect not.

Perhaps James finds the sentence odd for other reasons. Well, if the grammar is fine—by which I mean idiomatic— what could the fault be other than it is of a style that irks James? Does he, perhaps, find it odd that something can shut itself down? But it's clear to anyone who sees that message on their computer screen that *they* have caused Windows to shut down, that Windows is shutting down as a result of something they did (unless, of course, it was a bug). It is common practice in spoken and written English to leave out the agent if the agent is blindingly obvious. For instance, there is no grammatical or logical flaw in writing *The plane landed safely*. It doesn't need to be spelt out as *The pilot landed the plane safely*.

## Some usage is non-standard

Prescriptivists will tell us that if a word is labelled *non-standard* in a dictionary—such as *youse* and *brang* in the *Macquarie Dictionary* of Australian English—you should refrain from using it. They will probably tell you it's *incorrect* to use it and instances of it are *wrong*. Rather, *Standard English* is what we should be using. So what is Standard English?

> "Educated speech—by definition the language of education—naturally tends to be given the additional prestige of government agencies, the learned professions, the political parties, the press, the law court and the pulpit—any institution which must attempt to address itself to the public beyond the smallest dialectal community ... By reason of the fact that educated English is thus accorded implicit social and political sanction, it comes to be referred to as Standard English, and provided that we remember that this does not mean an English that has been formally standardized by official action, as weights and measures are standardized, the term is useful and appropriate." (Quirk et al. 1972, p. 16)

One can see how educated language might become elevated to the accepted standard. Societies have long recognised the need to teach their young how to write. Such a skill bestows much advantage on a person (not to mention on others around them). But if there are dialects in a society, which ones are to be taught: every dialect a child might encounter, some or just one? Those charged with making this decision will, of course, come from the educated classes. Moreover, being granted the right to make that decision—that is, to exercise power—strongly suggests that they will already belong to an advantaged or privileged group (for the powerful tend to delegate power only to those who are like-minded). Given the advantages that the skill of writing bestows, and the natural tendency we all have to preserve our own advantages, the language chosen as standard—the language that will be taught in schools—is thus very likely to be the language of those making the decision: the language of the educated elite. This becomes the written language foisted on all members of society, regardless of their native dialect. Thus young Yorkshire folk, for example, will be forced to abandon their dialect by Yorkshire-born teachers forced to follow a curriculum designed by folk of another dialect.

Speech, though, is more difficult to re-engineer than writing:

> "Standard English is the dialect which is normally used in writing, and which is spoken by the most educated and powerful members of the population ... [However, those] who speak Standard English [in England comprise] perhaps 7–12 per cent of the population of the country."(Trudgill 1999, p. 3)

Thus 100% of students in England's schools are taught to write Standard English but 88–93% choose to retain their native dialect when they speak.

> "Nearly all of the thousands of textbooks, grammars and dictionaries that have been compiled for the English language are ... about Standard English, *even though most people do not speak this dialect.*" (Trudgill 1999, p. 5, emphasis added.)

Is this diversity a significant hindrance to society? We noted in the last chapter that before the arrival of the printing press in England there was great linguistic diversity. Folk in Kent had trouble understanding folk from Essex just across the River Thames. If language serves as our primary means of communicating, and if the benefits of trade—in goods, services and knowledge—depends on communication, then surely we would want the folk in Kent to understand the folk in Essex—

and the folk from Sydney, Ontario, Tulsa and so on. And surely the only way to achieve this is by having one English which everyone adopts and understands.

But standardisation of *speech* is not the only way of ensuring effective communication and fostering a first-world economy:

> "Norway and Switzerland have shown that it is perfectly possible to develop modern, democratic and technologically advanced societies in which the vast majority of the population speak regional dialects, and are proud to do so ... [T]heir government and educational systems do not attempt to impose national linguistic conformity." (Trudgill 1999, p. 135)

As for standardising *written* English, the genie is well and truly out of the bottle. Standardisation across the various countries that now have their own version of English seems highly unlikely. Which English will we take as standard and, more importantly, how will its global adoption be enforced? Is America likely to give up *faucet* for *tap*; England give up *nappy* for *diaper*? Will Americans be forced to insert a *u* in *color* and the British to add a serial comma in run-on lists? The same fervent nationalism behind the furore in Britain over plans to adopt the euro and America's staunch resistance to metrication—two standardisations that would achieve commercial efficiencies—is likely to thwart any attempt to introduce a Standard International English. And why should economic gain take precedence over sovereign culture?

But what of standardisation within a country? The first question to ask is which group within a country should be chosen to be the exemplar group. In other words, whose writing style is to be used as the basis for the standard? We noted earlier that the so-called Standard English is usually considered to be the English of the *educated* classes. But why should that be? Perhaps in the days when most people did not get an education, a preference for educated English might have carried some weight. But today just about everyone in English-speaking countries gets an education. So, in those countries, the language of the educated is the language of *everyone*. It might be retorted that not everyone completes the education available to them. A complete education is one that includes a tertiary element. So perhaps it should be the language of *university-educated* folk that forms the Standard English in that country.

But to make the language of university-educated folk the standard would be to force the language of a minority on that of the majority. In Australia, for example, only 24% of the population has a bachelor degree. In the United Kingdom, the figure is about 27.2%.[10] To give a minority power over the majority would be to deny the democratic spirit that gave birth to, and maintains, modern civilisation (which is something to be cherished; not allowed to be diluted). Further, it sits oddly with other forms of expression where freedom is taken for granted. Would any poet, painter or composer accept that the style of expression preferred by a sub-group of poets, painters and composers should be adopted by all? Hardly. So why is it different with language? Why must my writing ape that of some professor of zoology or lecturer in nanotechnology.

It might be retorted that the language of the tertiary educated is richer and thus deserves to be our exemplar. But the language of, say, a university-trained engineer is likely to be richer than that of someone with no university training only in the possession of a hundred or so *engineering-specific* terms: *cantilever, spline bore, phase spectrum* and so on. Such possession is unlikely to help the engineer navigate the language of courting, describe pain to a doctor or understand a political essay better than someone with no university training. Likewise, does knowing the language of a trial balance and asset depreciation give an accountant better *general* language skills than someone who missed out on a university place?

---

10. For the Australian figure, see www.abs.gov.au/ausstats/abs@.nsf/Products/6227.0~May+2011~Main+Features~Attainment?OpenDocument. Viewed 11 November 2012. The UK figure comes from the 2011 census. See C. Bell, "Most people in the UK do not go to university – and maybe never will", http://www.theguardian.com/higher-education-network/blog/2013/jun/04/higher-education-participation-data-analysis. Viewed 26 August 2014.

Does a voracious reader of literature who has no university degree necessarily have poorer language skills than a dentist whose sole reading since graduating has been newspapers and magazines? In a word: the completion of tertiary education is a poor marker of language skills. Editors struggling with the tortuous confusions common in the drafts of scientific papers and engineering reports will attest to that.

Indeed, the language of the tertiary educated might not be richer than non-standard English. There are many non-standard words—words shunned by the educated and influential—that serve a useful purpose. Take, for example, the word *youse*. Dictionaries tell us that *youse* is non-standard in Australian English. Yet contemporary English does not have a distinct second-person plural pronoun. Instead, *you* is meant to do the work of both singular and plural and thus carries with it the risk of ambiguity. The alleged non-educated folk in Australia have noted that and have filled the gap with *youse* (much as the folk in America have who use the non-standard word *y'all*). Clearly, the language of the alleged uneducated can be richer, and less prone to ambiguity, than the language of those who prescriptivists would extol. Even a cursory flick through Eric Partridge's *A Dictionary of the Underworld* cannot fail to convince one of the wonderful creativity and colour of the so-called common tongue.

> "Unless we rid ourselves of the idea that speaking anything other than Standard English is a sign of ignorance and a lack of 'sophistication', much of what linguistic richness and diversity remains in the English language ... may be lost." (Trudgill 1999, p. 136)

If the well-educated class does not provide an adequate model for a Standard English, which group in society does? Editors? Journalists? Teachers? Or perhaps the question is misguided. Perhaps we should be asking why *any* group should be granted the privilege of determining what English is declared standard in their country. If a society decides that only one variant of English can be taught in schools, then perhaps it should be the English of the majority. (In a democracy we accept the vote of the majority, so why not the language of the majority?) Then again, why should only one variant of English be taught? And if it is, why should other variants be derided?

> "The fact is that all dialects ... are equally grammatical and correct. They differ only in their social significance and function ... There is nothing linguistically superior about Standard English. It is not more 'pure' or more correct than other forms of speech. It is not even legitimate to claim that it is more 'acceptable' than other dialects, unless we specify *who* it is acceptable to. There are very many people who find Standard English highly unacceptable, at least in certain situations. The superiority that Standard English has is social." (Trudgill 1999, p. 13f.)

Thus in the Standard English approach to acceptable language, speakers and writers are judged by *attitudes*, not by the effectiveness of their communication. In other words, they are judged by prejudice, not by science. The least said about that the better.

## Change is necessarily diminution

> "Historically, a language is best conceived, like a species or an art style, *as a population of variants moving through time*, with differential selection pressures operating on different variants. A language is an heterogeneous system, where some categories exist in only one form, and others are sets of more and less common variants. And new variation is constantly being created. Sometimes the variation is unstable, and simply vanishes; sometimes it remains stable for centuries. But often—and this is what creates history—one variant is gradually selected at the expense of another." (Lass 2006, p. 45)

Pedantry is often a symptom of conservatism: an uneasiness with, or fear of, change. Such uneasiness can arise from many causes: laziness at having to adapt to something new, fear of being left behind or reluctance to accept that erstwhile authorities could have been wrong. But a common cause, and one openly admitted by many, is the belief that change diminishes or weakens a language. The argument might be put that language is like a physical system, and thus subject to the Second Law of Thermodynamics: the entropy or disorder of any system increases with time. With each change, entropy increases, and the power of a language to communicate is thereby impaired. This view is quite misplaced. Are we to say that the language of, say, the eighteenth century is better than the language of the twenty-first century simply because English has changed since then? Does anyone—pedants included—really want to adopt the English of the eighteenth century? And why stop at the eighteenth century? If change is necessary diminution, then let's go right back to the beginning of English. Any takers?

If change necessarily leads to diminution, to linguistic entropy, we should be surprised that, after 1600 years, English still survives as a language. And we should be further surprised that it has become the *lingua franca* of the world. So perhaps change—which has been with English forever—is not a cause of diminution, but a necessary precursor of strength and longevity. Indeed, some changes have significantly improved language. We have already mentioned the appearance of spaces between words in the eighth century. This was certainly not diminution, but improvement. Indeed, the gradual appearance of punctuation vastly improved the language. Once upon a time, Western languages had no punctuation. It eventually became clear, mainly to scribes copying earlier texts, that old texts were open to several interpretations. There needed to be a way of fixing a text to one and only one meaning. Thus grew a practice that we now call punctuation. This was a change, a linguistic change. To argue that all change is necessarily diminution is to argue that the advent of punctuation diminished language. This can hardly be sustained.

"As the number of different [punctuation] symbols increased, the refinement in the signals provided by punctuation marks made it possible for a reader to identify more easily the relationships between the elements of a sentence, and to determine the precise function of each of these structures in communicating the sense of a text." (Parkes 1993, p. 3)

Next consider neologisms. It is difficult to imagine where we would be if new words were not allowed into the language. New ideas and new products demand new words. A word for *transistor* was not needed a century ago; it is now if we are to avoid a long string of simple words that together describe a transistor (assuming that this was even possible).

It is not just new words for new things. New words for old things—or old words newly inflected—enrich the language. British English of the 1970s had no verb equivalent for *author* (Parkes 1993, p. 12). Pedants might frown on it, but *authored* is now well established in British English. It is difficult to see how a new synonym can diminish a language. How dull would literature be if we had at our disposal only one word for every thing.

And just as *Homo sapiens* excel at creating new words, we excel at chopping them up, splicing them or both. Our instinct, it seems, is to squeeze as much communicative potential into the shortest form possible (an instinct that does not, alas, readily extend to constructing sentences).

"language ranks highest which goes furthest in the art of accomplishing much with little means, or, in other words, which is able to express the greatest amount with the simplest mechanism."[11]

Truncating words has been an acceptable practice in English for many centuries. To truncate a word is to shorten it (most commonly by removing initial characters). For example, *omnibus* was the word commonly used for what we now call a

---

11. J. Aitchison 2001, p. 252, quoting Danish linguist Otto Jespersen.

*bus*. Over the course of the twentieth century, the original word became truncated, a change even prescriptivists seem happy to accept. Indeed, *omnibus* has almost entirely dropped out of common usage. Another example is *perambulator*. This has dropped out of common usage altogether, having been replaced by its truncated form: *pram*.

Sometimes both the original term and a truncated derivative remain in common use. *Telephone* is an example. It has been truncated to *phone*, and while both versions are in common use, more English users prefer the shorter version than the longer. Likewise *aeroplane* (or *airplane*) and *plane*, and *railway* (or *railroad*) and *rail*.

The causes of truncation and the reason why some words get truncated and others not—why, for example, hasn't *communication* been truncated to *cation*—is open to debate, but what isn't debatable is that truncating words improves the efficiency of communication. Truncation requires fewer characters to be typed by writers, and in some cases less vocal effort from speakers. Since no meaning is lost in truncation, and since the efficiency of communicating is improved, truncation can hardly be called diminution.

Some parents and educators frown on textese, the truncated form of English common in the text messages of youngsters (and increasingly so in the text messages of adults). Some examples: substituting *B4* for *before*, *THX* for *thanks* and *HAK* for *hugs and kisses*.

David Crystal, Honorary Professor of Linguistics at Bangor University, writes:

> "All the popular beliefs about texting [namely, that it is "wrecking our language"] are wrong or at least debatable. Its graphic distinctiveness is not a totally new phenomenon. Nor is its use restricted to the young generation. There is increasing evidence that it helps rather than hinders literacy. And only a very tiny part of the language uses its distinctive orthography." (Crystal 2008, p. 9)

Further:

> "There is a curious ambivalence around. Complaints are made about children's poor literacy, and then, when new technology arrives that provides fresh and motivating opportunities to read and write, such as email, chat, blogging and texting, complaints are made about that. The problems associated with the new medium—such as new abbreviation styles—are highlighted and the potential benefits ignored." (Crystal 2008, p. 157)

Crystal notes that we have been shortening words and expressions in English for centuries. Take the Latin initialism *pm* (a shortened form of *post meridiem*) for example. This was first recorded in English in 1666. Initialisms and acronyms are common in English: NB, RIP, AWOL, ETA, SNAFU, AKA, FYI, ASAP, DVD and so on. So too are contractions (such as *Mr, Dr* and *Sgt*) and abbreviations (such as *Prof., exam.* and *vet.*). Given their unavoidable exposure to well-established shortened words, it is difficult to tell whether those who complain about textese are prescriptivists (which would invite the charge of hypocrisy) or mere conservatives (thus inviting the charge of closed-mindedness).

Rather than deriding youngsters for their text-talk, perhaps we should be admiring them—admiring them for their ingenuity in devising ways to pack so much information into the limited canvas offered by SMS and Twitter messaging (typically 140 characters). *Gr8* is three characters, a saving of two over *great*. And there is no reason to think that *8* (or any other number) could not become a character in the standard English alphabet. Alphabets are not fixed. No logical imperative demands that the English alphabet stay as it is. Indeed, the English alphabet has changed throughout its history, adopting some new characters (such as *j* and *v*) and dropping others (such as & and ꝉ). So what is to stop *8* becoming an alphabetic character should its use as one become widespread? The fact that *8* is currently a numeral rather than an alphabetic character is no barrier to it serving both purposes. Many books are published with the preliminary sections numbered using the Roman numbering system. In these books, *i*, *v* and *x* are used both as alphabetic characters (as in *vexatious*) and as numbers (1, 5 and 10 respectively). So there is precedent—widely accepted precedent—for multi-purpose characters. The use of *8* as an alphabetic character might strike many of us as odd and unconventional, but to ban everything that is odd and unconventional is, by definition, to ban creativity, novelty and freshness. Should we have banned dodecaphonic music? Or pointillism? Or blank verse? How dull life would be—if such banning were indeed possible.

Still, it would be fanciful to think that all change is for the better. For example, the imminent demise of the en dash could well be seen as diminution.[12] However, the history of the English languages shows us that the loss of a useful word or device is invariably met by the creation of a new one:

> "language has a remarkable instinct for self-preservation. It contains inbuilt, self-regulating devices which restore broken patterns and prevent disintegration." (Aitchison 2001, p. 169)

And that might not even be necessary if already there is sufficient redundancy in the language to compensate for the perceived loss. For example, the ill-fated en dash in *Melbourne–Sydney route* could even now be replaced by *Melbourne-to-Sydney route*.

To sum up: there is no reason to think that English is not capable of adopting changes for the better (and of compensating for changes for the worse). A parallel with

---

12. The demise of the en dash (and its big brother, the em dash) is no doubt due to the ill-thought-out design of the common computer keyboard. No keys—not even function keys—were allocated to the two dashes despite these punctuation marks being in wide use. Curiously, keys were made available to programmers to help them debug programs (*Pause* and *SysReq*, for example), tasks that could have been done with combinations of common keys. Thus a minor need (ease of programming) was given preference over a major need (communicating with conventional punctuation). Fortunately, the dashes are still available from the keyboard, but in such a roundabout way that many users avoid them or choose to use hyphens instead.

another self-regulating convention should make this clear. Like any natural language, no-one owns morality nor has the authority to control it. And like one's own language, one has a vested interest in maintaining some core moral conventions. Compare *I don't want you to harm me, so I won't harm you* with *I want you to understand me, so I will use a language we both share*. And morality too has changed over the centuries. Are we worse off morally speaking because of that change? Few, if any, now believe that human slavery or the stoning of adulterers is morally justified. The repugnance the vast majority of people feel towards such practices is *moral* repugnance. It is not a delusion. It is, rather, a feeling that has gathered strength over many centuries (sometimes as the result of much argument). Our erstwhile acceptance of such barbaric practices has been transformed. We are now revolted by them. It is clear that the world is a far better place for it being rid of the harm they inflicted. We have, in other words, become better moral beings over the centuries. While we cannot assert this generally, we can assert that, on balance, life in the twenty-first century is less anxious, less brutal, less unforgiving than it was a thousand years ago. One is now less likely to have to flee every so often from marauding armies, or to be left to die on the side of a road, or to be sent in chains to a foreign country to break rock or pick tobacco day in and day out. No-one forced this moral betterment on us. It grew out of the collective spirit of society. There is no reason to think that other un-owned and uncontrolled conventional systems (such as natural language) cannot likewise change for the better through the undercurrents of collective spirit.

## Chaos is just around the corner

"If every word or device that achieved currency were immediately authenticated, simply on the grounds of popularity, the language would be as chaotic as a ball game with no foul lines." (Strunk & White 2000, p. 52)

There are at least two ways of interpreting this statement:
- accepting what is popular can lead to linguistic chaos
- unauthenticated change can lead to linguistic chaos.

Let's take each in turn. First, what does *popular* mean? To be popular something has to be regarded with favour or approval. But by how many? *Madama Butterfly* is a popular Puccini opera—popular amongst the handful of those who appreciate opera, but certainly not popular with the general population (the majority of whom have never heard it or of it). Rice is a popular foodstuff and—unlike *Madama Butterfly*— popular with the vast majority of the human race. Language users comprise a large chunk of any society—probably every single non-infant member—and so the popularity of a "word or device" can perhaps be judged by how many in society *as a whole* regard it with favour and approval. In other words, rice rather than opera is the better analogy. Thus the objection in question can be reframed as: accepting language use that the *majority* do not regard with favour and approval can lead to linguistic chaos.

In Australia, *youse* is a word with limited currency. Few regard its use with favour and approval. It is not a popular word. But how might we judge *youse* if 51% of the population used it and approved of it? What about 90%? First, would there be linguistic chaos? Well, *youse* is now common in Irish English and Irish English did not descend into chaos as the word became more and more popular (Trudgill 1999, p. 92). The meaning of *kid* as a child or young person took a while to gain favour and approval in Britain and Australia. That use was derided for decades by pedants who insisted that *kid* could only mean a young goat. Did the widening of meaning drag us closer to linguistic chaos? Of course not.

Second, what other yardstick for accepting language use do we have other than common use (that is, popularity)? We have already noted that calls to the authority of Standard English, or to logic, or to necessity hold no water. Today we accept the word *pram* in favour of *perambulator* because it is the most common word used for that sort of baby carriage. *Pram* progressively gained favour and is now common usage. Note that we did not wait for it to be authenticated by some academy or government department. Nor has its rise to common usage—to popularity—dragged English towards linguistic chaos. Thus unauthenticated change need not lead to chaos (the second interpretation of the objection at the start of this section).

However, our interpretation of Strunk and White's objection is that unauthenticated change *can* (not necessarily *will*) lead to linguistic chaos. Surely without some authority whose job it is to regulate language, it will decay into babble. On the contrary. *Homo sapiens* have such a deep-rooted need for language that they do not allow it to decay. Through our unconscious adoption of communication conventions, we maintain a system that largely serves our needs. The system appears to be regulated but it is us who is regulating it, though rarely do we see this. So we have no need for an external, authenticating body to regulate our language. We do it ourselves.

This is how it works. *A* wants to interact with *B* (for whatever reason: to borrow, to trade, to get a job, and so on). For *A* to succeed in getting his or her needs understood by *B*, it is in *A*'s interests to use a language that *B* will understand. For *B* to succeed in having his or her needs understood—to earn interest on a loan, buy some food or employ the right person—it is in *B*'s interests to use language that *A* will understand. A job applicant who uses made-up language in a job application risks failing to sell themselves, and a recruiter who uses made-up language in a job advertisement risks failing to attract the right sort of person. And *A* may need to interact with *C*, and *D* with *B* and so on, thus unknowingly helping to maintain a shared language. We are predominantly social beings. We need others to make life satisfying. But a personal, made-up language will confine us to a lonely and unsatisfying life. Thus our interest in, our need for, a *shared* language, for only with a shared language do we maximise our chances of gaining the wellbeing we seek. This is why languages do not descend into chaos. Some might die out—which is occurring now at an alarming rate—but this has more to do with pressures from dominant languages and from population decline. Languages don't die out from neglect or internal decay. The purpose they serve is too great.

This does not mean, of course, that every mature speaker of a language understands everyone else in their particular language group. There is a core set of usages that we all adopt. Outside that core are peripheral usages: the jargon of a particular profession, pillow talk, texting, pidgin and the like. Eavesdrop on the pillow talk of lovers and, although it is clear that the lovers understand each other, you are likely to find it baffling. Just because these particular forms of language are on the periphery of communication doesn't exclude them from being forms of English. They simply have a more limited currency. Theirs is a minority usage, not a majority usage. A physicist writing for other physicists can use the widely unknown jargon of physics just as a lover can use seemingly baffling pillow talk in a love letter.

But most of what gets written is not written for such a circumscribed audience as one's partner or fellow scientists. Rather, journalists, novelists and writers of books such as this one are writing for a general audience. If an author wants to communicate with a general audience, it is clear that they will need to avoid minority usages. This reinforces the prevalence and importance of core English. And it also brings us, in a roundabout way, to a further challenge that could be read into Strunk and White's objection at the start of this section, namely, that accepting language use that any *minority* regards with favour and approval can lead to linguistic chaos. Chaos won't occur because most written texts will adopt the usage of the majority. Writers have a vested interest in doing so. Intending to communicate with a *general* audience would be self-defeating if the author only used the language of minorities. And what we have said about writing applies equally to speaking. What interests are served in using heterodox language in attempting to buy a train ticket, woo a partner or answer a question at a job interview?

## Universal grammar supports prescriptivism

There is a branch of linguistics that seeks to uncover *universal* features of language. Noam Chomsky is perhaps the best-known of the linguists who work in this field. Chomsky founded the generative school of language, which contends that all the grammatical sentences in all languages can be generated from a single set of universal rules (Chomsky 1957). Moreover, these rules are innate. They are written into the biology or psychology of *Homo sapiens*. Could this view—known as *universal grammar*—give some support to prescriptivism? Might not Chomsky's claim that "deep-seated formal conditions are satisfied by the grammars of all languages" (Chomsky 2006, p. 99) warrant, if not the entire prescriptivist program, at least some aspects of it? For if there are universal rules governing the structure of sentences, then perhaps there are universal rules governing language use (or at least some language use).

Three problems bedevil this suggestion: to all intents and purposes, universal grammar is untestable; if universal grammar were true in the only sense that might support prescriptivism, then prescriptivists would have nothing to argue against; universal grammar does not apply to those issues of language that most worry prescriptivists.

A claim that some feature of language is universal—that is, found in all languages—will have little scientific merit unless *many* languages are analysed and compared. But few of the world's 6000 or so languages have had their structures fully described. Thus any claim to have discovered features shared by *all* languages needs to be treated as a mere hypothesis.

What compounds the difficulty in justifying Chomskyan universalism is the possibility that any seemingly universal feature could change over the long-term. No linguist denies that most facets of a language do change: vocabulary, morphology, syntax, pronunciation, semantics, and so on (Finegan et al. 1992, p. 231). If that is so, then it is possible that *any* feature of language might change, even those found—if any are—to be shared by all or most languages. Biology and psychology will no doubt continue to evolve and in doing so create novel capacities. What we do with language in the future might outstrip what we can now do. In other words, an apparent universal perceived at one time might be absent when looked for at another time. Thus the search for universals makes sense only on the untestable assumption that beneath the continual evolution of language lay features that never change.

It might be retorted that this is an issue for all the sciences. Indeed, as the Austrian philosopher Karl Popper rightly pointed out, it is its *falsifiability* that makes a scientific claim scientific. In other words, if it is impossible in principle to adduce evidence against it, then a claim is not the proper subject of scientific enquiry.[13] So the fact that Chomsky's claim that there are universals might one day be overturned is no argument against it. In fact it elevates it to being a genuine scientific claim. Even so, there is still the issue of *practical* verification. A claim might pass as scientific by being falsifiable—and Chomsky's is[14]—but it will have little scientific merit until numerous supporting instances have been observed. Such instances are additive verifications, and they are necessary before a hypothesis can be elevated to a theory, and the theory elevated to knowledge. But with most of the world's languages yet to be fully analysed, and the need to observe *over a very long time* the stability of a feature before it can be truly considered universal, it should be clear that Chomskyan universalism is, *for all practical purposes*, untestable.[15] An interesting hypothesis

---

13. K. Popper, *The Logic of Scientific Discovery*, Taylor & Francis, London, 2005, p. 18. The book was first published in 1935.
14. The presence of children who do not develop the requisite capacity for language use would falsify Chomsky's view, as would variation in syntax between spoken language and written language. Indeed, such variation has already been noted. See C. A. Perfetti, N. Landi and J. Oakhill, "The Acquisition of Reading Comprehension Skill", in M. J. Snowling & C. Hulme, *The Science of Reading: A Handbook*, Blackwell, Oxford, 2005, p. 237.
15. Numerous untestable assumptions in Chomsky's nativist view of language (and that of Steven Pinker) are discussed in Geoffrey Sampson's *The 'Language Instinct' Debate*, Continuum, London, 2nd edn, 2005.

perhaps, but a mere hypothesis does not give justification to the claimed verities of the strong prescriptivist. To *insist* that people write in a particular way because some feature of language *might* be universal is a symptom of cognitive derangement. Thus the postulation of universal grammar provides no rational support for prescriptivism.

A second problem for the prescriptivist who looks to universal grammar for support is this: if our biology or psychology did limit our language use in certain ways, it would make no sense to call some instance of language use incorrect or wrong. It would be as silly as saying it is *wrong* that humans have, say, two hands. To see this, let $p$ be some type of language use (such as beginning a sentence with a conjunction). If our biology or psychology prevents us from saying or writing $p$, then there cannot be $p$-use to be labelled incorrect or wrong. On the other hand, if our biology or psychology allows us to say or write $p$, then a reliance on universal grammar to deny the legitimacy of $p$ would be contradictory.

Finally, recall that Chomsky's claim is only that "*deep-seated formal conditions are satisfied by the grammars of all languages*" (emphasis added). The patent differences between human languages clearly shows that everyday language use cannot be wholly determined by those deep-seated conditions. Acknowledging this, Chomsky draws a distinction between the surface structures and the deep structures of a language and makes it clear that the surface structure of a sentence no less than the deep structure can determine its meaning. Note that the two sentences below have identical deep structures— that is, identical grammars—but dissimilar surface structures:

[1] John washed the car; I was afraid someone *else* would do it.

[2] John washed the car; I was *afraid* someone else would do it.

The meaning of these sentences is given only by the stress the speaker or writer adds. In sentence [1], the speaker or writer is happy that John washed the car; in [2] they are not. Thus grammar

and meaning are independent. Chomsky goes on to say:
"It is not clear at all that it is possible to distinguish sharply between the contribution of grammar to the determination of meaning, and the contribution of so-called 'pragmatic considerations', questions of fact and belief and context of utterance." (Chomsky 2006, p. 97)

Were it not for the contribution of Chomsky's "pragmatic considerations", universalists would have difficulty accounting for the contemporary and historical variations in a language: current American English differs from current British English, which differs from Elizabethan English, and so on. For Chomsky the surface features of a language are not innate and thus cannot be universal. Yet it is the surface features of English—such as the placement of apostrophes and the unity of infinitives—that mostly worry prescriptivists.

Chomsky makes a further distinction between *competence*— being able to express ourselves according to biological determinants—and *performance*: being able to use our innately-guided language well (Chomsky 2006, p. 102). This distinction is another barrier to any attempt to justify prescriptivism by the existence of universal grammar. Universal grammar is concerned with competence; prescriptivism is concerned with performance. So long as one has normal brain and body function, one will develop language competence, but that's as far as biology and psychology goes. The way we use our language is instead culturally determined. Useful parallels are not hard to find. Take the human eye. It can only discern colour differences to a limited degree. That is a universal structural limitation on human perception. But that in no way limits visual artists to any particular *style* of painting or any particular palette of colours. Pointillism, for instance, cannot be dismissed as non-art because (let us imagine) it breaks some universal law about human perception. Or consider music. If we assume— erroneously—that all music is limited to the eleven semitones of the chromatic scale in each octave, does that in any way place boundaries on the *style* of music that can be composed? Stravinsky used the same chromatic scales as Bach, but the musical styles of these two undeniably great composers are quite unlike.

To sum up: universal grammar does not bolster the case for prescriptivism. Even if there are biological and psychological limitations to language capacity, the way we use that capacity is up to us. There is freedom within determinism.

## Etymological purity should be preserved

To many prescriptivists, the spelling of a word should reflect its ancestry. For them it is *wrong* for a spelling not to, and some crusty old favourites—such as H. W. Fowler or the *Oxford English Dictionary*—are wheeled out in support of this view. An example is the argument against the *-ise* spellings of words like *authorise* and *colonise*. The following quote from the *Oxford English Dictionary* makes the case for etymological purity:

> "The suffix, whatever the element to which it is attached, is in its origin the Gr. -ιξειν, L. *izare;* and, as the pronunciation is also with z, there is no reason why in English the special French spelling in *-iser* should ever be allowed. Hence, here the termination is uniformly written *-ize*.[16]

Should *never* be allowed? Regardless of the extent of *-ise* usage? This is strict prescriptivism of the highest kind. But does it survive even a cursory scrutiny?

We can quickly dispose of the second line of argument, the argument from pronunciation. Why can't *s* sometimes be pronounced *s* and at other times *z*? English has never been a strongly phonetic language and it does allow one letter to have two pronunciations. Take the two *c*'s in *accident*. The first *c* is identical to the *k* in *koala* and the second is identical to the *s* in *silly*. Or consider the different pronunciations of *i* in *iota* and *inkling*. There are many similar cases. Thus there is no reason why an *s* in, say, *organise* cannot be pronounced as a *z*. It

---

16. *The Shorter Oxford English Dictionary on Historical Principles*, Oxford University Press, Oxford, 1973, See the entry for *-ize*. See also Fowler, 1965, p. 314.

certainly is pronounced that way in *surprise*, a spelling that seems to ruffle no feathers at Oxford University Press.

Let's now consider the argument from etymology. The argument goes that *-ize* is the correct ending because these words originate from Greek or Latin (where the corresponding ending is *-izein* and *-izare* respectively). But no reason is given for why the origin of a word should dictate its spelling. If we applied the practice consistently, we would need to change the spellings of a great many words in common English usage, not just those that now end in *-ise*.

For example, the *s* in *island* would have to be dropped so as to reflect its Anglo-Saxon origin (Crystal 1987, p. 214). We would have to spell *cabbage cabbach* to reflect its Old French origin (*caboce*), in line with *spinach*, which also has Old French origins. Perhaps *exercise* should be spelt *exercice* in line with its Old French origin (*exercice*). There are scores of current words whose spelling is divorced from the spelling of their origin, words whose spelling goes unremarked. So why is etymology the key to the acceptable spelling of some words but not others?

The issue is not peculiar to English. Should Italian speakers write *vinu* instead of *vino* to more align it with its Latin ancestor *vinum*? For the same reasons, perhaps Portuguese speakers should write *vinhu* rather than *vinho*. Few languages would remain the same were we to apply the argument from etymology.

The prescriptivists' application of the argument from etymological purity thus harbours a tolerance for unhelpful inconsistency. But the argument fails for a more fundamental reason: why must we stop at the Greek or Latin roots of a word? Greek and Latin did not spring forth *sui generis*. Both are derivatives of earlier languages, going back to what linguists call Proto-Indo-European (Crystal 1987, p. 296). Perhaps the roots of Classical Greek words ending with *–izein* had quite different endings. Take the word *character*. It is derived from the French term *caracter*, so maybe we should drop the *h* in English. Just one moment. *Caracter* has its own history. It is derived from the Latin *character*, so maybe we had better leave the *h* in. Now *organise* might derive from the Latin *organizare*, but what did *organizare* derive from? And whatever it did derive from, what did its parent derive from, and so on? So if history is to be the source of correctness, we should go back not just to Greek or Latin, but to the precursors of Greek and Latin. The fact that we know so little about these precursors suggests that the argument from etymology is doomed.

And if we continue with the argument from etymology, how *much* must the current spelling of a word reflect its ancestors? Just in the ending? Why not include the beginning too, and the middle? Why not, then, just go back to the original word and disallow all spelling change full stop? Goodbye *gallop* and *fly*; hello *wala hlaupan* and *fleogan*.

To sum up: *selective* etymology is not a convincing way to justify particular spellings. Further, given our necessarily limited knowledge of the ancestry of words, reliance on etymology can only ever be selective and thus arbitrary.

## Writing was better in the old days

Language doomsayers are fond of quoting snippets of arid bureaucratese to bolster their belief that language has gone to the dogs. Here's a snippet reported by John Humphrys in his *Lost for Words*:

> "Nurses who will on every occasion, at every time, recognise that this person is different from the last patient and needs something new, something different that will ensure better care. It is about using the opportunities of our investment in the NHS to create new ways for nursing to do what it does best—within the values of the NHS." (Humphrys 2004, p. 211)

Inelegant, perhaps, but surely undeserving of the roasting that Humphrys gives it. One aspect of writing that doomsayers usually ignore or downplay is that there is more to it than just language. There is also *thinking*. That's what makes writing difficult for all but the preternaturally gifted—and especially so for those bureaucrats, managers and others who have far less time to polish their words than the haughty, sneering, armchair critics who lampoon them. We think, then write. And thinking takes time. If we're pressed for time at one end there will be sausage meat out the other. Thus to compare fairly the writing of today with that of yesteryear, we have to ask whether those employees who have to write today are given as much time to do so as those in the obviously less rushed world of the 1950s or earlier. I suspect not. Moreover, in comparing language skills across generations we need to be sure to sift out language-related faults from other faults in writing. As any editor will attest, much poor writing is not so because of poor grammar, spelling or punctuation. It is poor because it is ill-thought-out, poorly structured, overly repetitive, contains logical howlers and so on.[17] We also need to be careful not to judge writing as poor simply because we do not like the writer's style. Controlling for these non-language factors in any comparison of writing across the ages is extraordinarily difficult and makes the claim that writing in the old days was better than today difficult to prove. Perhaps, then, the doomsayers pessimism is unjustified.

Even if evidence did show that writing was better in the old days, is that a reason to return to the strong prescriptivism of the past? Do we really want our children to be taught rules that are prejudiced, illogical or false (such as those discussed in chapter 1)? And do we want them to go through life believing that language use can be correct or incorrect, right or wrong? Surely we want our children to leave school brimming with knowledge untainted by prejudice, hunches or superstition.

But there is a further flaw in the prescriptivists' argument here, in so far as it goes like this:

[1] When prescriptivism is the philosophy of language teaching, writing standards are high.

[2] Prescriptivism is not the philosophy of language teaching.

---

17. "For we may rest assured that whenever we express ourselves ill, here is, besides the mismanagement of language, for the most part, some mistake in our manner of conceiving the subject. Embarrassed, obscure, and feeble sentences are generally, if not always, the result of embarrassed, obscure, and feeble thought." Hugh Blair, *Lectures on Rhetoric and Belles-Lettres*, 1783.

[C] Therefore writing standards are not high.

We might accept the truth of the premises and the conclusion, but the argument exhibits a logical fallacy: the *fallacy of denying the antecedent*. A simple parallel should make the fallacy clear:

[1] When it rains, the grass is wet.

[2] It is not raining.

[C] Therefore the grass is not wet.

The premises and conclusion of this syllogism might currently be true, but the argument is nonetheless fallacious. It is fallacious because it is possible for the conclusion to be false when both premises are true: the grass could be wet not because it is raining, but because there is a gardener hosing it. Likewise it is possible for writing standards to be high (or higher than they are today) without prescriptivism being the philosophy of language teaching *even if we accept that prescriptivism can lead to high writing standards*. Perhaps there is a teaching philosophy that leads to even better results than prescriptivism. One possibility is *active descriptivism*. This philosophy—seemingly overlooked by the cultural warriors of the 1960s and 70s—is described in detail in the next chapter.

## Effective teaching requires absolutism

Another reason sometimes put forward for bringing back prescriptivism in the classroom is this: students don't take seriously what is portrayed as mere accidental conventions. Thus the best way to get youngsters to appreciate language, and to speak and write well, is to teach it as if the rules of language are absolute, inviolable, set in stone for all time and never to be broken. An implication of this view is that it is fine to teach falsehoods so long as the overall result is, by some measure or other, beneficial. The ends justify the means. This is no less morally objectionable than teaching students to believe in a punitive god in order to get them to behave in a courteous, civil and moral way. One can understand the value of behaving in a courteous, civil and moral way without needing to believe in a punitive metaphysical being. Likewise, one can understand the value of communication without needing to believe that the underpinning rules are absolute.

Teaching knowledge rather than falsehoods is what gives integrity to an education system. Teaching falsehoods has a tendency to *corrupt*, corrupt in the sense of bringing about a certain type of devaluing. The type of devaluing in question here is the type where a moral good is diluted or lost. Not all instances of devaluation are equal, and not all are worth lamenting. The value placed on regularly attending a place of religious worship—a church, synagogue, mosque or temple— has certainly dropped over the last century. There are reasons why this might be hailed as a good thing, not a bad. There is certainly no evidence that morality or lawfulness has declined as a result of such a devaluing. Likewise, the value placed on a distant monarch in the far-flung countries of the British Commonwealth has been on the wane, and there is no evidence of political, legal or moral dissolution as a result. But some devaluations can harm a society and its citizens. If schools and universities are no longer seen as places where knowledge is paramount—but where falsehoods are allowed into the mix so as to instil beliefs and behaviours unrelated to truth—then the general usefulness and perceived importance, of such institutions will wane. Information is vital to a society and its citizens. When information begins to be crowded out by misinformation or disinformation, we are all the poorer. Truth in the classroom should be mandatory.

As to whether students won't take language studies seriously unless grammatical rules are taught as if they were inviolable, surely the jury is still out, given that the descriptivism we are about to discuss in the next chapter has not been given a run in most English curricula. Anyway, do students refuse to take art and music seriously? There is no correct or incorrect art; no correct or incorrect music. Could anyone seriously entertain the idea that the brilliance of a Pablo Picasso or Igor Stravinsky needed the fertilisation of false beliefs?

\*

Much of what prescriptivists argue about language is simply wrong or illogical. Language use cannot be correct or incorrect, right or wrong. None of the counter-arguments considered in this chapter counter the arguments of the previous chapter. Epistemology and the philosophy of language both show that it is a category mistake to evaluate language in terms of correct and incorrect, right and wrong.

This does not mean, though, that language use cannot be *evaluated*, that one way of saying something cannot be considered *better* than another. The primary use to which we put language is to communicate. If draft *A* of a document fails to communicate its message—perhaps because of ambiguity or vagueness—while draft *B* does, then clearly draft *B* is better written than draft *A*. But this is a question of effectiveness, not correctness. Ambiguity can thwart the very purpose of writing. That is the reason to avoid it, not because instances of it are incorrect. These are issues we will return to later in this book.

# 4: Taking language seriously

"when beliefs are more important than people
we are beetles on our backs"[1]

We have seen that a good deal of what passed for English-language teaching in the first half of the twentieth century was merely the transmission of prejudice (and sometimes in its ugliest form: snobbery). Moreover, what was taught was often illogical (or at least supported by arguments of dubious logic) and sometimes downright wrong. A student didn't need a first-class brain to see that there were no scientific grounds for preferring *napkin* to *serviette*, that *and* at the start of a sentence could link the sentence to the one before it, and that verbs cannot possibly be limited to the so-called *doing* words. And yet all this was taught as if it were immutable fact, its purpose overshadowed by a soporific teaching style that preferred command over explanation. Meanwhile, across the corridor, science classrooms were buzzing with new discoveries and new ideas: DNA, lasers, computers, neutron stars, quarks, The Big Bang, hyperbolic space, quantum superposition and so on. Science was going places. It could not but inspire the curious and nettle the closed-minded. It was demonstrating the immense power of imagination, hypothesis, observation and experiment—and it was exciting.

Yet the study of language was giving us no new insights, cobwebbed as it was in the beliefs and practices of yesteryear. Students began to sense that conservatism was masquerading as knowledge and found it increasingly difficult to engage

---

1. From "infallibility", a poem by Claire Gaskin printed in Robert Adamson ed., *The Best Australian Poems* of 2010, Black Inc., Collingwood, 2010.

with the subject. Among them were the cultural warriors who would go on to become the new educational bureaucrats. Their own stultifying experience of the English classroom meant that change was inevitable. The need passed unquestioned. And one change stood out from the rest: the teaching of English would become less about the *mechanics* of the language—with its seemingly antiquated and groundless rules—and more about the *sociology* of language. Textual analysis, cultural determinism and critical relativism: these became the topics of the new English classroom. An essay on character development in the script of a television soap opera came to be seen as a more legitimate product for assessing language competency than, say, skill in choosing the appropriate pronoun to lead a relative clause. No-one at the time questioned the move. It was a product of the Zeitgeist.

There was, no doubt, some good in this new approach, not least of which was keeping otherwise restless and easily bored students engaged with the language. But a widely acknowledged result was a failure to adequately prepare students for the language-centric demands of the approaching digital age. Everyone in the 1970s was about to be become a communicator, either as a requirement of their workplace or in order to participate in social media (the magnetism of which is irresistible to many). Knowing how to dissect a character in the script of a soap opera might well be interesting. But if learning how to do so crowds out learning how to express what you find—or if earlier studies have not provided the necessary expressive framework—then the learning has been incomplete. The essay might be understood by the teacher who is now marking it and who took the class (understood, perhaps, only with a good deal of contextual assumption). But to others it might be impenetrable. The concepts in it might be familiar, but the way they are assembled might bog any careful reading in a quagmire of ambiguity and vagueness. That is ill preparation for writing a report that pleases an employer or a blog that convinces a potential follower. And that is the conclusion of many of those adults now crowding into remedial English courses: their English curricula let them down. They did not get what they now need: a sturdy framework for effective communication. Thus one unintended consequence of the cultural revolution of the 1960s and 70s was that the baby of communicative competency got thrown out with the dirty bath water of blinkered prescriptivism.

Can communicative competency be improved without a return to old-fashioned prescriptive pedagogy? That is the question we explore in the remaining chapters.

## Prescriptivism and conventions

In the previous chapters we considered language use through the eyes of prescriptivism. A strong prescriptivist believes that there are inviolable laws of language, laws that should never be broken. The gerund-grinders of the pre–1960s classroom were strong prescriptivists, and traces of strong prescriptivism can still be found in the work of contemporary writers on language such as Lynne Truss and John Humphrys. The notion of inviolability—with its corollary that individual language use can be correct or incorrect, right or wrong— elevates the so-called laws of language to the realm of mathematics and science. In this realm, statements can be true or false. Here *knowledge* is possible: knowledge of science, knowledge of mathematics; knowledge of grammar. If you ignore the laws of science, you will fall if you step off the edge of a cliff, for gravity always pulls you towards the centre of the Earth; if you ignore the laws of language, you will fail to communicate, for "there is no reliable way of communicating meaning [without them]" (Truss 2003, p. 20). This way of looking at the so-called laws of language is mirrored in the way prescriptivists present them: as *categorical* imperatives (*Do x*, or *Never do y*).

On close examination we find that the laws of language promoted by the strong prescriptivists have no epistemological credentials. First, there are no *routes* to knowledge about language use, no ways of proving that such-and-such a law is true or false. Knowledge is derived only by *a priori* or *a posteriori* means, and neither gives us the laws that strong prescriptivists believe in. Second, the imperative mood of those laws rules out—logically rules out—any possibility that they can be true or false. A categorical imperative—that is, a *command* that something must be done or not done: *Never start a sentence with a conjunction*, for example—can be no more true or false than an interrogative (*What is the time?*) or an exclamative (*Ouch!*).

Although the so-called laws of grammar cannot be true or false (and thus cannot be verified or falsified), what strong prescriptivists say about them to justify their alleged inviolability can. For example, the claim that the laws are necessary if communication is to be reliable can be verified or falsified. It can be true or false. And in the previous chapter we found that it was false. Breaches of many of the laws are not necessarily failures of communication. Every competent English speaker understands *We expect to more than double our profit next year* despite it breaking the prohibition on splitting infinitives. Conversely, following some such laws can lead to failures of communication. We showed that the way that prescriptivists insist we use the genitive apostrophe is one such case.

We can accept that there are patterns in language use just as there are patterns in the seasons and in the structure of bee hives. (Sentences contain verbs, a descriptive adjective precedes a definitive adjective, hyphens join prefixes to words, and so on.) But there is no need to postulate laws to explain these patterns (as we must if we are to explain the patterns we find in nature). For the history of a language shows that how people use it has less to do with *laws* that should be followed and more to do with *conventions* that happen to be followed. Language use, like etiquette, is simply a convention, and a convention is neither true nor false. Just as it makes no sense to say that the shaking of hands on being introduced is true (or false), it makes no sense to say that splicing prefixes and words with a hyphen is true (or false). It is just something that we commonly do.

A less extreme version of prescriptivism is *weak prescriptivism*. On this view the rules of language, although essentially a matter of convention, are worth treating as inviolable, for without them we would be worse off in some way (such as our ability to communicate would be severely diminished). Although they are more inclined to talk of invaluable *rules* than inviolable *laws*, weak prescriptivists are still fiercely protective of many aspects of language use. Like the strong prescriptivist, they insist that language should be used in particular ways regardless of common usage.

While strong prescriptivists express their claims as categorical imperatives (Do $y$), weak prescriptivists prefer the less forceful *conditional* imperative (If $x$, do $y$). Conditional imperatives can be true or false; can be verified or falsified. If we found an $x$ without an accompanying $y$, we would have falsified the imperative. For example, if $x$ is *successful communication* and $y$ is *don't split infinitives*, we would have falsified *If $x$ then $y$* by finding a split infinitive that did not impede communication.

The first hurdle for the weak prescriptivist is to provide a compelling antecedent for their prescriptions (that is, for the $x$ in their *If $x$, then $y$* imperatives). In chapter 2 we considered a number of possibilities—including the most obvious: *if you want to be understood by your audience*—and found all to be wanting.

A second hurdle is in explaining why we should follow some dearly held rules when they clearly serve no substantive purpose. We considered a number of these rules in chapter 3 (such as the rule governing the apostrophe of elision) and found that compelling reasons for adopting them are thin on the ground. Once we accept that the routines and repetitions of language use are merely the expression of a natural convention—as weak prescriptivists do—convincing others that they *must* follow these routines becomes especially difficult. Why must a convention always be followed? The wearing of black when mourning is a convention in some societies, but does that mean that a resident *must* wear black when mourning. For a woman to change her surname after marriage was once a strong convention in most Western countries. But did that make it a necessity for women to do so? Treating black Africans as saleable slaves was once a strong convention in certain countries. Did the conventionality of the practice give it justification? In other words, the value of a convention is independent of its conventionality. It must be established by some other means. Some conventions are good; some less so. But are any necessary? And here we need to draw a distinction between the need for a convention and the form the convention takes. We might accept that there is a need for some convention governing interpersonal communication (for without *shared* understanding no communication is possible). But that does not tie us to any *particular* convention. (If it did, *Homo sapiens* would have only one language.) Nor does it require us to resist change, even change to a useful convention. For there is no reason to think that the decline or loss of a cherished convention wouldn't be met by the rise of another convention to take its place. If writers consider it important or helpful to be able to do $x$ with writing, then there is little doubt that writers will do $x$ by whatever means is available. A thousand years ago, three dots were used to indicate the end of a sentence. It is useful to indicate the end of a sentence, which is why we still do it—but now with a single dot. The convention changed but the overriding practice hasn't.

The same is true in pictorial art and in music. The conventions adopted by Titian and Mozart were not the conventions adopted by Lucian Freud and Igor Stravinsky. Yet the works of Freud and Stravinsky are still works of art (indeed brilliant works of art). The ability to startle, move, uplift and unsettle was not lost in the transition from one set of expressive conventions to another. Do we see art critics call a brushstroke or colouring *incorrect*, insisting that the artist should have followed an earlier aesthetic? Do we see music critics calling a chord or fermata *incorrect*? The music might be dull, lacking structure or overly repetitious, but not incorrect (with students who copy the style in question given poor marks in music school). No. So why is it that language is judged to be correct or incorrect? The absurdity of the Apostrophe Protection Society is brought into sharp relief when one considers that there is no equivalent Realism Protection Society or Classical Harmony Protection Society. The notion that pictorial art and music should be conservative—should be unchanging—is self-defeating, if not contradictory. Art and music are forms of expression. So is writing. And just as artists and composers will continue to break conventions, writers will too. For writing too is an art form and just as deserving of creative licence. It is clear, then, that the weak prescriptivist shares with the strong prescriptivist a deep-seated conservatism. They want one set of conventions—usually the set they were taught at school—to be the only set allowable. The creative impulses that in large part define *Homo sapiens* are to be denied.

What is worth fighting for is the ability of language to be a means of communication (which, incidentally, is not under threat). What is not worth fighting for is the preservation of one way of communicating over other equally useful ways.

But the most difficult hurdle for both forms of prescriptivism is the elephant in the room: inevitable language change. Language is a convention and conventions change. How many conventions of 500 years ago are still conventions today, whatever walk of life? (Do men still wear wigs? Are scholarly books still written in Latin?) In deciding that it is important to hold on to some language use come what may, prescriptivists are implicitly rejecting what is undeniable: that the principle purpose to which we put language is to communicate. For if prescriptivists stubbornly hold on to so-called laws of language, or to conventions that are deemed especially important, they run the risk of communication failure.

To see how this can occur, imagine that we discover an *elixir vitae* (or manage to tweak our genes so as to engineer a remarkable longevity). We can now live for a long time, long enough to witness significant changes in the English language.[2] Suppose further that the changes are significant enough that a long-lived prescriptivist in the distant future, writing according to the apparently inviolable laws of English (or according to those conventions of the twenty-first century that were considered especially useful), is barely understood, if understood at all, by readers for whom the writing is intended. Could it rightly be said that our long-lived purist is, in this situation, a good writer? All the so-called fundamental laws of the language may have been followed and yet something essential is missing: the very thing that gives purpose to the act of writing—communication. Indeed, we don't even need to postulate preternatural longevity to make the point. Thanks to language change, understanding what our own grandparents wrote just 70 or 80 years ago can be a challenge (not to mention reading Shakespeare and Chaucer without a concordance). With the rate of language change on the increase—thanks to the web-inspired democratisation of publishing—it is conceivable that a writer who clings to the conventions of their primary school classroom will later in life use words and devices that contemporary readers will find mystifying. In a word, there will be communication breakdown. The writing will be self-defeating.

Let's flesh out this objection with some examples. Take, first, the pedants' insistence that *disinterested* means *impartial*. If they continue to use the word in that sense when most people take it to mean *uninterested*—which is likely to be the case in the next decade or two—then there is a strong likelihood of disrupted communication and even communication failure. To a writer wanting to communicate, it is not a question of what a word *should* mean, but what meaning is evoked when readers encounter the word. To write hoping to evoke a particular meaning (*impartial*) but use a word that will certainly evoke another (*uninterested*) is contradictory. The writing is self-defeating.

---

2. In fact, we don't need to rely on hypothetical magic or genetics know-how to prove our point, given that cryonics is now a viable technology. Just imagine a moribund purist coming off the ice in 400 years.

Another example: take the humble en dash (–). For a very long time the en dash was primarily used to indicate that two distinct entities are being treated as one, a task ill-suited to the hyphen:

> the Michelson–Morley experiment [an experiment conducted by two people—Michelson and Morley—as indicated by the en dash)]
>
> the Michelson-Morley experiment [an experiment conducted by a person with a double-barrelled surname, as indicated by the hyphen]

Thanks largely to the poor design of computer keyboards, the en dash (and the em dash) are now moribund. Perhaps in 50 years time, these dashes will have disappeared altogether from contemporary writing, replaced, one can already sense, by the open hyphen (that is, a hyphen with manually inserted spaces on either side of it). Will pedants continue to use the en dash even if it causes most readers at that time to scratch their head in bafflement (or misread it as a hyphen)? To repeat: to write to communicate but deliberately use language that hinders communication is self-defeating. Thus prescriptivism — if adopted consistently — is self-defeating.

To sum up: holding hard and fast to rules come what may will, in the face of inevitable change, thwart clear communication. But prescriptivists state that clear communication is their primary goal. Thus prescriptivism is a contradictory philosophy. Of course, prescriptivists are strongly opposed, sometimes vehemently opposed, to language change. But to base a philosophy on what won't happen — language stasis — is pointless, and to force it on others is authoritarianism.

## Descriptivism and conventions

The rejection of prescriptivism brings us to *descriptivism*. The first question to consider is what does the conventionality of language mean for the descriptivist? Everything, in fact. It is the descriptivist's starting point. The descriptivist approach is to consider what we *do* with language, not what we *should* do. It is a scientific approach to language use. Just as a scientist tries to fit an equation to a set of data-points, a descriptivist looks at a range of language use and tries to fit a rule to it. But the rule here is simply a description—perhaps at most an imperfect description—of current usage. The rule "*i* before *e* except after *c*" is a reasonably good fit to the spelling data-points of contemporary English (although there are data-points that fall off the line: *either, neither, seizure, beige* and so on). The rule *Place evaluative adjectives before descriptive adjectives and descriptive adjectives before definitive adjectives* strongly matches the data-points of common usage. And all that the descriptivist does with these rules is to invite people to follow them if they wish to follow contemporary English. Many of us do—since we want to be understood by our correspondents—and thus the descriptivist is doing us a service. But no-one is obliged to follow them.

So the first plank in the descriptivists' platform is that language use is not bound by inviolable laws or rules but is simply the manifestation of a convention. The arguments presented in chapter 2 strongly support this view.

The second plank is that the conventions that underpin language use will continue to change. This can't be proved. Still, the historical record shows that substantial changes have already occurred (again see chapter 2) and, given that no-one owns or controls the language, the chances of it not changing further seem remote. Human playfulness, the desire for novelty, the need to differentiate ourselves from others and our creative instincts seem certain to cause shifts in the language, as will the need to create terms for the things we are yet to encounter (such as new discoveries and inventions). Just as contemporary readers have difficulty reading Chaucer or Shakespeare without the help of a commentary or concordance, readers in the twenty-fifth century will no doubt need help reading Patrick White or Martin Amis. Perhaps the only thing that is constant in language is change.

The third plank in the descriptivists' platform is the claim that we primarily write to *communicate*. It is true that we use language for many purposes: to inform, persuade, amuse, deceive, conceal, move and so on. But in all these uses, some form of communication is involved. It is simply the way the communication is dressed that distinguishes, say, persuasive rhetoric from tear-jerking melodrama, fact giving from comedy, and so on. Prescriptivists also contend that the primary purpose of writing is to communicate, but they — unlike descriptivists — believe that it is only by writing according to fixed laws or rules that communication can succeed. But communication using language does not need fixed rules to succeed any more than communication via painting or music does (as chapter 3 shows).

Writing that communicates is also writing that shows respect for readers. Indeed, being true to purpose and showing respect are two sides of the same coin. One implies the other and vice versa. Readers want to understand what they are reading (not to mention understand it with the least effort). If someone commissions a report or buys a book, there is an expectation that they will understand what they get. Moreover, it is a *rightful* expectation if money has changed hands. For it is tantamount to taking money under false pretences for a writer to present a work as an informational text and make it available for sale, yet those who buy it cannot readily find the information they were expecting or understand it if they do. Thus writing that communicates is writing that meets the needs and expectations of readers. Such writing can also be a win for the writer. By meeting the needs and expectations of readers, it is likely to be judged good writing and the writer judged a good writer. If it is a report, the writer is more likely to meet their performance hurdles (and thus get a bonus at the end of the year); if it is a book, the author is more likely to get good reviews and thus earn more royalties than would otherwise be the case. Thus writing that is true to purpose — that is, communicates — can be a win–win: a win for readers and a win for the writer.

The fourth plank in the descriptivists' platform is the claim that *variation* in contemporary language use is legitimate. As a tool for communication, there is no reason to think that the English of one country or dialect is better than that of another country or dialect. An American can feel just as comfortable using a closed em dash to enclose parenthetic material as a Briton can using an open en dash for the same purpose. Likewise Australians can happily spell racquet *racquet* while the rest of the English-speaking world prefers *racket*. And Shropshire folk can legitimately call sports shoes *daps* while Essex folk call them *plimsolls*. There are no authorised adjudicators of what is better or best when it comes to particular variants of English, nor any obvious criteria by which such judgements could be made. The only criterion that might seem even remotely relevant is *expressive utility* or *richness* (but it would be a brave commentator indeed who would claim that, say, Oxbridge English is more expressive or rich than Ivy League English, or vice versa). Even so, if a term or device with no equivalent elsewhere appears in one variant of English, it will either be incorporated into other Englishes if it is deemed to have expressive utility or ignored if it is not. (The Englishes are not separated by impermeable barriers that prevent cross-fertilisation.) Thus an equilibrium of expressive utility is likely to be maintained among the Englishes. This renders any claim that one variant of English is superior to another incurably relativistic.

Putting these four planks together yields the descriptivists' manifesto: if you want to write to communicate—or in a way that maximises communicative potential—it is best to adopt the language conventions of your intended audience: best for readers and writers. By focusing on the *audience* for language, descriptivism can accommodate language variation and language change. A descriptivist will write differently for an American audience than for a British audience, and a sixty-year-old descriptivist will write differently to how they wrote when they were twenty—if conventions have changed in the intervening years. Using foreign or dead conventions—the logical outcome of consistent prescriptivism—is no less a barrier to communication than making up your own conventions. Prescriptivism, in other words, leads to language that is neither true to purpose nor shows respect for readers. Clearly, then, the better approach is descriptivism.

A preference for reader respect over rules is not to dilute the value of rules—*so long as they are understood as changeable conventions*. Descriptivism does not entail linguistic anarchy. Humans benefit from communication and communication benefits from there being shared conventions. It benefits if there is some convention that enables readers to see where one sentence ends and another begins. It benefits if there is joint understanding of what words mean. It benefits if there is widespread acceptance of the need for a punctuation mark in compound adjectives. And so on. Without conventions, and their ready adoption by writers, there would be little written communication—hence the self-regulatory nature of natural languages. For we all have an incentive to maintain what is beneficial to us. But it is an incentive that competes with ignorance (a poor understanding of relevant conventions), creativity (the need for novelty), admiration (the disposition to copy those we admire) and rationality (the desire to seek improvement). It is this multi-pronged competition that spawns many of the changes in language.

## Active and passive descriptivism

Descriptivism comes in two flavours: *passive* and *active*. Both assert that communication is paramount and contend that, in general, the best way to achieve it is by adopting the conventions of one's audience (whoever they might be). The difference between the two lies only in what is done when:

- there is no strong convention governing some use or other
- there is a strong convention but it is confusing
- a convention is waning.

A passive descriptivist simply goes with the flow, following the conventions of common usage and making no recommendations about language use. Where there is no strong convention governing some use or other, the passive descriptivist will do as they please (so long as it doesn't get in the way of communication). On the other hand, the active descriptivist will consider whether there might be good reasons—reasons that improve communicative power, for example—for preferring one usage over another. If there are, the active descriptivist will adopt the better usage in their own writing and may even seek to directly influence other writers. (The compiler of a style manual is likely to be an active descriptivist.) The goal is to coax change and, by doing so, turn a usage that is currently discretionary into a convention.

What form should quotation marks ideally take: single or double? This is the sort of question that might exercise an active descriptivist should there be no strong convention one way or the other. This is the case in Australian English at the moment, where both forms are widely used. A writer seeking advice on the matter—or corroboration that there is no strong convention—will probably consult a style manual, and the most authoritative one for Australian English is *Style Manual for Authors, Editors and Printers*. This manual acknowledges that, in the absence of a strong convention, its advice on quotation marks can only be a recommendation, and its recommendation is to use *single* quotation marks. To its credit, it gives a reason to support its recommendation, namely, that it is "in keeping with the trend towards minimal punctuation" (*Style Manual* 2002, p. 112). This is a defining feature of active descriptivism—giving *reasons* for adopting a particular usage. Naturally, where reasons are offered, there is an implied invitation to comment and challenge. (This is in stark contrast to the authoritarianism of strong prescriptivism.) And one challenge to the reason given for preferring single quotation marks should be obvious: even if we assume that consistency of use is important—which is implied by the recommendation—is the existence of a trend sufficient to justify following it?

Anomalous usage is mostly stillborn. It rarely survives beyond the text in which it appears. But sometimes an anomalous usage gains followers. The transmission might in large part be subconscious, but the result could be that the usage becomes a fad. (The capitalisation in business documents of what are deemed *important* nouns—even if they are not proper nouns—is a current example.) With enough critical mass of followers, a fad can become a trend, and a trend, if widely adopted, becomes a new convention. For example, there was once a strong convention in English that writers place a space before a semicolon and colon. Someone stopped adding this space (anomalous usage), others followed (creating a fad) and a trend was born. This trend gained enough critical mass—perhaps as a result of little more than herd momentum—to evolve into the space-omitting convention we all follow today. But other usages, fads and trends have died out without attaining the imprimatur of conventional usage. One example is the hyphen in street names often seen in Australian English 50 or so years ago (as in "123 George-street Sydney").

From the perspective of communicative power, not all trends are equal. Some are certainly worthwhile (such as the trend of omitting the apostrophe of elision). Others appear to add nothing to communicative power and do little more than distract readers. One example is the enclosing of a single adjective or adverb in parentheses, as in:

"His approach ... is to situate us exactly in the middle of the (logarithmic) spectrum of magnitudes ranging from the astronomical to the sub-atomic."[3]

This practice adds nothing to (communicative) potential and may have the opposite effect of distracting the reader. (Were you puzzled by the parentheses around *communicative* in the previous sentence?)

---

3. Richard Dawkins (ed.), *The Oxford Book of Modern Science Writing*, Oxford University Press, Oxford, 2008, p. 5.

Another trend that carries no value and is likely to distract is the use of a comma to splice independent clauses in a two-clause sentence, as in:

"There is no cure for Alzheimer's disease, it brings dementia and slow death to thousands of Australians every year." [*The Age* newspaper]

No doubt these particular practices could one day become conventional and do so without saddling readers with a loss of readability. However, some trends might not be so innocuous. Take, for instance, the gathering use of the hyphen for the unifying en dash. (Is *Michelson-Morley experiment* referring to one or two experimenters?)

What these examples suggest is that if we are to base a recommendation on a trend, it is important that the trend not be one that hinders communication. With that in mind, let's revisit the recommendation to use single quotes. Recall that the closing single quotation mark (') and the possessive apostrophe (') are identical. And there lies a problem. For a plural possessive apostrophe in a quotation enclosed within single quotation marks could be mistaken by readers for the end of the quotation. Consider the following fragment:

They would accept anything as legitimate scholarship as long as it sounded good and 'flattered the editors' ideological preconceptions—or should we say ideological misconceptions—to the contrary'.

Note the phrase 'flattered the editors' at the end of the second line. Many readers would initially interpret the possessive apostrophe as the end of the quotation. Then, when they get to the end of the sentence, they see what, on first thought, looks like an orphaned quotation mark. Perhaps, in bafflement, they will re-read what they have just read, or perhaps, being time-poor like many of us are, they won't. Thus there is the chance of interrupted or thwarted communication—all because of an infelicitous choice of quotation mark.

Seeing the potential problem, an active descriptivist might choose to place double quotation marks around quotations in their own writing, thus rendering our sample text:

They would accept anything as legitimate scholarship as long as it sounded good and "flattered the editors' ideological preconceptions—or should we say ideological misconceptions—to the contrary".

This solves the problem. It won't be unconventional, as there was no convention to begin with, merely discretionary usage. Nonetheless, should a strong convention in favour of single quotes arise—so strong that the use of double quotes would puzzle and distract readers—the active prescriptivist will abandon double quotes. Holding fast to a usage come what may is the intransigence of prescriptivism. It is entirely foreign to descriptivism. Prescriptivists and descriptivist alike might lament the loss of communicative power brought about by some change or other. But the descriptivist will not insist that an abandoned convention be followed. For a start such an approach is unhelpful in oiling communication. It also overlooks the fact that the English language is so rich of synonym and flexible of syntax—offering many ways to say the same thing—that the communicative power lost with the demise of one useful convention will almost certainly be offset by the rise of another to take its place.

Let's now consider the case where there is a strong convention but it adds nothing of communicative value and often confuses readers. In such a case, the active descriptivist— unlike the passive descriptivist—will ignore the convention. Take, for example, the genitive apostrophe in *two weeks' notice* and *five years' experience*. The genitive apostrophe is primarily meant to help us distinguish singular from plural. But the phrase *two weeks* (and also *five years*) is obviously, unmistakably plural. No competent reader will puzzle over it. So why the need for the apostrophe? The genitive apostrophe is also thought to help us distinguish a plural noun from a genitive noun. Notice the difference between *you must have two weeks free in June* (plural) and *you must give two weeks' notice* (genitive). It might be argued that these two cases could be confused if the latter was written as *you must give two weeks notice*. But the word that follows *weeks* makes the intended meaning clear. *Free* is clearly an adjective (so the preceding noun is obviously plural) and *notice* is a noun (so the noun before it must be a genitive). So there is no ambiguity. And if there happened to be a thing called a *weeks notice*, we would indicate plurality by writing *two weeks notices*, as we do with most compound nouns. Thus the apostrophe in *two weeks' notices* and *five years' experience* is adding nothing of communicative value.

It can also be confusing. This apostrophe is more commonly called the *possessive* apostrophe, which leads many to ponder where the possession is in *two weeks' notice* and *five years' experience*. The context is clearly *of*, not *for*, but is any possession indicated in *notice of two weeks* or *experience of five years*? Can *weeks* possess *notice* or *years* possess *experience*? Hence the apostrophe is confusing as well as redundant. It is best forgotten. To insist on it—to insist on *any* punctuation or distinction that serves no useful communicative purpose—is senseless authoritarianism. Just as biological evolution will probably see *Homo sapiens* shed the appendix—thereby improving the overall health of the species—language evolution will hopefully see the weeding out of those conventions that contribute nothing to the health of our writing.

Let's now consider an active descriptivist's likely response to conventions that are waning. Clearly, that response will depend on whether the change is beneficial or detrimental (with the unit for comparison being commutative potential). We'll begin with one that is sure to be considered beneficial.

Many students were, and some still are, taught that if a singular noun ends in *s*, we just add an apostrophe after the *s* to indicate possession, otherwise we add an apostrophe and an *s*. Thus, if marking singular possession, we are to write *The cat's whiskers are long* but *The species' distribution is unknown*. This erstwhile strong convention is on the wane—at least in Australian English (*Style Manual* 2002, p. 85)—with a trend underway to treat all possessive singular nouns the same *regardless of spelling*.

We have noted a number of times that the convention defeats the primary purpose of possessive apostrophes, namely, to distinguish singular from plural. For we typically mark *plural* possession by adding an apostrophe after the final *s*, (as in *my brothers' books*). Hence, by the erstwhile strong convention, *the species' distribution is unknown* could be read as referring to the distribution of one species or many species. In other words, it generates ambiguity. The current trend away from the convention avoids this ambiguity by inflecting *all* singular nouns with *'s* in the possessive. Thus the *species's distribution is unknown* is written to indicate that it is the distribution of a *single* species that is unknown. Prescriptivists might decry the trend, but the clarity added to the language should this trend become a convention would please any active descriptivist. An active descriptivist might not mirror the trend in their own writing if doing so was likely to distract or confuse their readers. But they are sure to encourage the trend to become a convention. (A passive descriptivist would not mirror the trend until it had become a convention.)

But not all changes to strong conventions are beneficial. It was once a strong convention to use first-line indents to indicate the start of a new paragraph. Many writers have abandoned this convention. Instead they use additional line spacing to indicate that a new paragraph follows, and all paragraphs are set flush against the left margin. An active descriptivist is likely to find this trend less appealing than the one discussed in the previous paragraph. It is clear that paragraphing is an invaluable device for alerting readers to a change of topic.[4] But if a paragraph falls at the bottom of a page and its last sentence finishes close to the right margin, there will be no cues for the reader to interpret the next sentence—starting unindented at the top of the next page—as

---

4. This somewhat obvious point is overlooked by the increasing number of newspaper editors who enforce a one-sentence-per-paragraph regime.

the beginning of a new paragraph. The first-line indent of traditional publishing overcomes this problem.

The problem also arises where you have block text—text set off from the main body of the paragraph (as in the following example):

> This is an example of block text, text set off from the parent paragraph but still part of the parent paragraph.

If space is the only guide a reader has as to when a new paragraph begins, it will not be obvious to the reader when the text below a piece of block text begins a new paragraph. (This particular block of text is not indented, which should make it clear to the reader that it is the continuation of the paragraph that began just before the block text—but only because of the convention adopted in this book of indenting new paragraphs.) Both passive and active descriptivists will continue to use first-line indents until the trend towards space and space alone becomes the convention (if it does). If it does, descriptivists will follow the new convention (but the active descriptivist will not have given up without a fight).

Another declining convention is in the use of the genitive apostrophe when the context is *for* not *of* (as in *the Captains parking space*). We noted in the last chapter—when discussing so-called necessary usage—that this trend reduces our ability to tell singular from plural. (Does *my brothers books* mean books for my *only* brother or books for *all* my brothers?) But we also noted that the prescriptivists' insistence on keeping the apostrophe for both possessive and non-possessive cases means that we cannot tell whether the context is possessive (*of*) or non-possessive (*for*). For example, does *my brother's books* mean books *for* my brother or books *of* my brother? Here, perhaps, is a field that is begging for the active descriptivist to make suggestions, and here is one: continue to use punctuation marks to help the reader see singular from plural but use different marks depending on whether the context is possessive (*of*) or non-possessive (*for*). For example, *my brother's books* would mean the books of my brother, *my brothers' books* would mean the books of my brothers, *my brother`s books* would mean the books for my brother and *my brothers` books* would mean the books for my brothers. (The character in the last two examples is the grave accent, found on many keyboards below the tilde, although any mark other than an apostrophe would do.) Another suggestion—and one that could be implemented immediately—is to avoid the non-possessive genitive form altogether. Thus write *the books for my brother* or *the books for my brothers*, forms that avoid apostrophes and thus ambiguity. This suggestion would also be useful in those cases where the apostrophe would invite not two, but three or even four, potential interpretations. Consider *Melinda's painting* where Melinda is an artist who is alive. Does this phrase mean a painting that Melinda owns (possessive genitive), a painting that I have bought for Melinda (objective genitive), a portrait of Melinda (subjective genitive) or a painting painted by Melinda (descriptive genitive)?

It should be clear that apostrophe use in English is a mess (and clear, too, that the purists' insistence that it be used in all genitive forms is a recipe for ambiguity). It is a punctuation mark best used with caution. Avoiding the genitive form where no possession is involved is a useful approach, and one that doesn't break any convention. It is likely to be the preference of descriptivists from both camps.

## Nudging change

Can the philosophy of active descriptivism influence language to any significant degree? The picture of language we have sketched in this book is of an unowned, uncontrollable beast (though one we happily take advantage of). Despite the haughty reproofs of prescriptivists and the earnest entreaties of the academies, language seems to do its own thing. If so, isn't active descriptivism doomed from the start?

Language might be a mere convention and appear to travel its own path, but that doesn't necessarily put it outside the influence of its users. A natural convention—the sort that language is—is not foisted on people. Rather, it develops from what people do. And what people do can be influenced by what they think. Some conventions have changed radically as a result of thought, discussion and debate (and occasionally blood on the streets). The once-strong convention that only males could vote in parliamentary elections was fiercely challenged in the late nineteenth and early twentieth centuries, the result being women's suffrage. The old male-only convention was dispensed with in its entirety, the equivalent of a paradigm shift in social customs. Most conventions change in a less radical way: schoolteachers gradually abandon the wearing of academic gowns in the classroom, women stop feeling compelled to wear a hat in church, correspondents begin dropping the once-common courtesy title *Esquire* from their messages, and so on. Revolutions aside, conventions mostly change slowly. But they do change, and that should give heart to the active descriptivist.

Perhaps it is not overly fanciful to think that the manner in which an active descriptivist writes might be mimicked by others, propelled by social media into a fad that spawns a trend that finally gives rise to a new and useful convention. But the probability of that happening is no doubt slim. Language commentators seem not to have the right degree of cool to be able to catch a viral wave to web stardom. Active descriptivists do, though, have other avenues of influence: they can influence the influencers. For instance, they can join a professional society—especially a society of editors—and engage in debate with like-minded people, perhaps publishing articles in the society's journal arguing for or against some practice. Fellow-members might include those who have some influence in deciding what recommendations appear in a national style guide. Publishing houses too can influence language. The internal style guides their copy-editors use to prepare manuscripts for publication may well influence subsequent readers. The logic is natural if not infallible: if it has been published this way by a reputable publishing house, then that way must be fine. But there is one profession where an active descriptivist can have significant influence: teaching. Teachers are by far best suited to honing the communicative skills of youngsters. Not only can they transmit to a new generation the contemporary conventions of the local language; they can also steer usage that is unconventional (deterring students from poor practices and encouraging them to adopt good ones).

There is no contradiction in giving teachers a role in moulding language skills while at the same time accepting that there is no correct or incorrect usage. For the conventionality of language in no way implies that we should not fuss over its quality. Nor does it imply that quality must be in the eye of the beholder, that one use cannot be better than another. For a start, we all have a need to communicate, so we will need to learn communication skills whatever the epistemological standing of the rules that make communication possible. Moreover, it is clear to most native speakers—prescriptivists and descriptivists alike—when a piece of writing is of poor quality. Obviously text *A* is better than text *B* if *B* but not *A* has aspects that obstruct communication (such as ambiguity, vagueness, contradiction and the like). These obstructions arise from a failure to appreciate the *mechanics* of writing (which we touch on briefly in the next chapter). A text can also be judged in other ways: as elegant, simple, coherent, prosaic, colourful, dull and the like. But these are meta-measures. They only come into play if the writing is already *mechanically good*, that is, it does well its primary job of communicating with others. They are issues to do with the *style* of writing and are not discussed in this book. For the descriptivist, mechanics is more important than style. (What good is knowing how to ice a cake if you don't know how to bake it?) So writing can be judged good or bad even if it cannot be judged correct or incorrect, right or wrong. It can be judged in terms of how well it communicates what it intended to communicate. And teachers are best placed to instil in the young the mechanics that yield effective communication. For their charter is not simply to teach rules of language use—many of which are unhelpful, as we've seen—

but to prepare students to be effective communicators. And that requires an assessment, on the scale of communicative power, of the value of each rule that could be taught. (One does not teach communication skills by teaching rules that generate ambiguity.) Thus, through the classroom, active descriptivism can influence the language of a nation. We return to the topic of language teaching in the final chapter.

Of the four approaches to language we have been considering—strong prescriptivism, weak prescriptivism, passive descriptivism and active descriptivism—only the latter offers any chance of engineering beneficial change. But the active descriptivist needs to be realistic. Language largely does its own thing. It is not fuelled or constrained by internal forces: by logic, consistency, origins, necessity, standardisation or whatever. It just is. It is not a random convention. Its rules do not pop into existence like quarks in a quantum vacuum. When it changes, it changes for a reason, but those reasons cannot easily be predicted or even understood. In this regard, it is akin to a chaotic system (such as the weather, or the stockmarket). Nonetheless, it can be nudged in certain directions (as John Dryden and a few others have succeeded in doing). Change begins somewhere, somehow. If, every so often, that somehow is an argument put forward somewhere by an active descriptivist, then the active descriptivism program will have been justified. Vive active descriptivism!

## Needs, morality and justice

Whether active descriptivism can make a difference to the way language is used makes for interesting discussion, but it is tangential to our main argument—that prescriptivism has lost its right to be the pedagogy of first choice. Not only is it unnecessarily authoritarian; its implicit conservatism thwarts its purpose. We have proposed descriptivism as a replacement (at least passive, but preferably active). To prevent writing from being self-defeating—from thwarting its purpose—it is best to adopt the language conventions of your intended audience, that is, language as it is actually used, not language as some think it should be used. That is the central plank in the descriptivist's program. But there is more going for descriptivism than the fact that it is a workable alternative to prescriptivism. A respect for the way language is actually used—that is, majority usage—could well be a moral requirement, a requirement that imposes obligations on parents, teachers and governments.

For too long the classroom spotlight has been shone on examples of correct and incorrect language. If there is no correct or incorrect when it comes to language use, then we need to dim that spotlight or move it elsewhere. Perhaps a better candidate for our attention is what is in our best interests when we decide on the language to use.

By instinct *Homo sapiens* seek some level of wellbeing. That level will not be the same for each of us, but it is certainly more than we find ourselves with at birth. As we mature we realise that we need others if we are to reach our desired wellbeing. We seek affection, love and protection; we seek goods more plentiful than we can eke out alone. We seek respect and maybe influence. But how do we make our needs known to others? And how might I convince them that in helping to satisfy my needs I will help them satisfy theirs (without which I might not get their help)? Body language—crying, grunts, pointing and the like—can only go so far. It lacks the richness and precision of verbal language. But if I am to make my needs and intentions known to others using verbal language, I need to use *their* verbal language. Otherwise what I say or write will appear as nonsense. Further, if I am to make my intentions known to the greatest number in my tribe, society or country—thereby *maximising* my chances of attaining the wellbeing I want—I will need to use (or at least want to know) the language of the *majority*. Thus a preference for majority usage is an insurance policy. It gives me confidence that I will be able to communicate with whoever I might need to communicate with. It is the natural outcome of instincts that drive us to seek our own wellbeing. And this same reasoning applies to every other person in society. They too will want to know the language that will help them maximise the chances of getting what they need in order to secure the level of wellbeing they want. The universality of this preference for majority usage is the mechanism that keeps all strong natural languages from sinking into anarchy and disintegration.

Of course, there will always be those who prefer to use the language of a sub-group (the language of the court, the upper class, academia and so on). If their needs are well met (and will continue to be met) by doing so, they will not be acting irrationally. But none of us can know *in advance* who we might need to interact with in order to gain the wellbeing we seek. In this respect, we start out behind a "veil of ignorance", a useful notion introduced by the American philosopher John Rawls.[5] Under this condition—that is, where we do not know who we will want or need to interact with—would it not be irrational to choose to learn as our principal language one other than that of the majority in our society? (Would we choose Elizabethan English when most others in our society are speaking twenty-first century English? Would we choose Jamaican English if we are living in New Zealand?) Of course, we don't get a choice as to the principal language we will learn (which might be the only language we learn). We are too young when that decision needs to be made, too young to know what is in our best interests. But we are, at that age, in the care of people who are morally obliged to act in our best interests, namely parents and teachers. And parents and teachers must also decide from behind a veil of ignorance what language you should be taught. Not knowing who you will most often need to communicate with, your guardians are obliged to choose the language of those you are most likely to need to communicate with. Most people spend most of their life in the country of their birth. Moreover, there is good reason to suppose that a youngster will encounter, and communicate with, people from all socioeconomic classes during their lifetime. The language that is common across all socioeconomic classes is majority

---

5. J. Rawls, *A Theory of Justice*, Oxford University Press, Oxford, 1972.

usage. Thus it is the language of the majority in their society that youngsters should be taught. In a word, adopting descriptivism is a moral obligation, implied by the obligation to act in the best interests of those in our care. A parent who sends their child to a school that will only teach a minority variant of English—say U-English—is not acting in the best interests of their child. What good is learning that *disinterested* means "impartial" and that a *serviette* is really a *napkin* if it proves to be the generator of noise in attempts to communicate with the wider society?

Majority usage will be evident in numbers: statistics, to be precise. Statistics will show us what is and what is not majority usage. If 90% of a nation put commas between adjectives only if they are of the same type, then that practice is unmistakably a majority practice in that country. It would also be a strong convention. If it was 55% instead, there may be some reluctance to call it a majority usage. Perhaps linguists had been observing the gradual decline of the practice. Perhaps by the time the results of their observations are published, the practice will have dropped below 50%. Hence the reluctance to call it a majority usage. But if it was 55% and it could be shown that the practice has been trending upwards for some time, perhaps there would be less reluctance to consider it majority usage even if we couldn't yet call it a strong convention. Still, these borderline scenarios need not worry us unduly. As long as there is a method for finding majority usage and comparing usage over time, we can have confidence that our instinct for clear communication can be satisfied. And such methods are well-established in the disciplines of linguistics and lexicography.

We need to be careful where we look for information about language use. There are myriad blogs, websites, columns and books that offer advice on language use, but most will only tell you how you *should* write. Few back up their recommendations with usage statistics. One rarely sees recommendations along the lines of: "now that 82.6% of Australians interpret *disinterested* to mean "uninterested" and only 17.4% interpret it to mean "impartial", the former is now the primary meaning of the word in Australian English" (a statistic that matches my own research). Instead we see claims that the use of *disinterested* to mean *uninterested* is wrong, incorrect or a misuse.[6] This is prescriptivism—most people's default position—and it is hopelessly flawed, as we've shown. If you want to ask how people *should* write, the only sensible answer is that they should write in ways that are not *self-defeating*. But the *should* here is only a conditional imperative: *if* you want to achieve the primary goal of language—to communicate—then you will more likely do so by adopting the language of those you are attempting to communicate with. If you don't know your audience, or you want to communicate with as many people as possible, then it is best that you resort to majority usage. But who can tell me what is the majority usage in any particular case? Who can help me separate primary meanings from secondary meanings, waxing meanings from waning meanings, parochial meanings from general meanings? Who has collected the statistics? Fortunately there are, in many countries, bodies that do just that: bodies of lexicographers and linguists.

## A National Language Record

The obvious need to know what majority usage is helps us dispose of a common retort made against the claim that there is no correct or incorrect language use. If nothing is correct or incorrect, the retort goes, then we can throw away the rule books and do what we like. On the contrary (with one minor caveat). Accepting that language use is neither correct or incorrect doesn't mean that we are going to do whatever we like. The need to communicate with others keeps us safe from solipsistic anarchy. But to communicate with others I need to know how they use the language. How do I learn that? Post-childhood, we will typically learn from teachers. But an ever-changing language means that what teachers learnt from their

---

6. See, for instance, www.dailywritingtips.com/disinterested-not-the-same-as-uninterested. Viewed 13 September 2014.

teachers might no longer be majority usage. So for teachers to avoid teaching out-dated usage, they need resources. And this is where rule books come into it. But the caveat is this. By *rules* we mean conventions and thus the rule books of interest cannot be the prescriptivist grammars of yesteryear, with their concern more for what should be done rather than what is done. The rule books must instead be the work of professional descriptivists, the linguists and lexicographers who treat the national language with the same sort of empirical respect and rigor as a botanist applies to a line of plant life.

Let us lump together under the rubric *national language record* (hereafter NLR) the grammars, dictionaries and style manuals that record how a country uses its language. Any hint of prescriptivism in the NLR should be more akin to the dispassionate argumentation of active descriptivism—of the sort discussed earlier in this chapter—than to the categorical pontifications of prescriptivists. Other than that, the NLR should be a purely *descriptive* guide to majority usage.

A government that does not fund, or actively support, the publication and periodic update of the NLR is negligent in its obligations: both to promote the wellbeing of its citizens and to protect sovereign culture. Without such a record, the teaching of language will become increasingly haphazard and anecdotal, and the capacity for effortless communication (and avoidance of miscommunication) will be compromised. We will get by, as English speakers did for centuries before lexicographers and linguists arrived on the scene. But we will be all the poorer as a result.

A government's obligation to maintain an NLR extends even further. Governments subject their citizens to various laws, and a failure to comply with a law more often than not attracts a penalty. It would be an injustice to impose a penalty for failing to comply with a law if the law was written in a way that the proverbial common man on the Clapham omnibus— our exemplar of majority usage—could not easily understand it. Similarly, it would be unfair if a government were to offer its citizens an entitlement (such as free dental care) if the offer is couched in language that only the privileged educated classes could understand.[7] Thus governments have an obligation to know what majority usage is and to use it in its dealings with the general public.

How might governments ascertain what majority usage is? There might already be dictionaries, grammar books and style guides available for consultation, but this does not absolve a government from the responsibility of ensuring that some subset of those publications constitutes an accurate NLR. (There are plenty of prescriptivist books about.) And if no such sub-set can be found, the government owes it to its citizens to create one. (It would be silly to postpone the machinery of government until some non-government body created the NLR.)

The need to communicate, together with the inevitability of language change, means that writing in a descriptivist spirit is more demanding than writing in a prescriptivist spirit. If prescriptivism was tenable, the language we learnt at school would serve us well throughout our life. Like our arithmetic times tables, we would learn it once and never have to worry about it again. But a natural language is not like that. The conventions taught fifty years ago may not be the conventions of today (and indeed many are not). Those who are constantly immersed in language may have absorbed the changes unthinkingly (such as dropping the space before a colon, limiting the spaces between sentences to one, dropping the hyphen in street names, replacing the colon–hyphen composite (:-) with the solo colon (:), and so on, all these being conventions in the last 80 or so years). Others may not be so fortunate and have to check every so often that what they are writing is contemporary English. And those who suddenly have to write—perhaps for a new job—may struggle, even if they were taught the conventions of their childhood. In other words, writing contemporary English well means that you need to

---

7. Similar arguments were put forward in the US in support of the *Plain Writing Act* 2010. A preamble to the Act states that "The purpose of this Act is to improve the effectiveness and accountability of Federal agencies to the public by promoting clear Government communication that the public can understand and use".

keep abreast of changes in the language since school days. That is the burden placed on us by the need to communicate. And it is a burden that parents must be especially aware of if they want to help their children with their English homework. (It is no help to be guiding a child's education according to the conventions you were taught when you were a child. "But I was taught $x$" is not a sound counter-argument to a new convention.) It is also a burden placed on governments: the burden of maintaining a national language record that citizens can consult to ensure that their communicative needs are met (and that governments can consult to ensure that their promulgations are just).

\*

In this chapter we finalised our demolition of prescriptivism as a serious philosophy of language use and teaching. We concluded that, if followed consistently, prescriptivism ends up bringing about the very communicative poverty it was meant to keep at bay. Descriptivism provides a stabler, more scientific, approach to language, with enough room to accommodate rational debate about the usefulness or otherwise of trends and conventions. We also emphasised the importance of being able to communicate with the majority of our fellow citizens if we are to reach our desired level of wellbeing. The urgency to seek and maintain some such level—the desire for self-betterment—is close to being a biological imperative. This imperative brings the study, and use, of language within the force-field of morality. What language *should* be taught if we want to maximise the chances that those in our care will gain the level of wellbeing they need? What language *should* be used if punishment, and the distribution of social entitlements, is to be just? Only the language of the majority—so-called *majority usage*—meets these biological and moral necessities. Descriptivism, then, is more than just a replacement for prescriptivism. It is a necessary corollary of *care* and *justice*, two constituents in that amalgam of concerns that comprise our common morality.

# 5: The bedrock of good writing

"The test of good or bad writing must surely be that of impact, of clarity, of ease of reading, not of strict adherence to conventional rules." (Cooper 1964, p. 82)

In previous chapters we emphasised that *communication* is the primary goal of language, a simple, perhaps incontrovertible, claim that is overlooked or downplayed by many (language pundits included). That we write to communicate is the *axiom* from which many of our arguments have taken their shape. One such argument—a simple deduction, in fact—is that writing is likely to be self-defeating if it does not take into account the language of the intended audience. For it would be contrary to purpose—in a sense, *contradictory*—to attempt to communicate with another but deliberately use language that baffles them or gives them an impression other than what you intended. For example, if you write to someone in French but they do not speak French, then your attempt to communicate with them has failed. You should have used their language. And what applies *between* languages applies equally *within* languages. If you use a variant of English that puzzles or misleads your readers, then you might fail to get your message across. And if you do it deliberately, your writing will be intentionally self-defeating (and thus irrational). You might, for instance, be convinced that a certain word (say, *disinterested*) has just one correct meaning (*impartial*) and decide to use it only in that way. You are, in other words, a fan of prescriptivism. But if your audience interprets it to mean *uninterested* (as most do these days, at least in Australia), then your communication will have failed. Indeed, *you* will have failed: failed in your attempt to communicate. Similarly, if I insist on using *suspenders* to mean a garment for affixing ladies' stockings (the strong British meaning) but I am writing for an American audience, they will likely think I am talking about over-the-shoulder straps that hold up trousers. Confusion and misunderstanding are highly likely. Thus our conclusion that any form of prescriptivism that refuses to accept language change and language diversity necessarily leads, at some time, to writing that is self-defeating. And since prescriptivism, by definition, cannot accommodate language change or diversity, the prescriptivist approach to language use—namely, that there are laws or rules that *must always* be followed—must be abandoned and replaced with a form of descriptivism.

The need to take into account the language of the intended audience gives us a good start in unravelling the necessary features of good writing. From it we can derive our first principle:

> *Principle of familiarity*: to prevent readers from being distracted from your message by unfamiliar usage, use language in ways that the majority of your intended audience will understand.

But much more than familiarity is needed. Consider this famous sentence: "Colorless green ideas sleep furiously". Noam Chomsky used it to show that grammar and semantics are different things (Chomsky 1957, p. 15). The syntax, grammar and punctuation of the sentence are fine, but the meaning? Well, there isn't any. The sentence—and any other nonsense string you can think up that adopts conventional syntax, grammar and punctuation—proves that you can know all the so-called rules of language and still fail to communicate. It justifies us in giving precedence to the principles of communication over the so-called rules of syntax, grammar and punctuation in any serious study of what makes writing good writing. Chomsky's sentence makes it clear that in addition to familiarity, good writing must deliver *meaning*. Moreover, any vehicle of meaning—for example, a clause or sentence—must deliver *one* meaning and it must be a *precise* meaning. In other words, as well as making sense, good writing must also be free of *ambiguity* and *vagueness*. This gives us our next principle of effective communication:

*Principle of clarity*: to ensure that readers get your intended message, avoid nonsense, ambiguity and vagueness.

We might have written a clear text—one free of nonsense, ambiguity and vagueness—and have used language that is familiar to our intended audience, but still our attempt at communicating might fail. It might fail if we overlook the *context* in which the audience might read our text. For that context could include aspects that will compete for the attention of our readers, aspects such as *demands* and *distractions*. Consider firstly competing demands. Despite the immense labour-saving potential of computers, most of us are time-poor. The leisure dividend most of us hoped for never materialised. It was converted instead into profits. Moreover, we appear to be working more than we did before the advent of the computer (which will strike many as paradoxical). No-one, it seems, has an empty in-box, work is taken home on the weekends, recreational leave is delayed and personal stress is on the rise. This is the unfortunate backdrop against which we must frame our attempts to communicate. The more words there are to read, the longer it takes to read them. That is a truism. In a climate of time-pressure, a reader who detects too much verbiage might become alienated from the text and disengage from it. They sense that it is needlessly, discourteously keeping them from other pressing demands. They might abandon their reading (even if they would be better off if they had persevered). In a word, communication breakdown has occurred—the antithesis of the very goal that prompted the writing in the first place. Thus the wise writer assumes that their audience is demand-stressed and time-poor, and chooses to write economically. For by doing so—by avoiding verbosity, redundancy, nominalisation and other forms of bloat—they increase their chances of being read.

It is true that sometimes we don't want an author to be economical with words. The author of a novel, for example, might be such a brilliant anatomist of character, setting and plot that we don't want the book to end. Likewise, a poem may be so luscious of word-music that we want more, not less:

"I have seen them riding seaward on the waves
Combing the white hair of the waves blown back
When the wind blows the water white and black."[1]

"It is spring, moonless night in the small town, starless and bible-black, the cobblestreets silent and the hunched, courters'-and-rabbits' wood limping invisible down to the sloe-black, slow, black, crowblack, fishingboat-bobbing sea."[2]

But if what you are writing is informational rather than fictional, and you suspect—as you must—that your intended readership is time-poor, writing *economically* becomes a practical necessity. If you want to communicate but deliberately take 20 pages to convey what could have been conveyed in 15, your readers may not have the time to read all that you have written (including the more useful or important information they were hoping to find). In that case, you have engineered communication breakdown. Your writing was self-defeating. Other demands on your readers' time have out-competed your wish to communicate with them. That may not be entirely their fault; some of it must lie with you.

As well as competing demands there are competing distractions. The magnetism of cheap gadgets capable of doing the seemingly impossible, the loneliness-breaking offerings of social media, the ready access to global television and other awe-inspiring inventions combine to tempt readers away from reading (or at least from careful, unbroken reading). Writers need to accept that reports and books will never out-compete the dazzle and lure of technological wizardry. Thus their best

---

1. The penultimate stanza of *The Love Song of J. Alfred Prufrock* by T. S. Eliot.
2. From Dylan Thomas, *Under Milkwood*, Phoenix, London, 2000, p. 3. First published in 1954.

approach, if they want their works to be read in full, is to adopt the philosophy of minimalism, that is, writing economically. It is simply a practical necessity in this time-demanding, gadget-distracting 24/7 world we find ourselves in.

Writing economically might also be a *moral* necessity. We all have a finite number of hours in a lifetime, and we all want time away from study and from the office. We want—and need—time to engage in activities that give our life special richness and significance, whatever they might be: time with our friends and family, time to hike through the bush, time to visit galleries, and so on. I suspect that on reflection most people would assess time as the asset they value over all others. (If the word *asset* carries too much of an economics overtone for your liking, then think of time as your most valuable *possession*, a possession that is a birthright.) Most of us have other assets, assets more tangible than time, but of less intrinsic value. We might have a classic car, a collection of first-edition books, a plasma television, expensive jewellery, and so on, and we would feel aggrieved if some such asset was stolen or damaged. (We might have some of these assets insured so as to lessen the sense of loss in the event of theft or damage.) But just how valuable would that car or book collection be if we had no time to drive or read. The value of all possessions presupposes time, thus elevating time to the most valuable possession of all.

Now the theft of a tangible asset—such as a car or a painting—is a moral issue. Who can deny that? But if so, then so must be the theft of an even more valuable asset: time.[3] Morality is largely concerned with the prevention of harm to others: physical harm, mental harm or being made worse off. By having time taken from us, we are made worse off. We now have less time to do the things that are most valuable to us. It is a moral issue. Thus readers have the right to feel aggrieved at

---

3. Time might be an *intangible* asset, but that doesn't necessarily rule it out of the moral sphere. There are other intangible assets that owners have a moral right to, such as copyright, patents and goodwill.

having to plough through large tracts of scarcely penetrable verbiage in order to get the information they need. They are having their time—a finite resource of great value—stolen from them, time they could be putting to better use.

Let's clothe this idea with some detail. Suppose you have written a 50-page report and every sentence in it has three superfluous words (a feat that is easily achievable). If we assume that the average length of a sentence is 18 words (James 2007, p. 354), your report effectively contains just 42 pages of substance. That is, the accumulated verbiage—all those unnecessary words—accounts for about eight pages. A reader might take 40–45 minutes to plough through that verbiage, time they would not have needed to devote to the report had it been written with concision in mind. Thus you have stolen time from every one of your readers. (It doesn't matter that readers might not notice that their time is being stolen. It is still a moral issue, just as taking money from the wallet of a blind person is still a moral issue even if they will never know that money has been taken, and even if they have more money than they need.)

Thus there are moral as well as practical reasons why economical writing is essential. In the ever-demanding, non-stop, multi-channel world in which most of us live today, the demands on our time are often excessive. If we want to increase our chances of being read and getting a message across, we should assume that our intended audience is time-poor and that our communication is likely to be one in a pool of many communications each competing for the attention of our audience. Moreover, even if our readers have time to read what we have written, it is immoral to assume that we can take up as much of their time as we like.

This brings us to our next principle of good writing:

*Principle of economy*: to maximise your chances of being read, avoid verbosity and other forms of bloat that will steal time from your intended readers.

Familiar, clear and economical writing can still fail to communicate if the cognitive burden it places on readers is too great. We attempt to process a sentence in our short-term memory (also known as our *working memory*). Cognitive science has shown that such memory is limited (Cowan 2010, p. 52). It is unlikely to cope with a complex, multi-clause sentence on one reading. (Indeed it cannot cope even with certain short sentences, as we will see in a moment.) The sentence will need to be read twice, maybe three times, before it is fully understood. In this time-poor world in which we live, will all our readers have time to do that? Possibly not. To assume that they will when there is a good chance that they won't is contradictory. It leads to self-defeating writing. Moreover, the moral issue we discussed above in considering the time thievery implicit in verbiage applies just as equally here. So another important principle of successful communication is this:

> *Principle of conceptual lightness*: limit the complexity of sentences so that they can be understood by the intended audience on a single reading.

In communication studies, much is made of the concept of *noise*. Noise is anything that is likely to distract the receiver from the message the sender intends. Some noise is outside the writer's control: a flickering fluorescent light, for example, or the sound from a neighbour's television. These might block the message or, if attention is only diminished, cause it to be misinterpreted or only partly understood. But some potential noise is within the writer's control. For example, if informational writing engages the emotions of readers, there is a good chance that they will take their mind off the message and ponder why it has been written in the way it has. Paternalistic, sexist or culturally insensitive writing is likely to do just that, as might humour, sesquipedality and a poor choice of tone. Thus another useful principle of communication is this:

> *Principle of neutrality*: to prevent readers being distracted from an informational or factual message, adopt an emotionally neutral style.

As with non-neutral writing, *inconsistent* writing can distract readers, especially where two terms are used for the one thing. For example, if a writer uses both *ciliary neuralgia* and *cluster headache* in a report intended for a general audience, there is a good chance that some readers will think the author is talking about two things when in fact only one is being discussed. Elegant variation—that is, introducing synonyms for the sake of it—might be a tool that contributes richness and vitality to fiction writing, but in informational writing it can easily mislead. So another sensible principle of communication is this:

*Principle of consistency*: if a reader might be misled or distracted by inconsistency—whether of vocabulary, spelling, punctuation or style—avoid it.

Leaving aside the moral concerns that time-thievery raises, the six principles of communication we have outlined above are not *categorical* imperatives. They are *conditional* imperatives (in other words, practical necessities). *If* you want to get your message across—as we mostly do when we write—*then* you need to pay attention to potential obstacles: things that could thwart or dilute communication. These principles will do that. And taken together they suggest the following subsuming, over-arching principle, which I'll call the *principle of communicative efficiency*:

Always write in a way that maximises communicative efficiency with respect to your intended audience, where maximum communicative efficiency is the attribute a piece of writing has when no other way of expressing what is expressed would express it with greater efficiency.

Note that we have couched this principle in terms of *efficiency* not effectiveness. (The former implies the later, but not the other way around.) A 50-page report might be effective in the sense that a reader might eventually get to understand everything that is in it. But if it takes them 45 minutes longer than is strictly necessary to do so—because of verbosity, redundancy, tautology, padding and so on—the writing is not efficient. It might even cause reading to be abandoned. And given the paramount importance of communication, that is precisely what writers don't want to happen.

I hasten to repeat that I am not talking here about *all* forms of writing, but only factual or informational writing. Scientific writing, technical writing, academic writing and business writing fall into this group. Fiction writing, copy-writing, writing chatty letters to friends and lovers, poems and the like are clearly outside the scope of this principle. In these forms of writing, some of our principles are less important, such as economy and neutrality. (A novel, poem or love letter that did not engage the emotions would have failed in its purpose.)

There is nothing mysterious about the derivation of the principle of communicative efficiency. We want to communicate. That part is obvious. It is the very purpose of writing and speaking. We might be lucky in communication: a reader might understand precisely what we intended to convey. But if we want to remove the luck, we need to clothe our communication in a way that minimises the effort on our readers' part—so that they don't have to struggle to understand us—and minimises the likelihood that they will be distracted from the message by how we have clothed it. Too much effort and too much distraction might do more than dilute the communication: it might cause the reader to stop reading altogether. If this occurs we have unwittingly engineered communication breakdown, thwarting the very purpose of writing.

Thus writing that meets the principle of maximising communicative efficiency is simply writing that:

- gets its message across to intended readers
- gets its message across with the least effort on the part of intended readers and
- gets its message across with the least distraction on the part of intended readers.

We now have six sub-principles of good writing, all derived from our fundamental axiom that the goal of writing is to communicate with an audience. No doubt there are others we could derive, but to keep this book to a manageable size we'll stop at these six. Still, two other principles are worth a brief mention. These relate to *reader engagement* and *cognitive lodgement*.

We maximise reader engagement by adopting a style of writing that will keep readers wanting to read (or at least won't cause them to nod off). Varying sentence types and sentence lengths, letting pronouns take some of the load off nouns, giving the agent of verbs prominence in the sentence, employing metaphors and similes, varying strong non-specialist terms, letting the context carry some meaning, and much more contribute to reader engagement.

Cognitive lodgement is a measure of how likely it is that what someone has read will stick in their brain (that is, find its way into long-term memory). There are textual and non-textual features that affect cognitive lodgement. For example, noun clusters—strings of consecutive nouns—quickly build a barrier to cognitive lodgement. Your choice of font can also affect cognitive lodgement. Publishers have always suspected what Colin Wheildon proved in the 1980s: that comprehension of texts set in a sans serif font (such as Arial or Helvetica) is substantially lower than comprehension of texts set in a serif font (Wheildon 2005, p. 47). The practice currently popular in commerce and industry of using a sans serif font for all written communication is a hidden drag on productivity.

From the importance of maximising communicative efficiency—that is, of maximising the ease with which a message is communicated—we can easily derive some of the core attributes of good factual writing. Leaving aside issues of reader engagement and cognitive lodgement, these attributes are simply those that our six sub-principles will, if followed, give to our writing, namely familiarity, clarity, economy, conceptual lightness, neutrality and consistency. We will now consider each in a little more detail.

## Clarity

Although earlier we discussed familiarity before clarity, we will start our finer analysis with clarity. For clarity is, in fact, the primary attribute. Clear writing couched in unfamiliar language could eventually be understood; familiar language that lacks clarity might never be understood. For the same reason, clarity trumps the other attributes. What good is an economical, neutral or consistent document if it is marbled with nonsense, ambiguity or vagueness?

Writing that exhibits clarity not only makes sense; it is precise, clear and definite. There is no uncertainty about what it means. More than that, it is writing where what the reader interprets is exactly what the writer intended to convey. That is, it succeeds in getting its message across. Hence, writing that has clarity is free of nonsense, ambiguity and vagueness. Alas, these are diseases of writing that are often difficult to avoid. Their eradication—especially ambiguity and vagueness—typically takes up most of a reviewer's or editor's time.

### Nonsense

Nonsense comes in three main flavours: *unexplained inventions, category mistakes* and *contradictions*. Unexplained inventions are baffling words ("The sky is *plit*") or syntactically chaotic structures ("Mat sat the the on cat"). Category mistakes occur when an attempt is made to relate concepts that cannot logically be related. As we proved in chapter 2, there is a category mistake at the heart of prescriptivism (namely, the application of the concept of correctness to language use). Chomsky's "Colorless green ideas sleep furiously" is another example. Ideas cannot be coloured; nor do they sleep. To suggest that they do is nonsense. Fun in a kids' book, perhaps, but a sure sign of cognitive disorder in serious adult discussion.

Chomsky's sentence is also an example of a contradiction, for something cannot be colourless and green at the same time. Another example is this statement from the International Olympic Committee (IOC):

"On average, each potential viewer around the world consumed 3.5 hours of Winter Olympics coverage."[4]

The purpose of this rather extraordinary statement is, no doubt, to subtly sow in the mind of those who might be thinking of advertising during the next Winter Olympics an idea of revenue greater than what is realistically achievable. It takes advantage of the sad fact that greed usually trumps reason. But the statement defies logic. It is internally contradictory. A *potential* viewer cannot consume anything. The document in question defines potential viewers as "all individuals over the age of four who have access to television". The following parallel should draw out the silliness, the contradiction, in the IOC's statement:

> Each *potential* shopper—being anyone in the world over the age of four with money to spend—*spent* on average £1000 at Harrods last year.

If everyone in the world over the age of four *did* buy something at Harrods last year, perhaps the average amount spent would be £1000. But then they would no longer be *potential* shoppers.

## Ambiguity

> "[ambiguity] means 'capacity for dual interpretation', which leaves the reader swinging between two possible meanings for the same string of words."(Peters 2007, p. 41)

Ambiguity can be ephemeral, acute or chronic. Ephemeral ambiguity is inter-sentential ambiguity that can usually be resolved by re-reading the sentence and thinking about its possible meanings. An example: *The doctor, whose wife is dead tired of all the talk about a family reunion* will, if read one way, lead to cognitive dissonance. Is it the doctor or the wife who is tired of all the talk about a family reunion? If you assume the

---

4. From a report published by the International Olympic Committee on the Torino 2006 Olympic Winter Games. See www.olympic.org/Documents/Reports/EN/en_report_1087.pdf. Viewed 20 September 2104.

former, the sentence will make sense; if the latter it won't. But re-reading the sentence will help you get the intended meaning, which would have been clear if the parenthetic material had been closed: *The doctor, whose wife is dead, tired of all the talk about a family reunion.* Ephemeral ambiguity is always inter-sentential (or, in a multi-clause sentence, inter-clausal). You don't need to go beyond the sentence to work out the intended meaning.

Acute ambiguity occurs when the meaning is not immediately obvious and cannot be determined by re-reading the sentence. However, the context, or further explanation, eventually enables the reader to work out what the writer meant. On the other hand, chronic ambiguity occurs when there is nothing to make the writer's meaning clear: neither context nor further words. *She is a very old friend* is an obvious example of a sentence that is acutely or chronically ambiguous. Is the friend a nonagenarian? Or have you known her for a very long time? The problem is not one of ephemeral ambiguity. You cannot determine the intended meaning by re-reading and rethinking the sentence. Perhaps you will work out the meaning from the context or when you read on; perhaps you won't.

If ambiguity is detected, it will slow down communication. The reader will need to look for clues as to what the intended meaning is (assuming they are interested and have the time to do so). If ambiguity is not detected, the sentence might be read in the wrong way (that is, in a way that the author did not intend). The ambiguity might only come to mind when material read much later in the text appears odd or contradictory. The reader might then re-read (but again only if they are interested and have the time). And where the ambiguity is not detected, the wrong interpretation is made and subsequent material does not cause bafflement, then the ambiguity has caused the reader to be misled. Thus ambiguity can disrupt, sever or divert communication. It does not fare well against the principle of maximising communicative efficiency. Writing in ways that force readers to pause or re-

read is, by definition, not efficient. Any re-reading is time-loss and thus time-thievery. Then again, given how time-poor many of us are, the baffled reader might not re-read. So communication is either inefficient or it fails altogether. Thus ambiguity is best avoided unless the context makes it crystal clear at the time of reading which meaning is intended. But in that case there is no real ambiguity—except in isolation.

There are many types of ambiguity. We will list some of the more common ones.

- *Lexical ambiguity* occurs when a single word or expression in a sentence can be understood in more than one way. An example:

  *My aunt can't bear children.* [Is the aunt intolerant or infertile?]

- *Structural ambiguity* occurs when the syntactical structure of the sentence allows for two competing interpretations. An example:

  *"The Prime Minister ... reminded all Australians that they owe so much to the more than 100,000 troops who died in battle during the delivery of his Special Address."*[5]
  [Did the troops die before or during the Prime Minister's address?]

- *Pronominal ambiguity* occurs when a pronoun could be interpreted as referring to more than one thing (and hence possibly not the thing that the writer had in mind). An example:

  *We attached the Gazmasta to the Teleon, but it still wouldn't work.* [Which item needed to be fixed?]

- *Relative clause attachment ambiguity* is similar to pronominal ambiguity but in this case it is a relative clause rather than a pronoun that the reader could associate with the wrong noun in the sentence. (A relative clause—also

---

5.  *New Scientist*, 22 September 2007, p. 64.

known as an adjectival clause—is a string of words modifying, or providing more information about, a noun.) Consider this example:

*Someone shot the butler of the actor who was on the balcony.* [The relative clause is "who was on the balcony". Is it describing the whereabouts of the butler or the actor?]

- *Relative clause ambiguity* occurs when it is not clear whether a relative clause is restrictive (that is, necessary to the intended meaning) or non-restrictive (that is, parenthetic, and thus could be omitted from the sentence without changing the meaning or truth of the sentence). For example:

*The insects which were resistant to DDT all developed cancers.* [Did all the insects develop cancers? Or just those that were resistant to DDT?]

- *Detached modifier ambiguity* occurs when a modifying phrase or clause and the thing being referred to are separated in a way that may confuse readers. For example:

*Falling heavily, the clothes were soon saturated by the rain.* [What fell heavily: the clothes or the rain?]

- *Undifferentiated ambiguity* occurs when a reader is unable to clearly determine which words or expressions are being used to refer to something. This usually occurs when the writer fails to provide adequate typographical cues. An example:

*The first performance of Noah in London caused a mini-riot.* [What is the name of the film? *Noah* or *Noah in London*?]

- *Telegraphic ambiguity* arises when a word or group of words necessary to distinguish between two competing interpretations is omitted, as in:

*That was the chap I heard about at Melbourne University.* [Who was at Melbourne University: you or the chap?]

This form of ambiguity is frequent in writing that has been overly influenced by the clipped English of Power-Point-speak.

- *Phantom-possibility ambiguity* occurs when unnecessary information appears to limit or restrict the current discussion to one of a number of possibilities when there is, in fact, only one possibility. An example could be:

  *To test the hypothesis using a spectrometer* ... [If the hypothesis was not tested in any other way, the words "using a spectrometer" create a false impression—the phantom possibility—that elsewhere in the text there will be a discussion of *other* ways in which the hypothesis was tested.]

- *Agentless ambiguity* occurs when the reader needs to know who the agent is but the agent is suppressed, as in the following example from a computer user manual:

  *The record is returned to Data Entry status if it is necessary to correct any errors.* [Who returns the error to Data Entry status: the operator or the system?]

- *Genitive ambiguity* occurs when one noun modifies another but the context does not make it clear what the relationship between the two is. We have already discussed problems that arise from a common use of the genitive apostrophe. (Does *my brother's books* mean *the books of my brother* or *the books for my brother*?) But the genitive case is also apparent in cases of simple attribution (that is, where the first noun specifies an attribute or quality of the second, a case sometimes referred to as the *attributive genitive*). Consider *steel bin*. Is it a bin made *of* steel or a bin *for* placing steel shavings and off-cuts?

- *Semantic-bleed ambiguity* occurs when a unit of information in a sentence is assumed to be qualifying or relating to an earlier unit when it is not. In other words, the semantic intent of one unit of information bleeds into an earlier unit. For example:

*After weighing the stems were removed and the flower heads dried.* [Some readers will think that the first unit of information ends after "stems"; others will think it ends after "weighing". The second unit of information actually begins with "the stems". Those who initially read the sentence as if the second unit of information begins "were removed" will have encountered semantic bleed. The best that can be said about this example is that at least the ambiguity is ephemeral. A comma after "weighing" would have prevented the ambiguity.]

## Vagueness

*vague* (n.) Of statements, ideas, etc.: couched in general or indefinite terms; not precisely expressed; lacking in definiteness or precision; indefinite. (*Oxford English Dictionary*)

The rejection of vagueness should be self-evident, whatever the type of factual writing. We write to communicate. That is, or should be, our prime intention. But we do not communicate if we use terms and expressions that are imprecise. Imprecision is, by definition, non-communication. Vagueness is often more of a problem than ambiguity. Ambiguity can be temporary (that is, ephemeral or acute); but vagueness is usually irresolvable (and thus chronic). The words just don't tell us anything (or, if they tell us something, it is not enough to enable us to conclude anything of substance). Here are some examples:

*If there had been no activity for a long time, we proceeded to ...* [But how long is a "long time"?]

*Keep paragraphs short.* [But short of what? Sentences, clauses or words? And how short?]

*The current 'seeped' though the substrate.* [But if it didn't literally seep, how did it get through? Why is the author telling the reader not to interpret *seeped* literally, thereby expecting the reader to work out what they had in mind when they wrote the word?][6]

## Familiarity

The principle of familiarity—*always write in ways that will be maximally familiar to your intended audience*—is easily justified. If you are writing to communicate—as we mostly are—it will be self-defeating if you use words, idioms, punctuation, symbols and so on that might distract or baffle. If you have a deep urge to show off the richness of your vocabulary, then by all means do so—in some form of writing other than informational writing (the writing we are principally concerned with in this book). One does not inform by using language that hinders the informing; nor does one inform efficiently using language that slows the reader. And in the time-poor world we all share, if you don't inform efficiently you might not inform at all, or inform only partly. Thus to achieve your goal of informing, you should write in an audience-centric manner, that is, write for your audience.

Familiarity can be *implicit* or *explicit*. Implicit familiarity is what writing will have if it is written entirely according to the conventions that the audience adopts. Words, idioms, punctuation marks and the like are used exactly as the audience would expect. Explicit familiarity is provided by the author to give readers an explanation of what some possibly unfamiliar term or device means. A glossary, for example, gives explicit familiarity. A note at the start of the document alerting readers to special meanings is another case. (Two more examples: a note at the start of a user manual explaining that text set bold is text the user will see on the product and a note at the start of a report stating that the apostrophe of elision has been deliberately omitted.) Of course, writing can display a mix of implicit and explicit familiarity.

Writers can be as creative as they like in devising ways of imparting explicit familiarity. But if you intend instead to rely on implicit familiarity, you would be wise to use:

---

6. Quotation marks used in this way are sometimes called *scare quotes*, but perhaps a more apposite term would be *lazy quotes*.

- familiar vocabulary

  Why use *utilise* in a document aimed at a general audience when there is a more familiar, more frequently used equivalent that would be understood by all readers regardless of whether English was their first, second or third language (namely, *use*).[7] Why use *faucet* if you are writing for an Australian readership?

- familiar meaning

  Engineers and scientists are prone to using common words to mean something other than their common meaning. An example is the word *universe*. Consider the following headline to an article in the popular-science magazine *New Scientist*: "What the universe before ours was like". To most people, the universe is everything there is, was and will be. There simply cannot be a universe before our universe. Another example is *chaos theory*. This is poorly named for it describes difficult-to-predict systems that are nonetheless just as strictly deterministic as any other physical system. There is no chaos in these systems at all, just a difficulty in tying them down to neat formulas.

- familiar grammar, spelling and punctuation

  There is no point in surprising your readers with heterodox syntax, spelling or punctuation, or with syntax, spelling or punctuation that applies to an English other than that used by your intended audience (such us *enroll* for an Australian audience or *red, white, and blue* for a British audience). Unless explicitly flagged in advance, heterodox language will distract readers, breaking their reading and potentially breaking the communication.

---

7. A good proxy measure of the familiarity of a term is its frequency of use in general writing. Useful word-frequency tables are maintained by Professor Mark Davies of Brigham Young University. See www.wordfrequency.info.

Authoritative style manuals are your best guide to the grammar and punctuation practices of various English-speaking countries. For example, consult *Chicago Manual of Style* for advice on current American English, *New Hart's Rules* for advice on current British English, or *Style Manual for Authors, Editors and Printers* for advice on current Australian English. Consult authoritative dictionaries for advice on spellings and meanings.

## Economy

Lack of clarity and familiarity wastes readers' time, but even if what you write is clear and it is written in familiar language, time can still be stolen from your readers if you saddle your writing with verbosity, triviality, redundancy, tautology or nominalisation.

*Verbosity* occurs whenever a string of words is used when a single word (or a shorter string) would suffice. Some examples: you write *at this point in time* instead of *now*, *has the ability to* instead of *can* and *owing to the fact that* instead of *because*.

*Triviality* occurs when the writing states the blindingly obvious, as in:

> Connect the unit to mains power. Use a wall socket that is accessible. [As if it was possible to use a socket you couldn't access!]

*Redundancy* occurs when you use words to do work that is already being done by other words in the sentence, as in *There are four different flavours*. [If they weren't different, you would have one flavour, not four.]

*Tautology* is a type of redundancy where a word repeats the meaning of another word used in the sentence. The writer is in effect repeating themselves, and consequently wasting readers' time. Two examples:

> Limbitin is to be taken orally through the mouth. [So what does *orally* mean?]

The features you selected are currently being installed. [If they are *being* installed, it must be something that is happening *currently*.]

Nominalisation is turning a verb into a noun or noun phrase and replacing it with an irrelevant verb (usually some grey, all-purpose verb that has nothing to do with the action that is being expressed). For example, you want to write:

We studied the effect of DDT on brassica vegetables.

but find yourself writing instead:

We undertook a study of the effect of DDT on brassica vegetables.

A relevant verb (*studied*) is converted into a noun phrase (*a study of*) and replaced by a verb unrelated to study (*undertook*) Nominalisation always introduces unnecessary words and, if not reined in, will deaden most readers' enthusiasm for reading. It is one of the forms of writing now forbidden to writers of public service documents in the United States.[8]

## Conceptual lightness

The principle of conceptual lightness recommends that we limit the complexity of our sentences so that they can be understood by our intended audience *on a single reading*. We are clearly not writing with communicative efficiency in mind if we force readers to re-read. It is worth discussing this principle in detail as there is a widespread misconception that sentential complexity can be measured by word count. It is a misconception that is easily disproved.

Many a language pundit is convinced that the number of words in a sentence should fall within a particular range. Some also contend that sentences should not have more than a specified number of words. For example, Dr Anetta Cheek tells us that we should "aim for an average sentence length of

---

8. See *Plain Writing Act 2010*, signed into law on 13 October 2010.

between about 15 and 22 words". Moreover, we should "avoid sentences of more than 40 words" (Cheek 2010, p. 10). Dr Neil James, Director of the Plain English Foundation in Australia, is also convinced that average sentential word-count is an important consideration in good writing: "a 15–20 word average is *fundamental* to writing well" (James 2007, p. 244, emphasis added). Further, James hints that 35 words is probably the maximum we should include in a sentence: "if your content is complex, or if you need to include a subsidiary point, you will want to go over 18 words—perhaps even stretching towards 35 words".

The view that sentential word-count is an important consideration in writing well has such a long history that it is surprising that it has received little critical attention. The view does have *prima facie* plausibility. We do get lost in long sentences. We attempt to make sense of a sentence with the mechanisms of our short-term (or working) memory. That memory is limited by our biology. If a sentence we are reading surpasses that limit, ideas we read earlier in it are pushed out of memory and we forget part of what we have just read. We will need to process the sentence in parts and this will require re-reading (perhaps a number of times). The respectful writer—keen to communicate while imposing the least effort on readers—will try to avoid making readers re-read, and will do so by ensuring that the sentences they write do not exceed the capacity of our short-term memory.

The common view is that we do this by limiting our word count. Yet experiments that challenge this view are simple to construct. In my writing classes over the last few years I have displayed on a screen a simple 11-word sentence. The sentence remained visible for six seconds (more than enough time for the sentence to be read by any competent reader). Students were asked to read the sentence just once and then to write down its main points. They were told not to fuss about reproducing the sentence exactly as it was presented, but just to jot down its gist. I then displayed another 11-word sentence for six seconds. Again students were asked to jot down the main points. Here are the two sentences:

[A] The United States of America has reluctantly signed the peace accord.

[B] The hot, treeless plain is covered in dark, smooth, elongated rocks.

I then gathered the cards the students had written on and tallied the number of points that had been correctly recalled. Despite the sentences being of identical word-count and of comparable vocabulary, average recall scores—that is, the average number of correct responses given—were markedly different: sentence [A], a little over 89%; sentence [B], just 33.9% (from 519 students). If word count is a critical factor in reader comprehension, then surely these sentences should have yielded similar recall scores. The explanation for the discrepancy is simple, and it does have to do with the limits of our working memory.

The notion of a limit to working memory was made popular in a 1956 literature review by the American psychologist George Miller. Miller thought the limit, averaged over diverse stimuli (such as words, numbers, sounds, etc.), was *seven* distinct chunks. Subsequent research indicates that the average is closer to four:

> "the capacity of short-term memory ... is known to be quite small, only about four chunks." (Kintsch & Rawson 2005, p. 224)

> "a central working memory faculty is limited to 3 to 5 chunks for adults." (Cowan 2010, p. 52)

To psychologists, a *chunk* in the act of verbal comprehension is a basic unit of meaning. Moreover:

> "the basic units of meaning are propositions. Propositions are n-tuples of *word concepts*, one of which serves as a *predicator*, and the remaining ones as *arguments*, each filling a unique semantic role. The predicator specifies a relationship among the arguments of a proposition. For

instance, in the proposition (LOVE, Experiencer: GREEK, Object: ART) there are two arguments, GREEK and ART, and the predicator LOVE; in English this proposition could be realised with the sentence *The Greeks loved art*. It is important to note that the arguments of a proposition are *concepts* rather than words." (Kintsch et al. 1975, p. 196)

In this example, the basic unit of information has the S–V–O structure, that is, subject–verb–object: The Greeks (S) loved (V) art (O). But there are other equally basic structures. For example, S–V (as in "Emily laughed"), A–N (that is, adjective–noun, as in "bacterial infection") and A–V (that is, adverb–verb, as in "loudly abused").

What cognitive science tells us, then, is that if we want our readers to understand our sentences from one reading, we need to limit the basic units of information in them to no more than four. And this explains the result of the experiment I described above. To see how, dissect each sentence into its constituent chunks:

[A] The United States of America has reluctantly signed the peace accord.

Two chunks: <USP> and <SR>—that is, (a) the United States of America has signed the peace accord and (b) the signing was done reluctantly.

[B] The hot, treeless plain is covered in dark, smooth, elongated rocks.

Six chunks: <P, C, R>, <P, H>, <P, T>, <R, D>, <R, S>, <R, E>—that is, (a) the plain is covered in rocks, (b) the plain is hot, (c) the plain is treeless, (d) the rocks are dark, (e) the rocks are smooth and (f) the rocks are elongated.

The variance in rates of recall—89% for [A] and 33.9% for [B]—is due to the fact that the sentences, though of identical word count, have significantly different chunk counts. Sentence [A] poses little cognitive strain on our working memory because it has just two chunks, well within the four-chunk limit. On the other hand, sentence [B] forces the reader to attempt to squeeze six chunks into a four-chunk slot and, as a result, some chunks escape. In the experiment, 78% of students correctly recorded both chunks of information in sentence [A] whereas only 1.9% correctly recorded all six chunks in sentence [B].

A fixation on word-count—average or maximum—is thus misleading. I could write a document with an average sentence length of between 15 and 20 words—a so-called "fundamental" average—no sentence is longer than 35 words, the vocabulary is familiar (as is the grammar and punctuation) and yet every reader will have to read every sentence at least twice to fully understand it. All I need do is pack more than four chunks of information into every sentence. My writing meets the pundits' guidelines, but it could hardly be considered good writing.

So length does matter—*so long as we are measuring the right thing*. And the right thing is not words, but chunks: the basic units of information that one is trying to impart to readers.

As we've seen, short sentences can be unreasonably burdensome on readers; conversely long sentences—longer than the limit recommended by many pundits—can be a breeze, so long as the chunk limit is kept to four or less. Here is an example:

> The Democratic People's Republic of Korea is smaller than the People's Democratic Republic of Lao, the People's Democratic Republic of Lao is smaller than the Republic of South Africa, the Republic of South Africa is smaller than the Democratic Republic of the Congo and the Democratic Republic of the Congo is smaller than the United States of America.

The logical structure of this 58-word sentence is very simple: A < B, B < C, C < D and D < E, and its apparent wordiness does not impede its immediate comprehension. This is because the concepts are simple—mere countries—despite their names being multi-word compound nouns. It is pertinent here to repeat the last sentence in the quote above from Kintsch:

"It is important to note that the arguments of a proposition [that is, a basic unit of information] are *concepts* rather than words."

## Neutrality

Our emotions are arguably as great an asset to us as our intellectual faculties. A life devoid of love, excitement, amusement, joy, curiosity and hope would be dull indeed. These are some of the so-called positive emotions. But there are negative emotions too, such as anger, fear, sorrow, disgust, disappointment and aversion. Some negative emotions serve us well as biological defence mechanisms (fear, for example). Others seem little more than anomalously self-destructive.

When we read fiction, we expect the writing to engage our emotions. Indeed, the writer of fiction will endeavour to stir our emotions. The intention is to make an emotional response carry some of the meaning or plot so that it can remain unwritten but implicit. It is there for the reader to infer. Miss it and you've missed part of the theme or story. On the other hand, informational writing shuns the emotions. The occasional positive emotion is accepted as unavoidable. A reader's pleasure at having found the information they had been looking for is not something that writers can prevent. But writers of informational texts can prevent stirring up negative emotions in their readers. And this is important because negative emotions distract the reader from what they are reading. Readers stop seeing the message and start wondering why what they have been reading was written that way. The writer has thus unwittingly engineered a breach of the principle of communicative efficiency. There is noise in the communication, and the reader is paying attention to the noise and not the message. The message itself is likely to be delayed while the reader sorts out their emotions, or the message might be overlooked entirely. Thus the writer of information texts—cognisant of the benefit of communicative efficiency—will prefer neutral writing—writing that intentionally avoids engaging the emotions of readers.

Neutral writing is writing that avoids paternalism (for instance, unnecessarily treating readers as less educated than they are), gender exclusion (sexist writing) and cultural insensitivity (ridiculing or belittling a race or culture). An example of writing that fails by these measures is the following, written by Pulitzer Prize–winning author Natalie Angier:

> "America's scientific eminence is one of our greatest sources of strength ... [so] let's cosset the scientists of today and let's home-grow the dreamers of tomorrow, the next generation of scientists. For by fostering a more science-friendly atmosphere, surely we would encourage more young people to pursue science careers, and keep us in fighting trim against the ambitious and far more populous upstarts India and China."[9]

Angier's injudicious use of the word *upstarts* is likely to offend a large portion of her Asian readers, many of whom will take their mind off the message and ponder instead the unflattering attitude of the author. The prognosis is likely to be communication breakdown.

Another aspect of writing that can engage the emotions is *tone*. The tone of writing (and of speaking) can be positioned somewhere along a spectrum that ranges from highly informal to highly formal. An ill-considered tone could affect communication no less than unfamiliar usage. The careful writer will attempt to anticipate the likely emotional responses in readers from using various tones and then choose the appropriate one. If, for example, I write a love letter in majority usage rather than in the intimate, familiar language my lover and I use when conversing, then my lover would no doubt suspect that I was going cool on the relationship. This might not be the impression I wanted to create—unless, of course, I really did want to break off the relationship. Thus I

---

9. N. Angier, *The Canon: The Beautiful Basics of Science*, Scribe, Carlton North (Australia), 2008, pp. 9–10.

will adopt a different tone for the same audience if the context is different: informal and intimate at one time; neutral and cool at another. Another example: suppose I write a business letter to a customer with news that I suspect will disappoint them. I am, say, turning down a loan application. I risk miscommunicating if I use highly informal language (the sort I might use in an email to a close friend). My letter might not be taken seriously, or the recipient might find the tone disrespectful and stop reading before the end has been reached (where I offer another potentially attractive source of funds). The tone has engaged the emotions in an unintended way and generated noise in the communication, blocking the entire message I wanted to get across. Similarly you lower your chances of getting a reply from the Queen or Governor-General if your letter to them is littered with slang and colloquialisms. On the other hand, an email to a friend written in the formal tone you would adopt if writing to the Queen or Governor-General is likely to be considered a joke. Linguists use the term *register* to refer to the spectrum of tones ranging from the highly informal to the highly formal. Maturity in writing is reached when a writer learns where on the register to pitch their tone in order for their communication to have the best chance of succeeding. (This is a skill that may require adjustment if the social stratifications in societies continue to dissolve, as they have over the last 50 or so years.)

## Consistency

Consistency is important in informational writing, but some editors and writers are overly obsessed by it. If we are writing with our audience in mind—rather than to please the God of Pure Platonic Forms—then it is only inconsistency that our readers are likely to detect and be puzzled by that we need fuss about. Such puzzlement is most likely to occur with vocabulary, and especially so if the writer has a penchant for *elegant variation*. Elegant variation is the unnecessary, and often distracting use, of synonyms:

"It is the second-rate writers, those intent rather on expressing themselves prettily than on conveying their meaning clearly ... that are chiefly open to the allurements of elegant variation ... The fatal influence is the advice given to young writers never to use the same word twice in a sentence—or within 20 lines or other limit ... [The effect of changing a word for a synonym] is to set readers wondering what the significance of the change is, only to conclude disappointedly that it has none." (Fowler 1965, pp. 148f.)

Consider this quote from a computer user manual:

"Insert the mouse cable into a spare USB port ... Now insert the printer cable into a spare USB jack."

Port? Jack? The novice reader is likely to think that there are two types of USB sockets—ports and jacks—when there is only one (or when the same type was intended).

Another example:

"The Governor of the Reserve Bank, Glen Stevens, reassured business with his prediction that the economy will still grow this year ... This is the second time in as many months that the Central Bank has cut official interest rates."

Reserve Bank? Central bank? Are these the same entities? Some will know; others will be confused.

Elegant variation is unlikely to be a problem with common or non-technical synonyms, especially if the synonymy is strong and there is no competing connotation. Hence words such as *but*, *hence* and *assume* could be swapped with *however*, *therefore* and *suppose* respectively without causing cognitive dissonance in most mature readers. And doing so might add just enough variety to keep the wandering reader engaged.

Inconsistent punctuation can also distract, prompting the reader to waste time wondering whether there is special significance in the use of one particular mark when another was expected. For example, if you have mostly been using closed em dashes to enclose secondary material but occasionally use open en dashes, the careful reader will notice the difference and wonder whether it is significant:

> "We compared the results of the first experiment—which was conducted in the northern hemisphere—with those of the second experiment – which was conducted in the southern hemisphere – and were surprised to find …"

Minimising the growth of unwanted significance is one reason for writing with consistency as a goal. Another reason is that inconsistency—if noticed—looks sloppy and unprofessional. A perception of sloppiness spreads easily and can even turn malignant. Readers might judge the quality of the content of a document on the basis of the quality of its presentation. Poor presentation, poor content. That might be an unfair judgement, but it's one that you have no control over once your work has been published.

\*

There is much more that could be said about the six attributes we have merely touched on above, and much more to good, efficient writing than simply ensuring that these attributes are present. We have already mentioned the importance of reader engagement and the judicious choice of font. There are also the important structural issues to do with sequencing and balance. (Is the material ordered in a logical way? Do topics of equal importance get equal treatment?) The rhetorical flavour of a document can also affect readability and influence how readers engage (or disengage) with it. Still, we have said enough to show that although language is a moveable feast, there are aspects to the way we use language that can be viewed as static and inviolable, in so far as we use language to communicate. The way we punctuate parenthetic material might change over time, but the need to avoid ambiguity, vagueness, obscurity, verbosity, bloat, alienation and inconsistency will burn on just as strongly as it always has. Teaching these ever-present attributes of successful communication should be the core task of English language teaching. The ever-changing surface rules should be of secondary concern (though still of importance). Ditching the lot through suspicion of the shaky verities of yesteryear was a mistake of the cultural warriors of the 1960s and 70s. What was needed was not abandonment of English language teaching, but a reprioritisation of concerns based on a simple fact: the goal of writing is to communicate. We come back to this topic in the final chapter.

# 6: Can the quality of writing be measured?

"words are by nature incurably fuzzy" (Aitchison 2001, p. 125)

We have seen that writing—or at least the *way* we write—cannot be correct or incorrect, right or wrong. To judge it as such is to fall into the quicksand of a category mistake: the trespass of a concept into an area where it cannot, *logically* cannot, belong. It would be akin to judging a glass of wine as right-angled or a child's behaviour as salty. We have also argued that writing can, nonetheless, be judged. It can be judged by how well it meets the writer's intentions in seeking to communicate. It can also be judged by the respect it shows for the audience's needs, especially the need not to have their time stolen from them). There can, in other words, be poor writing and good writing. In the last chapter we saw that there are many criteria by which we can judge the communicative potential of writing. Is it free of ambiguity and vagueness? Does it use language that will be familiar to its intended audience? Will it clog a reader's cognitive machinery? Will it eat into the scarce time most of us have for reading? And so on. There are so many criteria and sub-criteria that one might be forgiven for wishing that there was some simple proxy measure of the quality of writing, some formula or algorithm that quantified just how readable a piece of writing is.

There have been attempts to provide a way of measuring readability. Some word processing software will give you a readability score (being an assessment of how easy it is for readers to read the document that is currently on the screen). An example is shown in figure 6.1, taken from a recent version of Microsoft Word.[1]

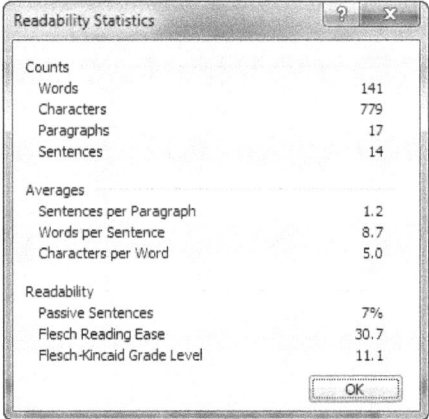

Figure 6.1 Sample readability statistics in Microsoft Word

*Readability* has two general senses, one applying to document design, the other to language. Readability as it is applied to document design is concerned with such matters as line length, leading, white space, font type and the like. Readability as it is applied to language is concerned with *comprehensibility* or *understandability*:

> "*Readability* means *understandability*. The more readable a document is, the more easily it can be understood…" (Samson 1993, p.58)

Another quote:

> "[Readability is] the efficiency with which a text can be comprehended by a reader, as measured by reading time, amount recalled, questions answered, or some other quantifiable measure of a reader's ability to process a text..." (Selzer 1983, p. 73)

---

1. To see your scores for a particular document, you will need to have selected **Show readability statistics** on the **Proofing** tab of the **Options** window and then run a grammar check of the document.

And one more definition of *readability*:

> "[the] sum total (including all the interactions) of all those elements within a given piece of printed material that affect the success a group of readers have with it. The success is the extent to which they understand it, read it an optimal speed, and find it interesting."[2]

In this chapter we are focusing on readability as it pertains to language, not as it pertains to document design. And this is the variety of readability that the readability formulas purport to measure.

Readability formulas are gathering in popularity, and in places that matter:

> "Today, reading experts use the formulas as standards for readability. They are widely used in education, publishing, business, health care, the military, and industry. Courts [in the USA] accept their use in testimony." (DuBay 2007, p. 5)

Organisations in the USA have been successfully sued by plaintiffs claiming that they have been disadvantaged by an inability to understand certain public documents.[3] To protect themselves against such litigation, many bodies—commercial and government—now have specific guidelines on the minimum readability required of their public documents. The result is that what was once an academic curiosity in cognitive science has been turned into a tool for profit-making. Companies abound that, for a fee, will help you improve your readability score. And to know if your readability has improved you need a test. So, just like intelligence tests, readability tests have become mainstream. The question of

---

2. From E. Dale and J. S. Chall, "The Concept of Readability", quoted in William H. DuBay, *Smart Language: Readers, Readability, and the Grading of Text*, Impact Information, Costa Mesa, CA, 2007, p. 6.
3. For example, Tampa General Hospital and the University of South Florida paid a US$3.8 million settlement to a group of people who claimed that a consent form they signed exceeded their reading ability. Cited in DuBay 2007, p. 2.

whether a better readability score translates into better readability is no longer considered a mere hypothesis. If Microsoft Word gives you a readability score, then readability formulas must, surely, have the imprimatur of scientific rigour. Or so many think.

Just as there is a variety of intelligence tests, there is a variety of readability tests. In fact, the history of readability research is littered with over 200 readability formulas, all of which appear to be *text-based*: that is, readability is considered a function of the text being read and has nothing to do with the reader. These tests consider as important such features as the average number of words per sentence, the average number of syllables per word, the number of single-syllable words, the number of polysyllables, the number of words not on some predetermined list of so-called *easy* words, and the like. For example, the Gunning Fog Index measures, in a sample of 100 words, the average number of words per sentence and the number of words of more than two syllables, and the Simple Measure Of Gobbledegook (SMOG) measures the number of words of more than two syllables in a sample of 30 words.

## The Flesch reading ease score

Probably the most influential of all the readability formulas is the Flesch reading ease formula, named after Rudolf Flesch. This is the formula Flesch came up with:

Reading ease $(RE) = 206.835 - 84.6s - 1.015w$

where $s$ is the average number of syllables per word and $w$ is the average number of words per sentence (Flesch 1948). In most cases, the value of $RE$ will fall between 0 and 100: the higher the value, the more readable the text (or so the theory goes).[4]

The Flesch reading ease formula (hereafter FREF) is behind the main readability statistic in Microsoft Word. It has also

---

4. "...on a scale between 0 (practically unreadable) and 100 (easy for any literate person)". Flesch 1948, p. 229.

been tweaked for special uses (such as in the US Navy Readability Indexes). It also provides the raw input for another of the readability statistics that Microsoft Word generates: the Flesch–Kincaid Grade Level (which simply maps ranges of readability scores to particular levels of schooling in the US education system). Because of its special influence, most of our comments below will be directed at the FREF (although it should be clear that most of what we say will apply equally to any formula that derives a measure of readability from the properties of text alone).

At first glance, the FREF appears to have a degree of plausibility. It is undeniable that very long sentences *are* difficult to digest. By the time you have reached the end of a multi-clause sentence of, say, 50 or more words, you are often struggling to remember what you read at the start of the sentence. So it is difficult not to argue that the longer the sentence, the less readable it is.

But there is a fallacy lurking here that we need to be wary of. The undesirability of something doesn't imply the necessity of its opposite. Just because boiling hot food is not desirable, it doesn't follow that food should be served icy cold. Likewise, from the fact that long sentences are difficult to read, it doesn't follow that maximum readability demands the *shortest* possible sentence. A string of two- or three-word sentences is hardly likely to be maximally readable.

> The cat shook. It sat. It licked. It hissed. Then it slept.

is more difficult to absorb than the following longer version:

> The cat shook and sat. It licked and hissed and then it slept.

As a well-regarded style manual notes: "a string of short sentences can be irritatingly abrupt" (*Style Manual* 2002, p. 41). But the FREF gives a higher score the shorter the sentences. In other words, it encourages us to write very short sentences.

Now consider the importance of syllable count. On the face of it, polysyllabic words are more challenging than monosyllabic words. Most of us scratch our head, or disrupt our reading while we reach for a dictionary, when trying to read a medical book or book on philosophy. So a measure that reduces readability as syllable count increases, as Flesch's formula does, has *prima facie* plausibility.

But the relationship between readability and syllable count is superficial. It fails to acknowledge the influence that frequency of use has on a word's readability. There are numerous two-syllable words that are far more understandable than one-syllable words simply because we use them more often and have used them since childhood. For example:

> Mummy always washes the dishes after breakfast every morning

is obviously more readable than the equally long sentence:

> Electrons jump a level when hit by a photon

even though the former has a higher syllable count (18 as opposed to 13).

Indeed, a sentence can be short, with only monosyllabic words and yet be entirely obscure to the reader. For example:

> The work done was five ergs.

To many this sentence will be meaningless. There is no comprehension, no understanding. Only the scientifically-minded is likely to know that *erg* is a measure of *work* (in much the same way as *litre* is a measure of *volume*). But *The work done was five ergs* has the same number of words and syllables as the eminently readable *The cat sat on the mat*. By the FREF they are equally readable. Conversely, consider a tongue-twister like *hyperglycaemia*. This six-syllable word might baffle a healthy person, but to someone with diabetes, its meaning is crystal clear. These examples suggest that readability is intimately tied to conceptual familiarity (which is hardly a breathtaking discovery). If so, then text-only attributes—such as word length and syllable count—are not as important as Flesch believed.

On closer inspection the Flesch formula is seen to miss much of what makes a piece of writing readable. Unconventional grammar obviously gets in the way of understanding. It hinders readability. But it can still gain a high Flesch readability score. For example:

Sat the mat the cat on

is a grammatically flawed sentence. Encountering it would frustrate our reading. And yet it has the same number of words and syllables as *The cat sat on the mat*.

In fact, the FREF necessarily gives the same readability score however you re-arrange the words in a sentence: with grammar and sense in mind or otherwise. For example,

The on mat the sat cat

has the same number of words and syllables as *The cat sat on the mat* and thus should be equally readable on Flesch's view of readability. Indeed, it gets the maximum score: 100.

Punctuation, too, obviously affects readability. For example, if you write *Have a good holiday* when you should have written *Have a good holiday?*, then you are very likely going to confuse or mislead the reader. But the FREF gives these sentences the same score.

The FREF also gives the following sentences the same score:

Their numbers can be estimated using an airborne particle detector.

Their numbers can be estimated using an airborne-particle detector.

Omitting the hyphen in compound adjectives can create ambiguity if the context cannot clarify the intended meaning. (And the FREF, of course, is blind to context.) Is the detector in question a detector of cosmic rays tethered to a meteorological balloon floating in the stratosphere? Or is it a detector of carbon particulates fixed to the roof of a building?

The way text is styled can also affect readability, and yet style cues are ignored when all that is being considered is sentence length and syllable count. Consider this sentence:

You must see the film My time before it ends.

This sentence is ambiguous because the title of the film is not clear. Is it *My time* or *My time before it ends*? But the FREF makes no judgement here. Too bad if I interpret it the wrong way and later encounter cognitive dissonance as a consequence.

Now consider non sequiturs: sentences that begin down one path and end down another. For example:

> Unlike many other areas of business where errors can be adjusted at a later date, employees immediately notice errors in their paycheques.

Whatever readability score this sentence gets, its meaning is impossible to determine. We can at best guess it. Indeed, it is easy to concoct non sequiturs that score the highest possible readability score, such as:

> When the cat sat on the mat, the square root of nine was three.

Any formula that attributes maximum readability to that sentence is undoubtedly faulty.

And what of vagueness? What meaning can we effortlessly attribute to *If there had been no activity for a long time, we applied heat to the solution* and *The current "seeped" through the substrate*? Imprecision, vagueness and the lazy use of near-enough quotes are obstacles to readability and yet the FREF is wholly oblivious to them.

Transition words are words having two equal or near-equal primary meanings. They are words that are part-way through a transition from one primary meaning to another. One meaning is waxing while another is waning. For example, a *villain* was once a yokel but is now a scoundrel. A *girl* was once a young child (of either sex) but now is a female child. The words *villain* and *girl* underwent a transition, and while they were in transition, their use could have been ambiguous. And thanks to the internet, and the democratisation of publishing it enables, we now have more concurrent transition words than ever before. An example is *disinterested*. Its strongest meaning not so long ago was *impartial* and *unbiased*; nowadays we see it used just as often to mean *bored* and *uninterested*. And does *regularly* still primarily denote *periodically*? Or is its use leaning more towards *frequently*? What is a transition word at one time might not be a transition word at another time. But when a word is in transition, its use is likely to be ambiguous if the context is of no help. Obviously, a readability formula that concentrates on textual statistics and ignores semantics will fail to detect the ambiguity posed by a transition word.

How many syllables comprise a word is not always clear cut. The number depends on how the word is pronounced, not how it is written, and this, of course, can vary between the different English languages. For US speakers, *temporary* has four syllables and *medieval* three; but for many others the syllable count is three and four respectively. Other words with varying syllable counts are *extraordinary, comparable, gaseous, medicine, laboratory,* and there are many more. Any formula that emphasises the importance of syllable count but considers only written language rather than spoken must make assumptions about how words are pronounced. Such assumptions obviously introduce further imprecision into the calculation.

Finally, consider again the two eleven-word sentences we used in the last chapter to show that sentential word-count is not a good measure of the cognitive effort expended in processing a sentence:

[A] The United States of America has reluctantly signed the peace accord.

[B] The hot, treeless plain is covered in dark, smooth, elongated rocks.

What Flesch scores do our two eleven-word sentences get? Sentence [A], with just two chunks of information, gets a score of 41.8 while sentence [B], with six chunks, gets a score of 72.6. So the sentence that the vast majority of readers will have to read twice before they fully understand it is deemed more readable than the sentence that nearly everyone understands immediately on first reading. Clearly there is something fishy with Flesch.

## Correlation, volatility and validation

The arguments in the previous section should cast doubt on any claim that sentence length and syllable count—the only variables considered by the Flesch reading ease formula (FREF)—*define* or *cause* readability. Readability—the ease with which writing can be understood—is far too complex a notion. But could the score given by the FREF still be a good *indicator* or *predictor* of readability? An analogy: we do not define the concept of *temperature* in terms of the height of mercury in a thermometer. Rather, temperature is defined as the degree of hotness or coldness (and sometimes in terms of the average kinetic energy of the particles in a body). Nonetheless, the height of mercury in a thermometer has been found to be a very reliable indicator of temperature (at least on human scales). Indeed, the correlation between temperature and mercury level is as strong as can be. So, might textual statistics—sentence length and syllable count—be a good indicator of readability even though readability cannot be defined in terms of them? If so, a writer might reasonably use the FREF to evaluate the relative readability of various drafts of a document even though they might not write with textual statistics as their overriding guide.

This is indeed the claim of contemporary proponents of the textual analysis of readability. There is now widespread admission that many factors—not just sentence length and syllable count—contribute to readability and that writers should acknowledge those features when they are writing.

But despite this admission, many proponents argue that textual statistics are still the *best* indicator of readability, that if you calculate the correlation between other features of readability and comprehensibility the value you get is no better than if you calculated the correlation between textual variables and comprehensibility. In other words, an analysis of sentence length and syllable count is just as good as, but far simpler than, more complicated analyses.

"Critics of the formulas ... rightly claim that the formulas use only 'surface features' of text and ignore other features like content and organization. The research shows, however, that these surface features—the readability variables—with all their limitations have remained the best predictors of text difficulty as measured by comprehension tests." (DuBay 2007, p. 79)

But *best* does not imply *good*. At one time, the *best* way we had of estimating the number of stars in the universe was to look at the night sky and count them. But that, obviously, was not a very *good* technique. So how might we determine that the FREF gives a *good* way of indicating or predicting readability?

Any creditable psychometric test must have two important attributes: *reliability* and *validity*. A test is reliable if it gives the same or similar result each time it is applied to the same subject. Obviously, the FREF is a very reliable test. Every time it is applied to the very same piece of text, it will give the very same score. What of validity? A test is considered valid if it actually measures what it purports to measure. This is usually determined by comparing the results the test gives against those given by an independent test widely accepted as being a good measure of whatever is being tested. A strong correlation between the results is considered to give the test in question validity.

So is the observed correlation between readability *as independently measured by reputable tests* and readability *as measured by the FREF* strong enough to warrant its use as a valid indicator or predictor of readability? In a typical readability research project, participants are given a number of texts and their comprehension of these texts is assessed. Two methods are widely used:

- Participants are given a number of questions about each text, and the number of correct answers supplied is used to assign a level of difficulty to a text.
- Participants undergo a cloze test whereby they fill in words that have been deliberately omitted from the texts. (In a typical cloze test, every fifth word is omitted.) The number of correct words added to a text is used to assign a level of difficulty to that text.

Once each text in a bank of texts has been graded, the relevant textual statistics in each are calculated and fed into a readability formula. Researchers then determine the correlation between the level of difficulty of a text as determined by a comprehension test (or cloze test) and the score given by the readability formula.

Correlation is simply a measure of how one variable changes when another variable changes. The most widely used formula for determining what is called the correlation coefficient, $r$, produces a value between $-1$ and $+1$. If $r = +1$, when the value of one variable is high, the value of the other variable is also high; and when it is low, the other variable is correspondingly low. If $r = -1$, when the value of one variable is high, the value of the other variable is low, and vice versa. Values between $-1$ and $+1$ indicate a less than perfect correlation, that is, the relationship between the two variables is loose and it is impossible always to infer with confidence what will happen to one variable when the other variable changes. And if $r = 0$, the two variables are completely independent: when the value of one is high, the value of the other is sometimes high and sometimes low, and equally so.

So how do the readability values generated by the FREF correlate with the readability levels determined by comprehension and cloze tests? In his paper introducing the FREF, Flesch reported a correlation coefficient of 0.7047 (Flesch 1948, p. 225). Follow-up studies have found widely varying correlations. Some have found a result similar to Flesch, and others reported lower results: 0.64 and 0.5 (Selzer 1983, p. 75). In a 1998 study of tourism texts, Woods found a correlation between text difficulty as assessed by cloze tests and text difficulty as determined by the FREF of just 0.13 (Woods et al. 1998). This is close to indicting that there is *no* predictive validity at all. The authors likewise found no high correlation between cloze scores and scores on a number of other popular text-based readability formulas (FRY, SMOG and FORCAST). They also noted that the four readability formulas gave widely inconsistent results, with some formulas scoring a text as considerably difficult when others scored it as relatively easy. They concluded that:

> "The readability tests examined in the present study gave very inconsistent results and none of the tests did a very good job at predicting readers' responses [to the cloze tests] ... The results do not support the use of the readability tests analysed in this study (FRY, SMOG, FORCAST or Flesch's Ease of Reading test)."
> (Woods et al. 1998, p. 58)

Let's stay with the Flesch correlation for the moment and ask whether 0.7047 is strong enough to validate the FREF? A number of theorists have argued that it is not (Chall 1958). It might be true that such a value tells us that an inference from a high score on the FREF to high comprehensibility has a greater probability of being correct than incorrect; but it is also true that this inference will sometimes be incorrect. Still, doesn't a correlation coefficient of 0.7047 give us a *reasonable* degree of confidence that the Flesch reading ease score is useful?

It will be instructive to draw a distinction between *absolute readability* and *relative readability*. To ask whether a low Flesch score is a good indicator of low readability and a high Flesch score a good indicator of high readability is to ask whether the FREF is a good indicator or predictor of *absolute* readability. To ask whether the readability of a document is improved from one draft to the next if the Flesch score of the latter draft is higher than that of the former is to ask a question about *relative* readability. These concepts are quite different. If the FREF is a good indicator of absolute readability, it will have a high *predictive validity*. If the FREF is a good predictor of readability variation between drafts, it will have a high *comparative validity*. But, as we're about to see, low comparative validity is compatible with what is deemed by Flesch and his supporters to be high predictive validity. This might seem paradoxical, but only until we question whether a correlation coefficient of 0.7047 is really enough to give the FREF high predictive validity.

Let's start by considering whether the correlation coefficient Flesch found—and used to justify his claim that the

FREF has significant predictive validity—implies significant comparative validity. In other words, does a correlation coefficient of 0.7047 give us confidence to conclude that draft 2 of our document is more readable than draft 1 if the Flesch score of draft 2 is higher than that of draft 1? Table 6.1 below suggests that it does not.

Table 6.1 Correlation and volatility

| Validation | | 1st draft | | 2nd draft | | F change | M change |
|---|---|---|---|---|---|---|---|
| Flesch | Master | F1 | M1 | F2 | M2 | | |
| 25 | 35 | 25 | 35 | 30 | 30 | Up | Down |
| 35 | 20 | 35 | 20 | 25 | 35 | Down | Up |
| 42 | 25 | 42 | 25 | 35 | 42 | Down | Up |
| 42 | 40 | 42 | 40 | 40 | 62 | Down | Up |
| 65 | 50 | 65 | 50 | 50 | 52 | Down | Up |
| 55 | 45 | 55 | 45 | 45 | 50 | Down | Up |
| 60 | 65 | 60 | 65 | 71 | 51 | Up | Down |
| 65 | 50 | 65 | 50 | 50 | 60 | Down | Up |
| 68 | 50 | 68 | 50 | 56 | 70 | Down | Up |
| 75 | 80 | 75 | 80 | 80 | 70 | Up | Down |
| 30 | 30 | | | | | | |
| 25 | 35 | | | | | | |
| 35 | 42 | | | | | | |
| 40 | 62 | | | Predictive validity = | 0.705083 | | |
| 50 | 52 | | | | | | |
| 45 | 50 | | | Volatility = | 100% | | |
| 71 | 51 | | | | | | |
| 50 | 60 | | | Comparative validity = | 0 | | |
| 56 | 70 | | | | | | |
| 80 | 70 | | | | | | |
| Correlation = | 0.705083 | | | | | | |

Imagine that the first draft of each of 10 documents is subjected to the FREF and they get the reading ease scores listed in the **F1** column in table 6.1. Suppose further that the same documents are subjected to the FREF at the end of their next draft. The FREF scores for that draft are listed in column F2. Suppose now that the 20 drafts—the 10 first drafts and 10 second drafts—are subjected to a master test of readability (a cloze test, comprehension test or whatever type of test Flesch used to validate his formula). The score for each draft is listed in the **Master** column in table 6.1 beside its corresponding Flesch score. Importantly, we have deliberately chosen scores so that the correlation between the Flesch score and the master score turns out to be almost identical to the correlation Flesch considered sufficient to support his reading ease formula, namely 0.7047. (The scores in table 6.1 yield the slightly better 0.705083.)

Now to a surprising feature of these scores. For every Flesch score that went up between drafts, the actual readability (as measured by the master test) went down, and for every Flesch score that went down the actual readability went up. To see this, compare each **F1** score against its **F2** score and note the difference between the corresponding **Master** scores (**M1** and **M2**). Every change in a Flesch score brought about a change in readability *in exactly the opposite direction* to what the FREF would predict. (You can see this easily in the **F change** and **M change** columns: for every *Up* there is a corresponding *Down*, and vice versa).

Let us introduce the term *volatility* as the measure of the degree of directional variability in a sample of paired scores. Volatility occurs when one value in a pair increases (or decreases) and the corresponding value in a related pair of scores decreases (or increases). Maximum variability (measured on a scale of 0 to 100%) occurs when *no* increase (or decrease) in any pair in the sample is matched with an increase (or decrease) in a related pair. That's the situation illustrated in table 6.1. Thus the volatility of 100: maximum volatility.

Flesch's correlation of 0.7074 is certainly better than 0 so, on the face of it, it should give you some confidence that a low Flesch score does indicate low readability. If you are a fan of the FREF and got a low score for a draft of a document you are writing, you would no doubt consider polishing it up and checking it again against the FREF in the hope of getting a higher readability score. But this is where you can become unstuck. For as table 6.1 shows, Flesch's predictive validity is compatible with *maximum* volatility. If you get a higher Flesch score for your second draft, there is absolutely no reason for you to be confident that the actual readability has increased.

The confidence that a writer should be seeking is what I've called *comparative validity*: the likelihood that a higher Flesch score indicates a higher readability (and vice versa). When comparative validity is 1, volatility is zero and all increases in Flesch scores correspond to increases in actual readability (and vice versa). Writers can then be confident of improving the readability of their drafts if the FREF gives a higher score. But, as table 6.1 shows, the comparative validity is zero. No movement in Flesch score corresponds to an equi-directional movement in readability score. Writer confidence? Zero. A predictive validity of 0.7047 has misled us about the extent to which the FREF is useful.

You might retort that we concocted the scores in table 6.1. We did, but that is not relevant. All we have from Flesch is a correlation coefficient of 0.7047. This is meant to be an indication of the predictive validity of the FREF. The point is that the predictive power of a formula with a seemingly useful correlation coefficient of 0.7047 is compatible with indeterminate intra-score predictability (that is, maximum volatility). It is simply not enough to know that the correlation between two sets of measurements is 0.7047 to be confident that a rise (or fall) in a value of one measurement will more often than not correspond to a rise (or fall) in the value of the correlated measurement. The correlation is compatible with a *comparative* validity of zero. But this is the very sort of validity writers need to know and be confident of if they are going to rely on the FREF to judge the relative readability of drafts.

Flesch scores are used in the USA to determine the suitability of books for certain school grades. Our argument so far has had to do with comparing the Flesch scores on various drafts of the same document. But within the confines of our argument, there is no relevant difference between comparing draft 1 against draft 2 of the same document and comparing book 1 against book 2. If an educator finds that the Flesch score for book 1 is greater (or less) than the Flesch score for book 2, a predictive validity of 0.7047 should give them no confidence that the readability of book 2 is greater (or less) than book 1. At best, such predictive validity suggests that a low Flesch score is associated with a low readability level and vice versa. But even that supposition is questionable, as table 6.2 below suggests.

Table 6.2 Comparative v. predictive validity

| Validation | | 1st draft | | 2nd draft | | F change | M change |
|---|---|---|---|---|---|---|---|
| Flesch | Master | F1 | M1 | F2 | M2 | | |
| 56 | 35 * | 56 | 35 | 50 | 30 | Down | Down |
| 40 | 20 * | 40 | 20 | 57 | 35 | Up | Up |
| 26 | 25 | 26 | 25 | 42 | 42 | Up | Up |
| 43 | 40 | 43 | 40 | 62 | 62 | Up | Up |
| 70 | 50 * | 70 | 50 | 51 | 52 | Down | Up |
| 56 | 45 | 56 | 45 | 49 | 50 | Down | Up |
| 45 | 65 * | 45 | 65 | 52 | 51 | Up | Down |
| 55 | 50 | 55 | 50 | 59 | 60 | Up | Up |
| 49 | 50 | 49 | 50 | 68 | 70 | Up | Up |
| 79 | 80 | 79 | 80 | 61 | 70 | Down | Down |
| 50 | 30 * | | | | | | |
| 57 | 35 * | | | | | | |
| 42 | 42 | | | | | | |
| 62 | 62 | | | Predictive validity = | 0.70477 | | |
| 51 | 52 | | | | | | |
| 49 | 50 | | | Volatility = | 30% | | |
| 52 | 51 | | | | | | |
| 59 | 60 | | | Comparative validity = | 0.7 | | |
| 68 | 70 | | | | | | |
| 61 | 70 | | | | | | |
| Correlation = | 0.70477 | | | | | | |

Table 6.2 gives another dataset where the correlation is close to Flesch's 0.7047. In this case, the volatility is 30%, which gives us a probability of 0.7 that an increase (or decrease) in a Flesch score between drafts will correspond to an increase (or decrease) of readability. That's better than the previous dataset, you might think.

But table 6.2 also suggests that a correlation of 0.7047 or thereabouts is not even a very good *predictor* of readability. You can see this by noting that in 6 out of the 20 drafts, the difference between the Flesch score and the corresponding readability score is at least 20 points. (These are marked with an asterisk.) Given that the Flesch scale is only 100 points wide, a 20-point discrepancy is something to worry about. (In the USA, where Flesch scores are used to select the suitability of books for certain school grades, a discrepancy of 20 Flesch points could see a book suitable only for Year 4 students set on a Year 3 curriculum or vice versa.) Thus, with Flesch's observed correlation, we could be wrong 30% of the time in assigning a readability measure to a document based on the FREF. Indeed, it is possible for a predictive validity of 0.7047 to co-exist with 100% of scores being at variance by at least 10 points. It seems, then, that the predictive validity of the FREF is not really as strong as the formula's proponents have assumed.

Perhaps in recognition of the fact that a correlation coefficient of 0.7047 is compatible with significantly volatile data, current proponents of readability formulas have begun tempering their enthusiasm for them, now admitting that they can only be rough guides:

"[Readability formulas] ... are not perfect predictors. They provide probability statements or, rather, rough estimates ... of text difficulty." (DuBay 2007, p. 110).

But whatever correlation coefficient is obtained, the typical validation methodology that readability researchers adopt *overstates* the actual coefficient. The reason is that the methodology excludes certain types of material from being tested. And if these types weren't excluded, the testing would be of little value (as we'll now show).

Any study of scientific merit does not arbitrarily limit its data sampling. If you want to establish that *all* bodies fall with the same rate of acceleration, you do not limit your experiments to, say, metal objects. But the problem with relying only on the results of comprehension or cloze tests to determine the correlation between reading difficulty and readability statistics is that the data sample is necessarily limited. This is because those who devise a comprehension or cloze test can only use texts that are fully comprehensible (at least to them), otherwise they would not be able to determine if an answer provided by a testee is the correct answer. Indeed, they would find it difficult, if not impossible, to devise sensible questions in the first place.

But to avoid skewing the results, the data sampled must be extended to include texts that are *partially* comprehensible and even *in*comprehensible. Assessing the *degree* of comprehension a text offers would be an extraordinarily difficult challenge. Fortunately for our argument we can side-step that issue and concentrate, instead, on incomprehensible texts. These are much easier to find. A politician's speech might be a good place to start. But incomprehensible writing can also be concocted. We could write passages that are hopelessly ambiguous, or hopelessly vague. It is much easier, though, just to concoct nonsense strings, such as *The door is in love* and *Honesty is the largest integer less bilious than the smartest flooring wart.*

Samples of nonsense strings don't need to be tested for comprehension before they are subjected to the FREF. We know, by definition, that they have a comprehension value of zero (for they are nonsense). Now if the FREF is a valid indicator of readability (and thus of comprehension) then nonsense strings should get an FREF score of zero. (Recall that FREF scores range from 0 to 100, with zero indicating that the text is incomprehensible and 100 that it is fully comprehensible to any literate person.)

However, it should be clear that there can be no correlation whatsoever between the comprehension scores of nonsense strings and corresponding FREF scores. This is because we can concoct any number of nonsense strings with few words and few syllables (which would score high on the FREF: the first example above—*The door is in love*—scores 100) and any number of nonsense strings with many words and many syllables (which would score low on the FREF: the second example above scores 46.6). And if we are conducting the experiment scientifically, we need to include all types of nonsense strings: short, long, monosyllabic and polysyllabic. Thus a zero actual comprehension score can be matched to any value in the 0–100 range of FREF scores. *This clearly indicates a correlation coefficient of zero.*

So, for maximally comprehensible texts, the best correlation coefficient that testers can find between comprehension scores and FREF scores is 0.7047. And the only correlation coefficient possible for incomprehensible texts is zero. It follows that if correlation testing were to include samples of all types of texts—comprehensible and incomprehensible— the real correlation coefficient must be even less than the already unconvincing 0.7074 that Flesch reported (and perhaps even less than the insignificant 0.13 that Woods and her co-researchers found: see page 239).

## The irrelevance of readability formulas

Let's return to the fact that studies to establish a correlation between scores on comprehension tests and scores on the FREF must use texts that are maximally comprehensible to the testers. If they didn't, the answers testees give would have no value in determining a text's degree of difficulty. But how will those devising a test know that a candidate text is fully comprehensible? They can't subject it to a comprehension or cloze test to assess whether it is suitable to be subject to a comprehension or cloze test. Nor can they subject it to a readability formula, since the validity of the formula is the very thing they are trying to prove. So for testers to determine whether a text is fully comprehensible there must be some other criterion available for them to use, that is, a criterion other than a score on a comprehension, cloze or Flesch test.

So the methodology boils down to this: you start with a reputable criterion or test of comprehensibility (which, on our earlier definitions, would be a test of readability) to select fully comprehensible texts for a comprehension or cloze test. You then use the results from the comprehension or cloze test to validate a readability formula, finding that the best correlation coefficient you can find is about 0.7 (which is over-stated due to sampling limitations). That is, you start with a criterion that must give a good measure of readability and use it to validate a formula that can at best give just a rough estimate of readability. *Wouldn't it be so much better just to use the initial* criterion as our test of readability and forget about readability formulas altogether?

Paradoxically, some proponents of readability formulas come close to adopting this view. For example, after a long and favourable consideration of many formulas, the most that DuBay can say is:

> "When adjusting a text to the reading level of an audience, using a formula gets you started, but there is still a way to go. You have to bring all the methods of good writing to bear."[5]

But if we still have to bring all the methods of good writing to bear—that is, to concentrate on all those features of text that are essential for maximal readability—why don't we just concentrate on those features and forget about the additional task of applying the FREF?

DuBay's quite sensible advice would not be welcomed by those who argue that for workaday uses we need a simple proxy measure of readability, such as a text-based formula, because directly assessing readability is just too difficult and time-consuming. I suspect that those who take this line may have gone through schooling during that Dark Age of English language teaching: the latter quarter of the twentieth century. Assessing readability might be a multi-faceted task, but it is not especially difficult. Any reputable language manual is a good start. Indeed, many of the examples given in the previous section to discredit the conceptual linking of readability and textual statistics can guide us here, enabling us to distil some of the general features of readability. Moreover, we discussed some important features in the previous chapter. They include familiarity, clarity, neutrality, conceptual lightness and consistency, each of which is ignored by text-based formulas. Devising a text-based, reader-independent algorithm that will assign an objective value to each of these attributes is highly

---

5. DuBay 2007, p. 112. This seems to contradict DuBay's earlier claim that when you consider all the features of a text, textual statistics are still the *best* predictor of readability.

unlikely, and probably impossible. (For a start, familiarity is as much a function of the reader as of the text.) It may be time, then, to dispose of text-based readability formulas on the scrap heap of over-zealous quantification. There is no shortcut to determining the quality of your writing. You need to sift out the ambiguity, vagueness, foreignness, verbiage and the like on your own (or with the help of an editor). There is simply no app with any claim to scientific merit that will do it for you.

# 7: Learning the lingo

> "The defence of the English language ... has nothing to do with setting up a 'standard English' which must never be departed from [nor with] correct grammar and syntax, *which are of no importance so long as one makes one's meaning clear* ..." (George Orwell 1946, emphasis added.)

The purpose of this book is to reorient attitudes towards language. Prescriptivism is still the religion of most people, and there are enough language pontiffs about to keep its pews full. But like the religions of the church, temple and synagogue, prescriptivism can be strong only through faith—for there is no rational, logical basis to it. Like all natural conventions, languages are not guided by laws or rules. They fall outside the epistemological boundary that circumscribes fact, truth and reason. Nor will languages be shackled by strictures that thwart the creative impulses that define *Homo sapiens*. Humans will continue to recreate their languages as they have always done, however strident the fulminations of pedants.

A new attitude towards language implies the need for a new attitude towards the *teaching* of language. The prescriptive grammars of the classrooms of the past need to be re-evaluated. And most, we are certain to find, will need to be abandoned. In their place will be the national language record: a collection of descriptive accounts of how language *is* used, not how it *should* be used. These are the dictionaries, grammars and style guides compiled by active descriptivists. But these only take us so far. They will tell us how a society uses its language: the words it prefers, the punctuation adopted, its common idioms and the like. We still need to assemble those basic building blocks into a coherent, logical text. Grammar books—whether descriptive or prescriptive—will be of some help. But as Chomsky's "Colorless green ideas sleep furiously" shows us, grammar does not suffice to give meaning. A sentence with impeccable grammar might still fail to convey the writer's message, especially if it is rushed out with scant regard to the principles of efficient communication. We explored these principles in chapter 5 and found, in chapter 6, that there is no easy method—or method with scientific credentials—for quantifying the communicative efficiency of writing. Measuring purely textual attributes—such as word count and syllable count—is patently inadequate. Other variables must be brought into the equation, and some of these variables are not measurable (such as a reader's sensitivity to the topic, their acceptance of the writing's tone and the widespread fuzziness of meaning). Learning to be a good writer is not easy. Language is a massive, mutable beast. It gives us means both for writing well and for writing poorly, and there are no simple formulas that will tell us when our writing is good. Clearly, writing well needs to be taught. And how it should be taught is the principal topic of this chapter.

Today, many educationalists and politicians talk of a decline in numeracy and literacy. For those who appreciate that language is forever on the move—at best nudged but mostly uncontrollable—yoking numeracy with literacy is likely to cause some concern. Competence in mathematics involves mastering absolute truths. For example, 2 + 2 = 4, and that's the end of the matter. The answer will still be 4 next year and next century. But language is different. There are no absolute truths about language use. *Knave* can once mean a male child (as it did) and subsequently mean a rascal (as it now does). Numeracy entails mastering unchanging truths; literacy does not. Yoking numeracy with literacy, measuring them during primary school years—as many governments are doing—and lamenting a decline in both easily creates the impression that literacy must be taught in the same way as numeracy: as the imparting of absolute and inviolable rules, best taught by rote. But a return to this approach to teaching literacy is doomed to failure. It will—in all likelihood—lead to another rejection of language teaching once the subjectivity and variability of language is rediscovered. That is the paradox of prescriptivism. It creates its own enemies. The cycle will repeat as another band of cultural warriors will throw out the baby with the bath water. The teaching of literacy—when understood as the teaching of communication skills—can succeed without any assumptions of invariance or inviolability. It doesn't need to be, and shouldn't be, compared on equal terms with the teaching of numeracy. They are chalk and cheese. But one is no less deserving than the other of study and inculcation.

## Communication as part-science, part-art

To some readers, the remaining sections of this chapter might seem trite, covering ground that has already been discussed endlessly by educationalists. But in some countries there is a new entrant in the debate over what should be taught in schools: parents. In Britain and Australia, for example, moves are afoot to devolve to parents the power to make many of the decisions once reserved for bureaucrats and educationalists. The appointment of school principals is now made, in large part, by school councils composed mostly of parents. What is sold in the school tuckshop is another decision that is being devolved to school councils. More importantly—at least for our discussion— is that parents are being given more say in the make-up of curricula. Whatever the reason—the small-government ideology of neo-liberalism, an over-fervent love of democracy, or the laziness of politicians wishing to outsource a difficult portfolio—there are now people who may have none of the professional insights of university-trained educationalists making decisions about what gets taught in the classroom. These folk may have good cause to worry about their children's writing, and they may have been influenced by the loudest of the combatants in the language wars—prescriptivists such as Lynne

Truss and John Humphrys (whose views are a magnet to shock jocks media). This chapter is addressed primarily to these folk.

It might be trite, but true: schooling should be preparation for life. And a life without adequate communication skills will almost certainly remain unfulfilled. This is a two-way loss. First, a youngster's wellbeing will be less than they might have hoped for. (And do we not, as guardians, have a moral obligation to ensure the wellbeing of our children?) Second, society is deprived of the artistic, commercial or scientific achievements that might otherwise have flowered—but only if fertilised by communicative competence. Thus instilling communicative competence should be one of the primary goals—if not *the* primary goal—of the English curriculum.

That might be the goal, but what should be the approach? For a start, it is a wise philosophy to treat the classroom as a transit lounge for *knowledge*. Falsehoods should be detected at the border and denied entry. In other words, teachers should be sure that what they are teaching as truth is indeed true (and not myth, hunch, prejudice and the like). If a teacher cannot back up a claim, then the claim should not be made as if it is true. From a moral perspective it does not matter whether a claim that happens to be false was made unintentionally or not. If it is made unintentionally, it is a poor reflection on the state of the teacher's knowledge. They do not know well enough what they have been entrusted to impart. They are, in effect, passing themselves off as qualified to teach when they are not. (The certificate framed in their office tells only that some minimum amount of learning has taken place.) If the false claim was made intentionally, students are being deceived and misled. That is clearly immoral. Further, the unchallenged spreading of falsehoods—whether unintentional or deliberate—risks corrupting the integrity of the education system. If one falsehood is accepted, why not this other one. And that one. Before long the noble idea of the school as the primary source of knowledge has crumbled, replaced by that of a consumer training camp where curricula are set by commercial interests rather than educationalists, and ultimately determined by the influential and the wealthy. So if the mechanics of the English language is to be taught, it must be taught truthfully: as a set of parochial conventions that has changed in the past and will almost certainly change in the future. There is nothing to be gained by pretending that English is superior to other languages, or that one English is superior to another, or that any one English is the end of a spent evolution. English has gained its prominence, has become the *lingua franca* of the world, not because it is endowed with qualities lacking in other languages. It has done so by the accidents of fortune that allowed Great Britain to dominate and colonise vast swathes of the world. Likewise the English of London–Oxbridge, once considered the exemplar of Englishes, owed its prestige to the accident of fortune that saw London and its environs chosen as the seat of the English royal court. Had Leeds been chosen instead, perhaps the folk of north England would be ridiculing the speech of the southerners and not the other way round (as is still sadly the case). And that is the context in which English should be taught. What any English speaker has is an accidental mutation on a many-branched evolutionary tree. To call British English superior to American English, as many prescriptivists do, or educated English superior to bogan English, is about as sensible as calling a Labrador superior to a Golden Retriever.

Given that English—like all natural languages—is dynamic and uncontrollable, subject to random mutations and outside the boundary of what can be true or false, do we want it taught in the classroom? Should, indeed *can*, such a ramshackle thing be the subject of legitimate and worthwhile scholarship? Moreover, if knowledge and knowledge alone should be taught in the classroom and knowledge entails truth—a claim few would deny—then surely what cannot be true should not be taught. Thus, the argument might go, the conventions of the English language should not be taught.

We can challenge this claim with a simple change of emphasis: from *usage* to *communication*. The way we use language cannot be true or false, correct or incorrect, right or wrong. The conventions instantiated by practice lie outside the realm of knowledge. But the principles of communication introduced earlier do lie within the realm of knowledge. They lie behind every communication—indeed, they form the medium for its transmission—and they are subject to verification and falsification just like any scientific hypothesis. For example, a comprehension test can be given to two groups of people one of whom has been given texts to read that lack clarity, familiarity, economy or neutrality and the other texts that exhibit clarity, familiarity, economy and neutrality. If the second group consistently scores higher on the comprehension tests, the principles are scientifically verified.[1] They can be accepted into the transit lounge of knowledge and thus legitimately taught in the classroom. I doubt that we need to go to that length, for these principles appear to be axiomatic (if not true by definition or validly deduced from a definition). Isn't it incontrovertible that a sentence that lacks clarity—that is, it is nonsensical, ambiguous or vague—risks failing to communicate? Likewise a sentence that uses words and devices that the intended audience is not familiar with? And isn't it incontrovertible that a text that is too wordy or too complex to be read in the time the reader has will not be read in its entirety and thus some part of it will not be communicated? And surely writing that has the potential to distract—such as emotionally charged or inconsistent writing—risks failing to communicate? Thus the value of clarity, familiarity, economy, conceptual lightness, neutrality and consistency in fathering communication seems undeniable.

Moreover, one of our principles is the principle of familiarity: to prevent readers from being distracted from your message by unfamiliar usage, use language in ways that the majority of your intended audience will understand. Clearly,

---

1. The principles are also falsifiable, giving them the necessary hallmark of scientific statements. If the second group consistently scored lower on the comprehension tests, the principles would have been falsified.

to meet this principle we need to know how our audience uses its language, and any claim about that can be the subject of knowledge. Statements *about* language use can be true or false, even if prescriptions about use cannot. Consider these two sentences:

[A] Always end a sentence with a full stop.

[B] In Australian English, sentences end with a full stop.

Sentence [A] is a prescription. It is a command that is to be followed. As we saw in chapter 2, commands cannot be true or false (and are thus beyond the realm of knowledge). On the other hand, sentence [B] is a descriptive statement. It is an observation regarding how a group of English speakers uses its language. It can be verified or falsified and thus true or false. (Indeed, it is true.) So to meet a necessary principle of effective communication—the principle of familiarity—we need facts about language. So knowledge about language can, and should, be taught even though rules of usage cannot themselves be items of knowledge. Thus our demand that only *knowledge* be taught in the classroom is not incompatible with the claim that language use cannot be correct or incorrect, right or wrong.

Our point that knowledge about language use *should* be taught is worth emphasising, not least in order to counter the despair some feel when told that there can be no correct or incorrect language use. Placing the focus on communication rather than on rules does not mean that rules—understood as conventions—should not be taught. They should be—indeed, *need* to be—taught, but not as categorical imperatives: *Do [y]*. Rather, they need to be taught as conditional imperatives: *if you want to maximise your chances of communicating with [audience x]—that is, not write in a potentially self-defeating way—then do [y]*. For example, if you want to maximise your chances of communicating with a contemporary Australian audience, place a full stop at the end of each sentence. Similarly, if you want to maximise your chances of communicating with a contemporary American audience, use the word *faucet* not *tap*.

These are statements that can be true or false. Their derivation will take this form:

[A] You maximise your chances of communicating with [audience $x$] if you use the language that is most familiar to [audience $x$].

[B] The practice of [$y$] is the one most familiar to [audience $x$], that is, the one most commonly used by [audience $x$], it being their convention.

[C] Therefore if you want to maximise your chances of communicating with [audience $x$], then do [$y$].

Premise [A] is axiomatic (but also verifiable by experimentation). It is our principle of familiarity. Premise [B] can be checked against the national language record (or made the subject of rigorous surveys by linguists and lexicographers). And [C] follows logically from [A] and [B] together.

So science has a place in the English-language classroom. The observation of language use that linguists and lexicographers undertake is no less scientific than, say, the observation of animal behaviour undertaken by zoologists. And their observations, once confirmed, become knowledge that can be imparted in the English classroom. They provide truths that, in maximising communicative potential, will help students—and anyone else who uses the observed language—achieve the wellbeing they seek in a life that will include other people. But this knowledge—like all knowledge—is conditional. That is, it is subject to change if conditions change. It is possible that *tap* becomes the word used by Americans to refer to what they now call a *faucet*. (Unlikely, perhaps, but still possible.) If that did occur, the statement "if you want to maximise your chances of communicating with a contemporary American audience, use the word *faucet* not *tap*" would no longer be true. But this doesn't mean that we have moved outside the realm of knowledge and into worthless relativism. Even the knowledge gained from a so-called hard science like physics is conditional (that is, subject to change). For example, the speed of light is now a constant, but it was much greater during the period of inflation that immediately followed the Big Bang. It may yet change again for all we know. But this conditionality—the possible falsification of a statement that expresses the current speed of light—doesn't make the statement unworthy of being taught in the classroom at a time when it is true. If it did, the whole of science would be deemed worthless.

An approach to teaching English that focuses on how language *is* used rather than on how it *should* be used should make it easier for teachers and students alike, for many of the so-called rules beaten into students by the gerund-grinders of yesteryear can now be happily ignored. Students won't have their time wasted learning what an infinitive is if there is no need to worry about splitting them. Nor will they have their time wasted investigating whether a slug is a higher animal or a lower animal before deciding on which genitive treatment is acceptable. If a practice does not affect communication one way or the other and it is not strongly adopted in whatever English is being taught, it can be ignored. It is discretionary. It becomes a matter of style, discussed, perhaps in classes on rhetoric or creative writing, but of no importance in mastering the mechanics of the language.

Indeed, when the focus is more on communication than on rules, much of what prescriptivists have shackled us with can be set free into the blue sky of discretionary usage. For example, many students are taught that dangling participles and double negatives must *always* be avoided. In some contexts avoiding a dangling participle or double negative is a good idea. It removes ambiguity. But there are many cases where there is no ambiguity at all. As linguist Pam Peters points out, there is nothing at all confusing about "Having said that, it would be a pity to do it too often" (Peters 2007, p. 192). At the head of that sentence is a dangling participle, but it in no way obscures meaning. Another example from Peters: "He wasn't incapable of speaking" (Peters 2007, p. 228). There is a double negative in that sentence, but no meaning is thereby obscured. The rule that students *should* be taught is to avoid anything that does hinder communication. It is a blunt, lazy and eventually self-defeating approach to force on students supposedly *general* rules that, as often as not, do not hinder communication. It also cruelly exacerbates the neurosis of those who feel that there are so many rules governing so-called correct usage that they will never become good writers.

## The variant of English to be taught

We have argued that the rules—that is, conventions—of English need to be taught (along with the principles of efficient communication). Students need to know if such-and-such a usage is strongly conventional with the audience they are writing for (which is usually members of their own society). If it is, they are wise to follow it (for their chances of communicating are then the strongest). If there is no strong convention but one of a number of alternatives will least hinder communication, then that is the one they should adopt. Finally, if there is no strong convention and no one possibility would hinder communication, they should be entitled to do as they please. So the national language record of their society needs to be studied so that students can best make those decisions. But what if there are many variants of English in their society (as in England). Against the conventions of which variant should usage be judged? And which variant should be taught in the classroom?

If the language in the society is homogenous, the decision as to what variant is to be taught should be straightforward. It is, simply, the language of that society. No-one has the right to impose another language on a society. There would be blood in the streets if that was attempted (an example of which was the 1497 uprising of Cornwall against England after England attempted to outlaw the Cornish language: see Mills 2010). But what if there are variants of the language, that is, dialects. What variant is to be taught in the classroom? Behind this question lies an assumption that there should only be one variant taught. But as we've argued, no one variant of English is superior to any other. American English is just as legitimate as British English, and Yorkshire English is just as legitimate as Somerset English. If it is impractical for a society to teach all variants of its language—as it no doubt would be in such a heterogeneous country as England—then a choice must be made. Two ideas stand out as giving support to the view that it is the language of the *majority* that should be the primary language taught: majority by *number*, that is, not by wealth, education or influence. First is the ethic of democracy and the entitlements it bestows on us. Minorities have no ungifted right to impose their cultural preferences on majorities. Second, by being taught majority usage, students, when they seek the benefits of living among others, will then have the best chance of being able to converse effortlessly with the greatest number in their society.[2] Thus society meets its obligation to ensure the wellbeing of those who are in its charge. To concentrate instead on a minor variant—such as the U-English dissected by Nancy Mitford in her *Noblesse Oblige*— may disadvantage students whose later circumstances find them living a non-U life. On the other hand, teaching majority usage will advantage everyone, whatever their class.

We deliberately said that the majority language should be the *primary* language taught, the implication being that other variants could also be taught, if not to the same degree. There seems to be nothing lost and plenty to be gained by teaching youngsters something about the evolution of their language. Most countries attach value to the teaching of history (especially the history of their own country). It not only helps instil loyalty, but can, if taught objectively, also temper the hubristic excesses of patriotism. Likewise, teaching the history of the English language could temper the excesses of linguistic patriotism inherent in prescriptivism. If a student can see how English has evolved—sometimes for the better, sometimes

---

2. Note that we are talking about probability here. It might turn out that someone taught the majority language of their society spends the rest of their life living in their home village where a dialect is in use. But since we don't know *in advance* that this will be the case, we sensibly choose the option that is most likely to meet the communicative needs of people throughout their lives.

not—they are less likely to be aggressively pedantic about the language of their times. For to learn that English has continually changed in the past, and that there are no good reasons to think it won't change in the future, is to learn that there is nothing special about the English of today. Learning it might be invaluable, but what *is* invaluable is that we *have* a language, not any particular language.

As well as historical variation, contemporary variation should also be acknowledged in the classroom. A modern, moral, pluralist society does not ignore its minorities. It will acknowledge that there are people within it who have different beliefs (religious beliefs, moral beliefs and the like) and different practices (ways of conducting religious observance, avoidance of certain foods). Typically, students are taught about these differences. They are also encouraged to treat them with respect. Sadly this does not always carry over to differences of language. The British are not averse to sneering at the English of Americans and Australians, Australians poke fun at the accent of New Zealanders, Belgravians knock Cockneys, and both mock Liverpudlian Scouse. But such derision is groundless. No one English is superior to any other (other than as a means of gaining admission to a particular social class, which is not relevant to communicative potential). The belief that there is a superior English—and the indecent snobbery that follows—would disappear if students were taught that all languages are conventions, that conventions evolve to meet the needs of particular groups of speakers, and that no one set of conventions can be judged better than any other. (We have already noted that the Englishes will regain an equilibrium of communicative potential if one variant gains an advantage over another, thereby nullifying that advantage.) The fact that only one variant is taught in the classroom can be no more than a *practical* necessity. There might be no time to consider all variants. Or there might be little likelihood that students will need to converse with those who speak a variant. (What value is there in teaching an Australian child Jamaican

English?) But the important point is to drive home the equal legitimacy of all variants of English.

There are other reasons for inculcating the legitimacy of variation. First, the school playground can be hell for those who are different. Taunting, ostracism and bullying are, alas, still common, and the psychological damage caused is well documented. If one child's accent is considered equal to another's, that sort of psychological damage can be reduced. Second, teaching the legitimacy of language variation will prevent cognitive dissonance. By the time youngsters start school, they will have already been exposed to more than one variant of English. Australian children navigating American websites will encounter spellings, words, idioms and punctuation that they might not have encountered in books published in Australian English. Likewise, an American youngster playing an English computer game may encounter a language different from what they are used to. Encountering differences outside the classroom and yet being taught that there is only one correct English will only be confusing. How is it (a youngster might think) that so many are allowed to get away with using incorrect English? Such early confusion could easily spawn derision and lifelong prejudice.

Thus the modern English classroom will expose students to linguistic variety, explain that usage cannot be correct or incorrect and acknowledge that no one variety of English is intrinsically better than any other. At the same time, the variant of English that is primarily being taught is that used by the majority of members of that society. If a school is situated in an area where many folk use a variant different from the majority, it will benefit students if they are taught it too (or some of it). Thus a school in Merseyside might concentrate on majority English but include lessons on Scouse. Communicative need should be the determiner. Most Liverpudlians will communicate with other Liverpudlians even if, over a lifetime, they communicate more with non-Liverpudlians. But majority English, not Scouse, is the predominant English precisely because it is the majority variant. Most of what is printed will be in the majority variant and the majority variant is what most people will understand. Knowing it thus improves one's chances of maximising the benefits to be gained from having a shared language and society.

## Language and literature

So far we have focused on teaching the mechanics of the English language, that is, on instilling in students the skills necessary to communicate with others and to understand the communication of others. These are foundation skills. We could not get what we do out of the writings of others without an understanding of the basic mechanics: spellings, meanings, syntax and the like. These skills are best reinforced by reading, and reading a lot. Thus the modern English classroom will, as it has always done, set texts for students to read. But what texts are to be set?

Informational writing—largely non-fiction writing—is the form of writing most of us will encounter most of the time. For that reason, it would be useful to students if some of the texts they had to study were informational. Teaching students how to write a good expository or narrative report would be beneficial to those who go on to university or who find that they are required to write reports in their subsequent employment.

But an English education that focused on non-fiction or on vocationally oriented texts would be dull and tiresome. It would also waste an opportunity to enrich the emotional life of youngsters as well as an opportunity to fertilise the ground for future cultural inventiveness. Having the legitimacy of one's own tentative, unsure feelings corroborated in the fictional writings of others is a thrill many of us never forget. So too is the thrill in seeing that there are many more possibilities in life than might be suggested by the usually claustrophobic milieu of one's own family and its circle. *I am not that different; I can do what I like*—these are emotionally liberating discoveries literature brings to youngsters. So powerful are they that some novels stay with us for life. Studying the works of others also introduces youngsters to varieties of expressive style, some of which they might mimic as a way of strengthening their own confidence. It would be a churlish society that decided to withdraw the study of fictional texts—stories and poetry—from the primary and secondary curricula.

## Clear thinking

> "the world is full of arguments that seem to be good to the untrained eye but are in fact quite worthless." (Richards 1978, p. 35)

There was a time when students in Australian schools were taught *clear thinking*. It was part of the English curriculum in mid- to late-secondary years. It taught students the value of scepticism and how to weigh up the pros and cons of various arguments. It taught them to be alert to hyperbole and misleading statistics. It also taught them to be vigilant for logical fallacies: where premises are offered to support a conclusion and they do not. Some of the most common fallacies are the *fallacy of petitio principii* (assuming that which we are trying to prove), the *fallacy of affirming the consequent* (if A results from B and B is the case, then A must also be the case), the *fallacy of denying the antecedent* (if A results from B and A is not the case, then B is not the case), the fallacy of *post hoc ergo propter hoc* (if A follows B, A must have caused B) and the fallacy of *definitional fiat* (proving the point but only by redefining pivotal concepts). Such fallacies are not rare and they can turn up in places where you might least expect them. Here are some examples.

In a recent report from an Australian government commission, we read that:

> "Epidemiological studies show that most women with breast cancer have led relatively inactive lives. Therefore [society has] an obligation to attempt to break the car culture, as it deprives women of a health-giving activity: walking."

This is an example of the fallacy of *post hoc ergo propter hoc*: assuming that correlation implies causation. Even if inactivity has preceded breast cancer in 100% of cases, it does not follow that inactivity *caused* breast cancer. (Might there not be some genetic defect that causes both inactivity and breast cancer?)

Even the greats can sometimes slip up. In his book *The Grand Design*, cosmologist Stephen Hawking describes how the Scottish physicist James Clerk Maxwell discovered that light is an electromagnetic wave. This, supposedly, was Maxwell's reasoning:

[1] If a thing is an electromagnetic wave, it travels through space at speed $c$.
[2] This particular thing—light—travels through space at speed $c$.
[C] Therefore this particular thing—light—must be an electromagnetic wave.[3]

Either Hawking is misrepresenting Maxwell's proof, or Maxwell's proof is no such thing, for this line of reasoning is a case of the fallacy of affirming the consequent. The fact that two things share one attribute in no way implies that they must share any other attribute. If at the same instant I drop a vase and a hammer from the top of a tall building, at each moment of their descent their speeds will be identical (since, as Galileo showed, all objects fall to Earth at the same rate of acceleration). But that, of course, in no way implies that a vase is a hammer.

Marcus du Sautoy has a well-deserved reputation as a brilliant mathematician. He has written numerous books that many will think are attempting the impossible: to popularise mathematics. He does make some claims that will startle and intrigue many a young reader, but closer inspection shows that definitional fiat is sometimes at play. For example, in his book *The Number Mysteries*, du Sautoy tries to convince readers that a certain graph (a graph of a fractal) has a dimension of 1.26.[4] But he succeeds only by subtly redefining *dimension* in a

---

3. S. Hawking and L. Mlodinow, *The Grand Design*, Bantam, London, 2010, p. 91.

way that simply does not match our ordinary understanding of one-, two- and three-dimensional objects.

Hawking's book and du Sautoy's book both belong to the popular-science genre. Thus their poor or lazy logic has the potential to mislead many more than if their claims had appeared only in scientific or mathematical journals. Popularisers need to walk a slippery path between yawning simplicity and daunting complexity. It is a difficult act, and the temptation to oversimplify is no doubt strong. But to mislead is a moral lapse, even if unintentional.

Poor or lazy argument is not always unintentional. Most of us are swamped every day with persuasive rhetoric: claims mischievously presented as established facts, stunning graphs meaningless for the want of intervals along axes, comparisons spruiked without mention of baselines, and so on. Propaganda, demagoguery, subliminal brainwashing, doublespeak, advertising—each engineered to persuade us to accept this or to buy that. If left unchecked, this constant battery of misleading persuasion is likely to generate a citizenry incapable of determining for themselves what is in their best interests (not to mention the best interests of their society). A greater appreciation of logic—and of the subtle techniques of rhetoric employed by self-interested persuaders—would help students respond critically and rationally to the pressures of persuasion. And a rational citizenry is one of the essential pillars of a workable democracy.

Sadly, this is a pillar now under threat. Consider, for example, the current assault on science. We are living in a world of denialism, a denialism driven in large part by vested interests who own, or who can strongly influence, the media. They, and thus the unquestioning *we*, demand more of science than science can possibly give. Science shows us that we are subject to chaotic systems. These are deterministic systems that are just so complex, so prone to deviate with the slightest change in initial conditions, that their behaviour is virtually

---

4. M. du Sautoy, *The Number Mysteries*, Fourth Estate, London, 2011, p. 95.

impossible to predict beyond their next few steps. Climate, stock markets, volcanic activity, turbulence: these are all chaotic systems. And yet when scientists say they do not know *for certain* the outcome of a chaotic system—the weather, for example—whatever they do say about the system is ignored or lampooned. (And in some cases they are imprisoned for failing to predict what cannot be predicted with any certainty.[5])

Predictions within chaotic systems are notoriously difficult to make. Predictions within non-chaotic systems might be easier, but scientists are still reluctant to elevate their verified predictions to anything more than theory. There is always a chance—no matter how slim—that a theory will be falsified. Scepticism and challenge are welcome components of the scientific method. But this professional tentativeness gives those with what might be called *obsessive scepticism syndrome* a reason—a false reason—to doubt everything that scientists put forward. Scientists are mostly unconvinced that there is a causal link between the measles, mumps and rubella (MMR) vaccine and autism—and yet thousands of parents refuse to immunise their children because of an urban myth (propagated by a doctor with an undisclosed vested interest[6]). Only 3% of climate scientists are unconvinced that global warming is caused primarily by anthropogenic activities, but that is enough for climate change deniers to ridicule the empirical evidence gathered by the remaining 97%. Something is wrong here. Some gasket is blown, some head cracked in the cognitive machinery of contemporary *Homo sapiens*. How is it that the honesty of scientists in admitting that there is always a chance that some theory is proven wrong can be twisted into a view that whatever a scientist says is wrong?

It is clear that science has lost respect. Whatever the cause, it is also clear that without more research in the sciences, the

---

5. In 2012, seven people, including four scientists, were sentenced to six years imprisonment in Italy for failing to predict a 2009 earthquake in which more than 300 people died.
6. See V. Grech, "MMR Vaccination Complications – Is it Time to Lay the Myth to Rest?", *Malta Medical Journal*, 2005, vol. 17, iss. 2., pp. 17–20.

Earth and the multifarious lives it harbours are at serious risk. The looming prospect of a hostile climate, diminishing resources and vaccine-resistant viruses—to mention just a few—is unlikely to be prevented by arbitrageurs, bank executives and economists. Nor will it be prevented by shock-jocks who smudge the airwaves with their blinkered denialism. It will be prevented, if prevented at all, by committed, non-partisan thinkers: the philosophers and scientists who follow the argument and evidence no matter where it takes them. And if society is to benefit from these endeavours, its citizens—and especially its influencers—need to be skilled in understanding the strengths and weaknesses in the arguments that these endeavours prompt.

So how are we to develop a passion for critical thinking, a passion for screening out the unlikely, the absurd, the specious and the fallacious? Other than forcing philosophy into an already crowded secondary curriculum, the next best option is to reinstate clear thinking as a compulsory component of English. If it is legitimate to spend classroom time dissecting the character of Micawber or Anna Karenina—the conclusions of which will not affect the world one way or another—it is surely legitimate to spend time dissecting something that will: specious argumentation. After all, language is common to both.

\*

The predominant philosophies of the English classroom over the last 100 or so years have been *prescriptivism* and *relativism*. In the prescriptivist classroom, students were taught that the conventions of language use were inviolable rules. They were to be followed come what may, as they were necessary for logical thought and unhindered communication. The relativist classroom—inspired by the anti-authoritarianism of the 1960s and 70s, and by the spread of post-modernist thinking in many universities—declared that nothing was inviolable. Indeed, any aspect of language use was as good as any other and any critical assessment of language was mostly folly. We have argued that both approaches fail to provide students with the communicative prowess they will need if they are to have the best chance of maximising their wellbeing. Prescriptivism refuses to keep up with, or even accept, the evolutionary meanderings of language. Taken to its logical conclusion, it would have us using language that is foreign to our audience, an outcome that contradicts the very purpose of writing and speaking. Relativism ill-prepares students by largely ignoring or downplaying the importance of learning the conventions of contemporary English and the mechanics of efficient communication. Its predominance of late is the reason why so many people—even native English speakers—lack the confidence to write well in the workplace, and why so many feel the need to attend remedial language courses.

Both philosophies contain an element of truth. The relativists are right in that there is no correct or incorrect, right or wrong language use, but wrong to reject the study of the mechanics of language. The prescriptivists are right in thinking that it is important to study the mechanics of language, but wrong to mislead students into thinking that language use can be correct or incorrect, right or wrong. A third way is called for, and that is the philosophy of active descriptivism described in chapter 4. Here, imparting communication prowess is considered to be the primary goal of English language teaching. But English grammar is flexible enough to give us the means to communicate well and communicate poorly (or not communicate at all, despite our intentions). Thus students need guidance. They need to be taught the principles that enable them to communicate well. But these principles require an understanding of the mechanics of the English language— but it is the mechanics of the *audience's* English. And this may vary significantly from the mechanics set out in any prescriptivist grammar. Language changes. There is no way to stop it. We can try to influence it, but it will always be its own master. The active descriptivist acknowledges that change is inevitable and thus accepts that developing communication prowess requires keeping abreast of changes in the language.

In the active-descriptivist classroom, rules will still be taught. But they will be taught as changeable conventions. And while they are important, what will be given precedence is something else: developing communication prowess. (As we've noted a number of times, a sentence with impeccable, syntax and punctuation can still fail to communicate.) The reading of well-written texts will still be promoted, as doing so reinforces knowledge of the mechanics of the language, strengthens communication skills and provides an emotional richness that both inspires the young and stimulates cultural enrichment. Finally, the ways in which communication can be twisted will be examined, the goal being to better equip students to see through the fog of persuasion and become citizens capable of contributing to a rational democracy.

The order in which these topics are taught is an important consideration. We have spent much time arguing about the importance of communication, but the principles of communication we have outlined will, in all likelihood, confuse first-graders. We want to teach first-graders how to write, so little is gained by teaching them anything more than majority usage. Sample texts will help in this endeavour. But at some stage the parochialism of what has been taught needs to be explained. Many young students will have already seen that not all English speakers speak the same language. The confusion this might cause needs to be prevented, or resolved, early on. The principles of efficient communication can be introduced later, along with clear thinking. And all along, students should be encouraged to read texts that guide and enrich their emotional development. But eventually students should also be taught that they have a moral right to write as they please. We'll come back to this point in the epilogue.

\*

Language change in the past has been, if not glacial, then certainly slow. The internet will almost certainly cause the rate of change to increase. Now anyone with a computer and a modicum of technical knowledge can publish their thoughts.

This means that anyone could be responsible for introducing language change, whether knowingly or not. A seemingly innocuous blog or Twitter posting with anomalous usage could attract many readers—in web-speak, it could *go viral*—and, as a result, many readers of that post adopt the anomalous usage in their own postings. Others follow suit and the anomalous usage turns into a fad. With enough momentum the fad can become a trend, and the trend a new convention. (Notice the increasing usage on the internet of the open hyphen to mark out parenthetic material, a practice unseen in the pre-internet era. It is likely to become a new convention in the next decade.) Changes once took 50–60 years to cement into a new convention; now it's happening in a decade or two.

We argued in chapter 4 that governments have an obligation to maintain a national language record. When language changes, the national language record needs to be updated. But such updates are unlikely to filter through to the majority of language users. Most of us are not as keen as copy-editors to peruse the very latest dictionary, style guide or grammar book. And yet effective communication—if not efficient communication—needs to use *current* language if it is to meet the emotional and commercial needs of citizens. The thought of parents helping their children with their English homework is an endearing one, but only if the advice parents give matches current majority usage.

Periodic professional development will help English teachers keep abreast of changes in the language and thus help them to teach *current* majority usage. But what of others? The idea that people return to school every 10 or so years to have their English language knowledge updated—whether to help their children or to help them in their job—is somewhat fanciful. It won't happen. And yet the value of communication means that it is in everyone's best interest to keep their language skills up to date. Perhaps the only option is for governments to keep the general public informed by publishing a 5- or 10-year report on current language use. This should not be in the form of an obscure style guide—as is the case in Australia—but in the form of a publication that newspapers and television networks can readily absorb, summarise and discuss, all to the benefit of native users. It would also serve as a snapshot of one of any country's greatest cultural assets: its language.

# Epilogue

It is not uncommon for intimate friends to share a private language. They might have special terms of endearment or create private portmanteau words that invoke a shared sentiment. These words or terms have meaning for them but might be meaningless to an eavesdropper. Is this private language, this *unconventional* language, incorrect or wrong? Do prescriptivists have a right to criticise it and insist that the thoughts behind it be clothed in other ways?

Consider now a slightly larger group of people who decide to use language in a way that is not conventional—aeronautical engineers, for example. In that profession it is quite common to use the word *safety* as a verb (as in *Now safety the latch*). Few outsiders would use the word that way. Are we to say, then, that members of the aeronautical engineering profession have no right to use *safety* in this way? Is this an example of "plummeting standards [and] appalling ignorance", to borrow some of the vitriol dished out by arch-pedant Lynne Truss to those who use language in an unconventional way?

Let's move on to an even larger group of speakers, say the speakers of American English. Is it an example of plummeting standards and appalling ignorance for Americans to spell *colour* "color". Is it wrong of them to call a tap a *faucet* and to include a serial comma in run-on lists? These are, of course, rhetorical questions. No answers are needed.

Now let's go in the other direction: from countries to professional bodies to couples and finally to individuals. If countries, professional bodies and couples have a right to use language as they please, why is that an individual does not? Using language is a form of expression, as is painting and composing. Are artists obliged to paint in particular ways? Are composers obliged to compose in particular ways? Could some brushstrokes in Monet's *Water-Lily Pond* be incorrect or wrong? Could some bars in Stravinsky's *Le Sacre du Printemps* be incorrect or wrong? The absurdity of such questions prompts us to ask why writers are obliged to write in particular ways, as prescriptivists demand.

But haven't we been just as prescriptive in insisting that writers follow the principles of communication outlined in chapter 5? In other words, isn't the active descriptivism promoted in this book just as limiting as strong and weak prescriptivism? Not quite. First, the principles we outlined are quite general, unlike the specific usage rules prescriptivists insist on. An active descriptivist is, for instance, concerned that writing is clear—that is, free of nonsense, ambiguity and vagueness—but they do not fuss about how this is achieved. On the other hand, prescriptivists declare as wrong specific features of writing—such as missing genitive apostrophes, split infinitives and dangling participles—even if the writing is crystal clear. The difference is between the relativism of descriptivism and the absolutism of prescriptivism. How one era writes clearly might be quite different to how another era writes clearly. The descriptivist accepts this; the prescriptivist does not. Second, the principles of active descriptivism are *conditional* imperatives. Together they state that *if* you want to maximise your chances of being understood by your intended audience, *then* it is best if you follow certain principles: the principles of clarity, familiarity, economy and so on. They do not say that you *must* follow these principles come what may. In which case, I have a moral right to follow them or not follow them. A parallel: *if* you want to maximise your chances of getting a good return from buying shares in company $x$, *then* it is best if you study the performance and prospects of $x$. But that doesn't imply that I am morally obliged not to invest in $x$ if I don't study the company's performance and prospects. I am as free to make unwise investments as I am to make wise ones.

Third, and more importantly, I *can* meet the principles of communication outlined earlier and still write as I please. All I need do is to make my intended audience aware before they begin reading what my novel terms or devices mean. Suppose, for example, that I preface a document with "All conventional apostrophes of elision have been omitted in this document" and proceed to write *dont* rather than *don't* and *isnt* rather than *isn't*. I have alerted my readers to what I have done and thus the unconventionality of my practice should not distract them and get in the way of communication. They might find my decision odd, but they at least know what my odd words mean and can easily understand what I have written. There are plenty of precedents. A lawyer might, in the preamble to a legal contract, define terms in a way that, if left undefined, would baffle or mislead readers. The drafter of an act of parliament will also specify the meaning of those terms that are to be understood in unconventional ways, as do drafters of industry standards. The writer of a user guide will sometimes preface the guide with a *documentation conventions* section which sets out what, say, the bolding of text or the use of a mono-spaced font indicate, typographic cues that might remain a distracting mystery otherwise. Of course, any particular novelty might still distract readers even if it is explained. In other words, I might fail to meet my goal of communicating with as many of my intended audience as possible. But that doesn't detract from my right to introduce that novelty. Another parallel: my goal in making a particular investment might be to double my money in 10 years. I study the market carefully and am convinced that this goal is achievable. I make the investment. However, an unpredictable market crash comes along and thwarts my goal. Despite that, I still had the right to invest as I did. We all fail to meet some goals in our life, but mostly we are free to choose how we attempt to meet them.

The point we are labouring here is that the goal of communication is not necessarily thwarted by the use of unconventional language. Our principle of familiarity is not breached if we tell readers what to expect. Nor is the principle breached if it is blindingly obvious what the intent is of some new usage that is not explained. The purpose of the open hyphen would be blindingly obvious to a competent English audience when it encloses parenthetic material - it is simply doing the work more commonly done by a dash - just as the meaning of *two weeks notice* is blindingly obvious without the apostrophe. And no doubt the first reader of *C U L8r* in a text message would have understood its meaning unaided. Thus active descriptivism is compatible with the right to write and talk as we please.

None of this contradicts our emphasis on the importance of *teaching* majority usage. No-one can tell in advance what language or language variant will best help a youngster gain the wellbeing they eventually seek. Thus those charged with the wellbeing of a youngster—parents and teachers—need to choose from behind a Rawlsian "veil of ignorance". And from that position, the majority usage of the youngster's own country is the best choice. (Being able to communicate with the greatest number of people that one might need to call on for affection, goods, services, employment, care and the like is only sensible.) But that doesn't mean that we are then forever obliged to adopt the majority usage of our country. Sometimes failing to do so will be self-defeating; other times it will not. If you are a Liverpudlian writing for a Liverpudlian audience, you can use Scouse—a non-majority variant of British English—and be confident of being understood. And given that the principal purpose to which language is put is to communicate with others, what more relevant criterion of good writing can there be other than *being understood*. As Nicholas Hudson famously said:

> "... if everyone understands what we say, then the way we say it cannot be incorrect." (Hudson 1993, p. 98)

Playground bullying and social ridicule usually arise from difference: a difference in skin colour, in pronunciation or in the capacity to master the chaotic jumble that is the hallmark of all natural languages. The result is often an unhealthy desire to conform. Bullying and ridicule can also generate a neurosis that leads to withdrawal and sometimes hopelessness. They are, in other words, forms of psychological abuse. And the effects of that abuse can last a lifetime. Many being interviewed for a job, contributing to a tutorial or giving a speech are traumatised as much by the fear of saying something inane as the fear that how they say what they say will be judged poorly—judged, perhaps, as the coarseness of the uneducated or the patois of an under-class. Bullying extends to the workplace too. Many an adult student has reported that their reports are often torn apart by managers for reasons that are either not proffered or seem groundless. When I ask for examples of language that is corrected, it is clear that much of the criticism is about style, not language. (One student was told by his manager that the words *get* and *got* are never used in technical reports! Pure nonsense.) This vexatious editing only exacerbates stress in the workplace, especially among those who have English as a second or third language. It also generates an unnecessary language neurosis. This neurosis would vanish if there was wider recognition that no one way of speaking or writing has any more inherent legitimacy than any other. But for that to occur, we need to wrest away from pedants, sticklers and language snobs the presumed authority to foist on others what are little more than lazy pontifications. To that end was this book written.

In conclusion, a short poem that, I trust, captures the gist of this book:

### Youse

How strange that such a simple sound
Can rouse in some
Revulsion almost visceral—
A shuddering of the soul.

Its parts are nothing new but
Well established in the alphabet

Of sounds—*juz*—a soft concatenation
Yet together and from certain lips
In certain ears revolt.

"Illiterate", the complaint is heard
Although the utterer of the word
May never have been schooled
In all the fineries of palatial speech.
But whose fault is that?

Do we scorn those poor sods
Whose numerical dexterity
Leaves a lot to be desired
Whose sums and long division
Could so easily be decried?

No. And nor do we decry those
For whom the quark is a concept
Weird and dark, as is ergs, as is bosons;
Gravitons and photons.

It is just a matter of schooling, surely?
And ignorance is no laughing matter.

So why is it different with language,
Why does ignorance of words
But not of atoms and of surds
Cause so many of us to choke
In ridicule and belittlement?

Much of what we accept today
Came from the common folk
So should we rewind all of English
And strip out every vulgar link?
Or is there something else at play
In your choice of what is good
And what stinks?

Perhaps in words we see a way
To brand and mark, a simple way—
No fee required—to place ourselves
Above another, the them
That is not us. A snobbery so few
Admit, but so common as to

Make one think it springs
From sources somewhat deep, perhaps
A canny twist of DNA
That gives the utterer
Of dandy speech
An advantage I regret not having—
Considerably more sex?

But here's another twist:
This urchin word does not
Dilute nor does it blur
Our mighty language
Unlike so much else one finds
In the swamp of daily verbiage.
Indeed, it adds.
It fills a gap that's
Yawned for many centuries:
No second-person plural!
How could English have become so powerful
When it lacks what lesser tongues
Have had since birth?
And there lies the irony, that so
Useful and mellifluous a word
Could be so thunderously rejected.

It's not its freshness that offends:
New words are cuddled every day.
Who sniggers at *blog*?
Who frowns at *Blu-Ray*?
But these drop from the tongues
Of today's High Priests
The technocrats and their caucus
Drop one instead from the hoi polloi
And the pedants' shrieks are raucous.

Stop this bigotry at once!
It stinks so much of class.
Exclusion based on origin
Is nothing short of farce.

Do youse understand?

# Bibliography

Aitchison J. 2001, *Language Change: Progress or Decay?*, Cambridge University Press, Cambridge, 3rd edn.

Alford H. 1864, *Plea for the Queen's English*, Dick & Fitzgerald, New York.

Ayer A. J. 1956, *The Problem of Knowledge*, Penguin, Harmondsworth.

Burchfield R. 1985, *The English Language*, Oxford University Press, Oxford.

Chall J. S. 1958, *Readability: An Appraisal of Research and Application*, Ohio State University Press, Columbus.

Cheek A. 2010, "Defining Plain Language", *Clarity: Journal of the International Association Promoting Plain Legal Language*, no. 64, November 2010.

*The Chicago Manual of Style* 2003, Chicago University Press, Chicago, 15th ed.

Chomsky A. N. 1957, *Syntactic Structures*, Mouton, The Hague.

—— 2006, *Language and Mind*, Cambridge University Press, Cambridge, 3rd edn.

Cooper B. M. 1964, *Writing Technical Reports*, Penguin, Harmmondsworth, UK.

Cowan N. 2010, "The Magical Mystery Four: How is Working Memory Capacity Limited, and Why?", *Current Directions in Psychological Science*, vol. 19, iss. 1.

Crystal D. 1987, *The Cambridge Encyclopedia of Language*, Cambridge University Press, Cambridge.

—— 2006, *How Language Works*, Penguin, Camberwell.

—— 2008, *The gr8 db8*, Oxford University Press, Oxford.

Doyle D. 2003, *Grey Areas and Gremlins: A Grammar and Punctuation Refresher*, self-published.

DuBay W. H. 2007, *Smart Language: Readers, Readability, and the Grading of Text*, Impact Information, Costa Mesa, CA.

Finegan E., Besnier N., Blair D. & Collins P. 1992, *Language: Its Structure and Use*, Harcourt Brace Jovanovich, Sydney

Flesch R. 1948, "A New Readability Yardstick", *Journal of Applied Psychology*, vol. 32, iss. 3, pp. 221–233.

Fowler H. W. 1965, *A Dictionary of Modern English Usage*, Oxford University Press, New York, 2nd edn.

Hitchings H. 2011, *The Language Wars: A History of Proper English*, John Murray, London.

Hudson N. 1993, *Modern Australian Usage*, Oxford University Press, Melbourne.

Humphrys J. 2004, *Lost for Words: The Mangling and Manipulation of the English Language*, Hodder and Stoughton, London.

—— 2006, *Beyond Words*, Hodder, London.

James N. 2007, *Writing at Work*, Allen & Unwin, Crows Nest.

Khan J. E. 1985, *The Right Word at the Right Time*, Readers Digest, London.

Kintsch W., Kozminsky E., Streby J., McKoon G. & Keenan J. M. 1975, "Comprehension and Recall of Text as a Function of Content Variables", *Journal of Verbal Behavior and Verbal Learning*, vol. 14, iss. 2.

Kintsch W. & Rawson K. 2005, "Comprehension", in M. J. Snowling & C. Hulme, *The Science of Reading: A Handbook*, Blackwell, Oxford.

Lass R. 2006, "Phonology and morphology", in *A History of the English Language*, ed. by R. Hogg & D. Denison, Cambridge University Press, Cambridge.

Mills J. 2010, "Genocide and Ethnocide: The Suppression of the Cornish Language", in *Interfaces in Language* edited by J. Partridge, Cambridge Scholars Publishing, Newcastle upon Tyne, pp. 189–206.

Mitford N. 1956, *Noblesse Oblige: An Enquiry into the Identifiable Characteristics of the English Aristocracy*, Hamish Hamilton, London.

Moriaty M. F. 1996, *Writing Science through Critical Thinking*, Jones & Bartlett, Sudbury MA.

Murray-Smith S. 1987, *A Guide to English Usage in Australia*, Viking, Ringwood.

Orwell G. 1946, "Politics and the English Language", *Horizon*, April 1946.

Parkes M. B. 1993, *Pause and Effect: An Introduction to the History of Punctuation in the West*, University of California Press, Berkeley.

Partridge E. 1961, *A Dictionary of the Underworld*, Bonanza Books, New York.

—— 2008, *Usage & Abusage*, Penguin, Camberwell, 3rd edn.

*The Penguin Working Words: An Australian Guide to Modern English Usage*, 1993, Penguin, Ringwood.

Peters P. 2007, *The Cambridge Guide to Australian English Usage*, Cambridge University Press, Cambridge (UK).

Quirk R., Greenbaum S., Leech G. & Svartnik J. 1972, *A Grammar of Contemporary English*, Longman, London.

—— 1985, *A Comprehensive Grammar of the English Language*, Longman, London.

Richards T. J. 1978, *The Language of Reason*, Pergamon Press, Rushcutters Bay.

Sampson G. 2005, *The 'Language Instinct' Debate*, Continuum, London, 2nd ed.

Samson D. C. 1993, *Editing Technical Writing*, Oxford University Press, New York.

Selzer J. 1983, "What Constitutes a 'Readable' Technical Style?" in P. V. Anderson, R. J. Brockmann & C. R. Miller (eds), *New Essays In Scientific and Technical Communication: Research, Theory and Practice*, Baywood, New York, pp. 71–89.

Shrives C. 2011, *Grammar Rules: Writing with Military Precision*, Kyle Books, London.

Strunk W. & White E. B. 2000, *The Elements of Style*, Longman, Pearson Educational, Needham Heights, 4th edn.

*Style Manual for Authors, Editors and Printers* 2002, John Wiley & Son, Canberra, 6th edn.

Trudgill P. 1999, *The Dialects of England*, Blackwell, Oxford, 2nd edn.

Truss L. 2003, *Eats, Shoots And Leaves: The Zero Tolerance Approach to Punctuation*, Profile, London.

Wheildon C. 2005, *Type & Layout: Are You Communicating or Just Making Pretty Shapes?*, Worley, Mentone.

Whitney W. D. 1867, *Language and the Study of Language*, Trubner, London.

Williams J. 1980, "The Phenomenology of Error", *College Composition and Communication*, vol. 31, pp. 152–168.

Wood F. T. 1962, *Current English Usage*, Macmillan, London.

Woods B., Moscardo G. & Greenwood T. 1998, "A Critical Review of Readability and Comprehensibility Tests", *The Journal of Tourism Studies*, pp. 49–61.

# Index

## A

*a* or *an*? 27
a posteriori knowledge 71, 79–86
a priori knowledge 71, 73–79
active descriptivism 175, 268–269
   influencing the language 183
acute ambiguity 207
adjectives, in parentheses 177
agentless ambiguity 210
ambiguity 206
   acute and chronic 207
   and readability formulas 233
   types of 208–211
American English 63
*and* at the start of a sentence 33
apostrophe
   greengrocer's 125
   of elision 126–128
   of possession 43–46, 128, 182–183
   *See also* genitive apostrophe
Apostrophe Protection Society 52, 131
articles 27–28
artificial conventions 103
Australian English 63

## B

Betjeman, John 22
block text 182
British English 64
*but* at the start of a sentence 33

## C

categorical imperatives 89
category mistake 14, 88, 117, 205
Caxton, William 101
change
   communicating 270
   does it weaken a language? 152
   increasing speed of 269
   inevitability of 62, 169, 259
   why it occurs 57, 269
   will chaos result? 142–147, 148–151
Chomsky, Noam 86, 152, 196
chronic ambiguity 207
chunks, of meaning 217
clarity
   importance of 197, 205–211
   what to avoid 205–211
clear thinking 263–267
clipped English 210
cognitive lodgement 204
colons 61, 177
commas 61, 65

common usage *See* majority usage
communication
  competency in 165, 191
  efficiency of 202
  maximising the potential for 174, 254–256
  the goal of language 173, 195
  ultimate principle of 202
  *See also* principles of communication
communicative efficiency 202
comprehension, and readability scores 238
conceptual lightness 201, 215–220
conditional imperatives 89, 92
conjunctions, at the start of a sentence 33–36, 69
conservatism 56
consistency 202, 222–225
consonants 27–28
contemporary diversity 63–65
contradiction 205
conventions 55, 103–113, 172, 175, 192, 258, 260, 269
  and descriptivism 171–175
  and prescriptivism 165–171
  artificial 103
  natural 103, 105
  *See also* standards
coordinating conjunction 69, 75
Cornish language, fight for 258

correctness
  and intention 116
  definitions of 51, 98, 105, 106, 108
  relativism of 113
  *See also* conventions, knowledge
cultural insensitivity 221
cultural revolution 47–48, 165
curricula, parental influence over 251

# D

dangling participles 257
declarative sentences 89
deduction 71–73
descriptivism 12, 56, 171–175
  active 175, 183, 268–269
  and conventions 171–175
  first principle of 174
  passive 175
  teaching of 253–262
detached modifier ambiguity 209
dictionaries 102, 106, 191
  limitations of 115, 120–122
discretionary language 257, 275
diversity
  contemporary 63–65, 138
  historical 57–63
  legitimacy of 174
double negatives 64, 257
Dryden, John 36

# E

economy
  importance of 197–200
  issues with 214–215
educated speech 139–141
elegant variation 202, 222
elision 126–128
em dash 147
emotions, engaging 220–222
en dash 147, 171
etymology 157–158

# F

fallacies, of logic 263
familiarity
  importance of 196, 212–213, 254
  types of 213
first-line indents 181
Flesch reading ease score 230–235
Flesch–Kincaid Grade Level 231
fonts, serif or sans serif? 204
FORCAST 238
Fowler, H. W. 20, 156, 222
freedom, of language use 273, 275
frequency, of word use 213
FRY 238

# G

genitive apostrophe 43–46, 131–132, 182–183
  ambiguity in use of 132, 210
governments, responsibility of 191–193, 270

grammar
  and readability 233
  inter-English variations 64
  universal *See* universal grammar
Great Vowel Shift 59
greengrocer's apostrophe 125
Gunning Fog Index 230

# H

historical diversity 57–63
Hume, David 91
Humphrys, John 53, 54, 158, 165
hyphenation 129

# I

imperatives
  categorical 89
  conditional 89, 92
  derivable from declaratives? 91
incorrectness
  and mistakes 116–118
  connotation of 111, 112
  definitions of 113
indenting, of paragraphs 181
induction 71–73, 83
infinitives, splitting 39–43, 257
information, units of 217
internet 269
*-ise* or *-ize*? 156
*is–ought* problem 91

# J

James, Clive 135
justice and language 191

## K

keyboard design, and language change 147
Kintsch, W. 217, 218
knowledge
  a posteriori 71, 79–86
  a priori 71, 73–79
  conditionality of 256
  derivative v. primary 70
  in language studies 253–258
  necessary features of 70
  sources of 70, 71
  types of 71–86

## L

language
  acceptance of 107
  and class 21, 259, 260
  and freedom 273, 275
  and justice 191
  and knowledge 253–258
  and literature 262
  and logic 263–267
  and standards 100
  as convention 103–113
  better in the past? 158
  convergent pressures 151, 175
  discretionary 257, 275
  evolutionary view of 253
  improving 112, 176
  inconsistent 132
  influencing 183–186
  majority use 106, 188, 259, 276
  minority variants 260
  neurosis about 14, 258, 261
  non-standard 137–142
  origin of 103
  purpose of 95, 169, 171, 173
  register 221
  self-defeating 170
  self-preservation of 175, 179
  shared 150
  teaching of 253–262
  tone 221
  trends 178
  unnecessary 125
  variant to be taught 258–262
language change
  communicating 270
  does it weaken a language? 152
  increasing speed of 269
  inevitability of 62, 169, 259
  reasons for 57, 269
  will chaos result? 142–147, 148–151
language neurosis 277
Latin 38, 41
length, of sentences 215–220
lexical ambiguity 208
linguistic anarchy 175
literacy, testing of 250
literature 262
logic, teaching 263–267

## M

majority usage 106, 188, 259, 276
manuals, style 13, 191, 214
meaning
  changes in 60, 63, 234
  chunks of 217
measuring quality of writing
  *See* readability formulas

memory, capacity of 201, 217
minorities 260
mistakes 116–118
Mitford, Nancy 21, 259
mood 88
morality 14, 124, 188, 191–192, 199, 252, 273

## N

National Language Record 190–193, 270
natural conventions 103, 105
neither correct nor incorrect 111
neologisms 25
neurosis, language 277
neutrality 201, 220–222
New Zealand English 64
*Noblesse Oblige* 21, 259
nominalisation 215
nonsense 205
numeracy 250

## O

obligation
 of governments 191–193
 to teach 188
Orwell, George 249
Oxford comma 65

## P

paragraphing, indents or space? 181
parentheses 62
parents, influencing curricula 251
participles, dangling 257
Partridge, Eric 19–20
passive descriptivism 175
paternalism 221

pausing when reading 31
phantom-possibility ambiguity 210
Pinker, Steven 86, 153
Plain Writing Act 58, 192, 215
portmanteau words, apostrophes in 126
possessive apostrophe 43–46, 182–183
 *See also* genitive apostrophe
PowerPoint speak 210
prepositions, at the end of sentences 36–39
prescriptivism 55, 267–268
 and conservatism 56
 and conventions 165–171
 paradox of 251
 strong 56, 90, 92, 165
 weak 56, 167
principles of communication
 clarity 197, 205–211
 conceptual lightness 201, 215–220
 consistency 202, 222–225
 economy 200, 214–215
 familiarity 196, 212–213, 254
 neutrality 201, 220–222
pronominal ambiguity 208
pronouns 133
pronunciation 58, 156
 and punctuation 44
 in American English 63
 in Australian English 63
 in British English 63
*proper*, meaning of 115
punctuation
 changes in 60
 inter-English variations 65
 purpose of 28–32, 43, 44

## Q

quality, measuring *See* readability formulas
quotation marks 61, 178–179

## R

Rawls, John 188, 276
readability
 absolute v. relative 239
 correlation with comprehension 238
 definitions of 228
 score given in MS Word 228
 volatility of scores 241
readability formulas
 ambiguity missed by 233
 Flesch 230–235
 ignore chunk count 235
 irrelevance of 246–248
 problems with 231–235
 reliability of 237
 types of 230
 use of 229
 validation of 237–246
reader engagement 204
reasoning, types of 71–73
recall, of sentence contents 218
recitation 31
redundancy 214
register 221
relative clause ambiguity 209
relative clause attachment ambiguity 208
relativism 66–68, 267–268

## S

scare quotes 212
science, in the English classroom 254, 256
*scriptio continua* 30
semantic-bleed ambiguity 210
semicolon 62, 177
sentences
 length of 215–220, 230, 231
 mood of 88
 processing 201
 recall of 218
 types of 88
serial comma 65
serif or sans serif? 204
sexism 134, 221
Shakespeare, W. 25, 37
short-term memory, capacity of 201, 217
silent reading 31
Simple Measure Of Gobbledegook *See* SMOG
SMOG 230, 238
snobbery 94, 259
spelling
 changes in 59
 discretionary 116
 etymologically 157
 inter-English variations 64
split infinitives 39–43, 257
Standard English 10, 94, 137–142
standards 97–102
 explicit 99
 implicit 100
 *See also* conventions

strong prescriptivism 56, 90, 92, 165
structural ambiguity 208
Strunk, W. 21
style manuals 13, 191, 214
syllable count, and readability 230, 232, 235
synonyms, over-use of 222
syntax, changes in 60

## T

tautology 214
teaching
  and absolutism 160
  in a descriptivist classroom 253–262, 269
  structuring 269
telegraphic ambiguity 209
textese 145, 276
tone 221
triviality, in writing 214
truncation *See* elision
Truss, Lynne 14, 52, 54, 125, 128, 165

## U

U and non-U language 21, 259
undifferentiated ambiguity 209
units of information 217
universal grammar 86, 152–156
usage *See* language

## V

vagueness 211
variants of English
  contemporary 63–65
  historical 57–63
  in equilibrium 174
  legitimacy of 174, 258–262
  teaching of 258–262
*veil of ignorance* 188, 276
verbosity 214
verbs 25
vocabulary, inter-English variations 63
volatility, in readability scores 241
vowels 27–28, 59

## W

weak prescriptivism 56, 167
White, E. B. 21
words
  frequency of use 213
  maximum no. in sentences 215–220
working memory, capacity of 201, 217
writing *See* language
wrong 51

## Y

youse 107, 277

www.ingramcontent.com/pod-product-compliance
Lightning Source LLC
Chambersburg PA
CBHW071858290426
44110CB00013B/1202